PUBLIC PARKS

PUBLIC PARKS

THE KEY TO LIVABLE COMMUNITIES

ALEXANDER GARVIN

EDITED BY RONDA BRANDS

W. W. Norton & Company

NEW YORK • LONDON

IN MEMORY OF FREDERICK LAW OLMSTED

For information about permission to reproduce selections from this book, write to
Permissions, W. W. Norton & Company, Inc., 500 Fifth Avenue, New York, NY 10110

For information about special discounts for bulk purchases, please contact
W. W. Norton Special Sales at specialsales@wwnorton.com or 800-233-4830

Manufacturing by Colorprint
Book design by Jonathan D. Lippincott
Production manager: Leeann Graham
Digital production: J. Lops

Credits
Photographs and drawings are by the author except for those credited below.

Acknowledgment is made to the following for permission to use the illustrations on the following pages:

12: Used with permission from The Biltmore Company, Asheville, North Carolina; 19 (bottom): © Museum of London; 31 (bottom): Courtesy of the Library of Congress, J. S. Johnson Collection; 34 (top) © The Frick Collection, New York; 45 (right, second from bottom): Hargreaves Associates; 47 (top): *Minneapolis Park System 1884–1944*; 52 (middle): Oregon Historical Society; 60 (top left) Hem Tripathi; 62 (bottom): New York Public Library; 77 (right, top and middle): *Creating Central Park* (New York: The Metropolitan Museum of Art, 2008); 100: Richard Payne, FAI; 109: field operations; 110 (bottom): The Minneapolis Institute of Arts; 122: Chicago CartoGraphics and AGA Public Realm Strategists; 148 (top): Minneapolis Park and Recreation Board and AGA Public Realm Strategists; 177 (top): 34th Street Partnership; 179 (bottom): Chelsea Piers Sports and Entertainment Complex and Beck's Studio; 197 (top): Museum of the City of New York; 198 (top) *Greater New York Illustrated* (Skokie, Illinois: Rand McNally & Co., 1898)
and
127, 151 (left): Burnham and Bennett, *Plan of Chicago, 1909*; 106 (bottom), 123 (top), 125 (top left and right), 128: Chicago History Museum; 45 (left, second from top), 157 (top and middle), 161 (top and bottom), 193, 206 (top and bottom): City of New York/Parks and Recreation; 125 (bottom left), 143 (top), 144 (top): Frederick Law Olmsted National Historic Site, Courtesy of the National Park Service; 56, 94 (top left and bottom): Louisville Waterfront Development Corporation; 20, 36 (top): Museum of the City of New York; 65 (bottom), 66 (top): *UTSA Institute of Texan Cultures*

Library of Congress Cataloging-in-Publication Data
Garvin, Alexander.
    Public parks : the key to livable communities / Alexander Garvin ,
edited by Ronda M. Brands. — 1st ed.
        p.   cm.
    Includes bibliographical references and index.
    ISBN 978-0-393-73279-5 (hardcover)
    1. Urban parks. 2. City and town life. I. Brands, Ronda M. II. Title.
III. Title: Key to livable communities.
    SB481.G37 2011
    712'.5—dc22
                                        2010011146

ISBN: 978-0-393-73279-5

W. W. Norton & Company, Inc., 500 Fifth Avenue, New York, N.Y. 10110
www.wwnorton.com
W. W. Norton & Company Ltd., Castle House, 75/76 Wells Street, London W1T 3QT

0 9 8 7 6 5 4 3 2 1

Pages 2-3: Prospect Park, Brooklyn, 2008

CONTENTS

Chicago, 2008

ACKNOWLEDGMENTS

This book began as a friendly debate over which was the first public park in the world: the Derby Arboretum, as the English landscape architect John Hopkins maintained, or Birkenhead, which I thought was accepted history. John had been in charge of the restoration of the Derby Arboretum and took me there to make his point; a year later we traveled together to Birkenhead. Eventually we evolved a definition: It had to have been initially acquired for public use and designed for recreational purposes, and on that basis Derby, opened in 1839, was the first. But since it was initially open to the public free of charge only one day per week, I still clung to Birkenhead, which opened in 1843. But what about the Luxembourg Gardens in Paris, and the Englische Garten in Munich, neither initially designed for public recreation but both open to the public since the late eighteenth century? Or Hyde Park, originally a hunting preserve, which had been used informally by Londoners since the sixteenth century? As readers of the first chapter will discover, I decided the more appropriate question is, when did the concept of public parks originate? After extended conversations with the architectural historian and urbanist Robert Bruegmann, I came to the conclusion that this concept emerged over several centuries and became a primary governmental function in the mid-nineteenth century.

Thus, I must thank both John and Bob for the historical perspective that permeates this book.

I never write or lecture about places I have not been to, often numerous times. Over the years, Rick and Nancy Rubens have been my most frequent companions and informants on these visits. Carol Liebman first took me along the paths she had walked as a child in Louisville's Cherokee Park. Scott Stone accompanied me on two more trips to explore Olmsted's extraordinary work in that city. Rodney Yoder and J. B. Clancy wandered with me during several visits to Olmsted's Emerald Necklace in Boston, and Matt Jacobs and Anne Goulet joined me in some of my explorations of his work in Detroit and Buffalo. Robert Bruegmann has often guided me through Chicago's parks. When I decided to travel to Germany to see the Landschaftspark in Duisberg, Germany, Boris Sieverts was kind enough to give me a tour, and during our visit he helped me to develop the idea of *aesthetic sustainability*, discussed in chapter 12. My brother, George, helped me to sharpen my thinking about chateau gardens during a trip we made together to France. On my many trips to Pittsburgh I do not think I have ever failed to discuss Mellon Square with David and Susan Brownlee. During one of my walks around Washington, D.C., Bob Kaiser and Hannah Jopling introduced me to Meridian Hill Park. When John Meigs told me Philadelphia's Wissahickon Creek had to be in the book, I went there with him and decided he was right. Many others have accompanied me on visits to the places I have written about in the book. I am grateful to all of them for their insights and for the many challenges they made to my often inchoate thinking.

My thinking about park development is presented in chapter 4. It was deepened while I worked on the Beltline Emerald Necklace in Atlanta, Shelby Farms Park in Memphis, and Hinton Park in Collierville, Tennessee. Thus my approach to shaping development also reflects ideas that evolved as I worked with Jim Schroder, my major collaborator in Atlanta, and with Jeff Rader, Barbara Faga, Jim Langford, and Ed McBrayer. My thinking about park demand has been influenced by Laura Adams, Rick Masson, Barbara and Pitt Hyde, Teresa Sloyan, Calvin Anderson, Ham Smythe, John Charles Wilson, Ted Fox, and the many people I met while working on Shelby Farms Park. The notion that parkland acts as a framework for development, which I set forth in my book *The American City: What Works, What Doesn't*, was further clarified by working with Nick Peterson on a legacy plan for London's Olympic Park. My ideas about seizing opportunity evolved while working with Joshua Price, James Lewellen, and Chip Peterson on Hinton Park. I thank them all, and in particular Joshua Price, who collaborated with me on the design of Hinton Park.

Like most people who watched the shocking deterioration of American parks during the during the 1960s, '70s, and '80s, I consider stewardship an essential component of park planning, development, design, and management. Chapters 9 and 10 are specifically devoted to this subject, but the whole book is filled with ideas about stewardship that I learned from Elizabeth Barlow Rogers, Douglas Blonsky, Henry Stern, Adrian Benepe, Daniel Biederman, Tupper Thomas, Leslie Beller, and David Karem. I cannot thank them enough for their generosity in sharing with me the accumulated experience of decades devoted to park stewardship.

Whatever I have learned from these wonderful people, it is but a fraction of what I have gleaned from the work of Frederick Law Olmsted. This was possible because Charles E. Beveridge and the dedicated group of editors he assembled have produced eight volumes of what eventually will be the complete *Papers of Frederick Law Olmsted*, published by Johns Hopkins University Press. We all owe them our appreciation.

Charles Beveridge helped with some of the material on Olmsted. Steven Peterson advised me on the discussion of European gardens. Daniel Biederman, Tupper Thomas, and Leslie Beller provided material on Bryant and Prospect Park. David Lahm advised me on ways to make some sections more understandable to nonspecialists. I thank Matt Goldstein, Bob Bruegmann, and Rick Rubens for their good counsel on early versions of the text. Matt was invaluable; he found writings and images I was unfamiliar with, kept up an ongoing dialogue with me about the contents and organization of the book, and came up with what, in retrospect, was obvious: the decision to devote the concluding chapter entirely to Central Park.

Every book needs a publisher. When my dependable agent, Arthur Klebanoff, persuaded W. W. Norton to publish this book I was delighted. There is no better editor than Nancy Green, who has guided me throughout. Ronda Brands's restructuring of the text and Mary Bellino's copy editing transformed my manuscript into a book that is truly easy to read and understand. Mary's knowledge of landscape and garden history and her sensitivity to my thinking about parks not only helped to sharpen the text; they even induced me to change some of the images that illustrate it. I am grateful to these remarkable people for their invaluable assistance.

The illustrations in this book are as important as the text. I took virtually all the color photographs. The original maps were the result of my collaboration with Joshua Price. The wonderful layout was designed by Jonathan D. Lippincott. I thank Matt Goldstein, Steve Soroka, Christina Benson, Jason Mencher, and Sara Cedar Miller for helping me to track down historical images.

This book also is the result of help from so many others. The list is too lengthy to print. You know who you are and I thank you all.

PUBLIC PARKS

INTRODUCTION

Sir Joseph Duveen, perhaps the most spectacular art dealer who ever lived, always said of the value of a great work of art, "When you pay high for the priceless, you're getting it cheap."[1] The same is true of a public park.

Many people understand implicitly that public parks are an indispensable part of urban and suburban life, but too often parks are thought to be less valuable than roads, bridges, sewers, and water mains. That built infrastructure wears out and loses value with age; in contrast, parks, under responsible stewardship, become more beautiful and more satisfying as they mature. Unless the public is explicitly convinced that the money spent on public parks is an investment that grows in value, continuing to shape the development of entire metropolitan regions, parks will not receive the attention or the resources they require. Their role is so significant that it is impossible to understand fully the functioning of cities and suburbs or plan adequately for their future without a deep appreciation of parks and the way they affect every aspect of our lives. My aim is to clarify their value by exploring the origins and emergence of public parks and public demand for parks, defining their role and evolution, and examining public parks that function successfully as

ever-increasing investments that are essential to the well-being of all citizens, whether they live in cities or suburbs.

The man to whom this book is dedicated and who designed the earliest public parks in the United States, introduced the principles that still guide park development, and best articulated the role of public parks in metropolitan development was Frederick Law Olmsted (1822–1903), America's first truly professional landscape architect and perhaps the nation's greatest urban and suburban planner. He is best known for designing America's first public park, New York's Central Park, in collaboration with British-born architect Calvert Vaux (1824–1895), but the sum of his work is much more impressive than any single part. Olmsted built the premier landscape architecture and planning practice in the United States and left a remarkable written legacy: more than sixty thousand books, articles, reports, and letters. When he retired in 1895, the firm continued under the management of his son, Frederick Law Olmsted Jr. (1870–1957) and his nephew and stepson, John Charles Olmsted (1852–1920); John Charles was the son of Olmsted's brother, whose widow he married in 1859. The scope of the firm's work is awesome: six thousand projects across North America.

Frederick Law Olmsted by John Singer Sargent (1895)

Olmsted knew that as urban areas grew and parks became increasingly important, they would have to be more and more tightly interlaced with the metropolitan areas they served. He believed that parks "should, as far as possible, complement the town."[2] He conceived of parks as essential components of metropolitan living. That is a metropolitan planner's conception, taking the same comprehensive approach to urban and suburban planning to which I, as a planner, am committed.

More than a century has passed since Olmsted left the scene, yet he remains a towering genius. Nobody has had such a far-reaching effect on public parks. His remarkable legacy has been a continuing source of information and wisdom about parks, cities, suburbs, and their planning. Every chapter in this book includes material from that legacy: details, ideas, insights, attitudes, and observations.

I will also present the work of many other significant players in the American parks movement, and others still who have influenced that movement from abroad. We will look at the major parks in the United States from the nineteenth century until today, and some of the most influential private gardens and public parks in Great Britain, Italy, France, and Germany.

In 1850, when New York City was debating whether to create the nation's first public park, 23 million people lived in the United States, most of them in rural areas. One hundred and fifty years later, the country had become a largely suburban nation of 281 million, with nearly 100 million living in cities and towns with populations larger than 50,000. As the populations of the United States and the world continue to increase, so too will the importance of public parks, especially in the urban areas of the developing world, where most of that population will be concentrated and where investment in public parks has been woefully inadequate.[3]

Like Olmsted, I believe that parks play a major role in enhancing well-being and improving public health, incubating a civil society, sustaining a livable environment, and providing a framework for urbanization. The chapters that follow provide not only a history and description of that evolving role but also the background and information we must understand if we are to create great public parks for generations to come.

Creating parks involves making decisions about location, property acquisition, site adaptation, design, and development, and this book offers different strategies for all these activities. But a park's life really begins when it is opened to the public. Parks are forever changing as they grow and respond to the needs of generations of users, and so I also discuss different approaches to the stewardship, governance, and financing of parks and park systems.

Over the past two centuries public parks have become as central to contemporary life as airports, highways, and all the other components of the world's infrastructure. They constitute assets that must be sustained if we are to benefit from our growing investment. My final chapter is devoted to the ways in which Central Park was designed to be socially, functionally, environmentally, financially, politically, and aesthetically sustainable, and thus presents all the ingredients that go into creating great public parks.

Englische Garten, Munich, 2008. Large sections of this former military garrison were dug up to create a lake. Trees, shrubs, and grass were planted in the manner of the British landscape designer Capability Brown. It is now one of Europe's largest and most successful public parks.

ONE

THE EMERGENCE OF PUBLIC PARKS

Cities have always contained public open spaces that are available to all citizens free of charge. Among the earliest in the United States are the Plaza de la Constitucion in St. Augustine, Florida (1573), the Boston Common (1634), and the New Haven Green (1641). These areas are used today as public parks, although they were not specifically acquired or designed for recreational purposes. In Europe, landscaped estates owned by European royal or noble families have always been referred to as parks, and some of them became the forerunners of today's public parks. These private properties were, and in many cases still are, accessible to the public only on occasion and under circumstances defined by their owners. Most major cities also included royal parks, gardens or hunting preserves that generally were considered to be government-owned and therefore available—at least to a limited degree—to citizens who possessed "customary rights and privileges" of access. Londoners, for example, felt they had the right to use royal parks. In 1726 George II opened Kensington Gardens on Sundays, although "sailors, soldiers, and servants in livery" were excluded.[1] Legend has it that when his wife, Queen Caroline, asked Sir Robert Walpole what it would cost to enclose Kensington Gardens for her personal use, he replied, "Your crown, Ma'am."

Whether royalty, nobility, or commoners, people went to these early parks to have fun. The Tiergarten in Berlin was officially opened in 1649 to the simplest of pleasures: walking. When enough people gathered within privately owned parks, they sometimes sparked the establishment of commercial ventures that supplied them with further amusements. One of the earliest of these amusement-oriented parks emerged in suburban Copenhagen. Bakken, a natural spring at Klampenborg, north of the city, had been discovered in 1583, and by the late seventeenth century businesses sprang up that sold food, drink, and entertainment to visitors who came for the waters. Vauxhall Gardens, established in London in 1661, was initially a private property that charged no admission fee but offered food and drink for sale. Apart from beer gardens, which are still common in many German cities, the most well-known remaining examples of these commercial pleasure gardens are the Prater in Vienna and Tivoli Gardens in Copenhagen.

The Prater was royal hunting ground on the outskirts of the city that was opened to the public in 1766. It began as a place of business for coffeehouses and cafés and evolved into a full-fledged amusement park with a Ferris wheel (built in 1897) and other entertainments. Its popularity is matched only by Tivoli Gardens, which opened in 1843 and, like the Prater, is still in operation. For a price visitors can go to the theater, a café, or a restaurant or enjoy a ride on a carousel or a classic wooden roller coaster.

THE FORERUNNERS

The French Revolution opened France's royal properties to the public, and monarchs throughout Europe were soon under pressure to do the same. Transforming royal gardens and hunting preserves that had been places of recreation for a privileged few into public parks suitable for use by large numbers of people usually required substantial alterations. But two of Paris's most popular parks, the Jardin du Luxembourg and the Jardin des Tuileries, were easy to convert from palace gardens into public parks, and they still look very much as they did when they were first opened for public use. The 63-acre (25.5-ha) site of the Tuileries was occupied by tile kilns, called *tuileries,* from which the park's name derives. Queen Catherine de Medici commissioned a garden to replace them as part of the creation of the Louvre Palace, which began in 1564. Exactly a century later, Louis XIV had landscape designer and gardener André Le Nôtre (1613–1700) lay out the parterres at the Tuileries.

Despite insurrections in 1789, 1830, 1848, and 1871 and additions to and reconstruction of portions of the Louvre, today the Jardin des Tuileries still has the look of its original Le Nôtre design, but it is used in a very different manner. Children sail model boats in the circular pool, which contains a handsome fountain; tourists flock to the museums at the Orangerie and the Galerie Nationale du Jeu de Paume; office workers enjoy a bite to eat or a glass of wine at one of the cafés or kiosks. Here the seventeenth-century design elements (discussed in more detail in chapter 6) of axial vistas, allées of trees, floral parterres, and displays of sculpture coexist quite nicely with contemporary activities.

The Jardin du Luxembourg was created in 1612 for Queen Marie de Medici after she had acquired and remodeled the Luxembourg Palace as her residence. Jacques Boyceau de la Barauderie (1560–1633), the period's most famous designer of *parterre de broderie* (decorative plant or flower patterns cut into geometric shapes), initiated the design of Marie de Medici's formal garden with allées of clipped trees, geometrically shaped pools, and fountains.[2] Here, as in the Tuileries, the formal seventeenth-century design does not impede the park's twenty-first-century success as a well-used civic amenity. Every day the Jardin du Luxembourg attracts thousands of children and their parents, students from the Sorbonne, young couples, tourists, and neighborhood workers and residents. Like the Jardin des Tuileries, the Jardin du Luxembourg enchants visitors with the beauty of its original design, and these parks are all the more popular because central Paris has very little parkland designed specifically for public recreation.

Among public parks that began as the property of the nobility, the 922-acre (373-ha) Englische Garten in Munich, Germany's largest public park, had a most unusual origin. In 1789 Karl Theodor—Prince-Elector, Count Palatine, and Duke of Bavaria—decreed that military gardens be established in all garrison cities, including Munich. The idea was to provide soldiers with peacetime work as farmers and gardeners, as well as opportunities for recre-

Jardin des Tuileries, Paris, 2006. The Jardin de Tuileries, which was once an integral part of a grand palace, has become one of the city's most popular public parks.

Jardin du Luxembourg, Paris, 2005. The axial vistas, geometric floral plantings, and symmetrical organization of this seventeenth-century palace garden have become a cherished retreat for residents and workers in the surrounding neighborhood.

Englische Garten, Munich, 2008. This nineteenth-century German park is a lovely attempt to reproduce an eighteenth-century English garden, itself inspired by the work of Claude Lorrain, a seventeeth-century French artist who painted scenes of the landscape around Rome.

ation. In response to the opening of royal property to the public after the French Revolution, Karl Theodor decided that the garrison complex in Munich should also be opened for public use. The creation of the Englische Garten ultimately involved removing almost all traces of the royal garrison and hunting ground that once occupied the site. The earliest designs were prepared by Sir Benjamin Thompson (1753–1814), an Anglo-American physicist and the inventor of the wax candle, who entered Karl Theodor's service in 1784, and by the German landscape designer Friedrich Ludwig von Sckell (1750–1823).[3]

The existing military facilities, open fields, and woods were hardly touched when the Englische Garten was first opened to the public in 1792; the transformation into a public park took place largely after 1804, when von Sckell was appointed garden supervisor to the Bavarian court. Von Sckell, who had studied landscape gardening in England, sought to create something in the picturesque, naturalistic spirit of England's most famous landscape designer of that time, Lancelot "Capability" Brown (1716–1783). In the decades that followed the park's opening to the public, its boundaries were altered and streams that passed through the site were rerouted. At a strategic spot, a stream was made to look like one of the shallow, gurgling cascades that are common in Brown's work. A field at the far end of the park was dug up to create a large lake. Trees and shrubs were planted to exclude any visible signs of the surrounding city. A "Chinese" pagoda, inspired by the one in Kew Gardens, was added to the landscape in 1790. The architect Leo von Klenze (1784–1864) designed a circular temple, known as the Monopteros, for the park; although it was completed in 1837, it looked like one of the Greek and Roman structures the English nobility built on their estates, inspired by the paintings of Claude Lorrain (1600–1682). These exotic architectural fragments are charming incidental decorations. Most park users ignore them, spending

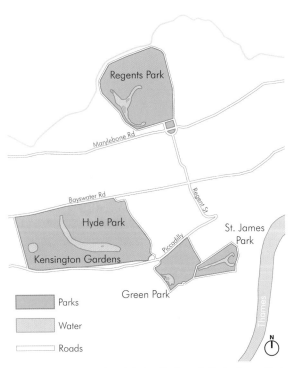

London. The earliest Royal Parks (St. James's Park, Green Park, Hyde Park, Kensington Gardens, and Regent's Park) were acquired by the Crown during the sixteenth and seventeenth centuries.

their time strolling along the paved walkways that wind through the open meadows and wooded scenery, sunning themselves on the manicured lawns, or chatting on benches while they keep an eye on their children playing nearby.

The Royal Parks of London also began as property of the nobility, and they remain so today. Lon-don's royal hunting preserves and gardens were originally managed by His Majesty's Commissioners of Woods and Forests. Since most of the territory owned by the royal family was not fenced in, it was available informally. The royal family retained ownership of these properties, and even today public access is technically a matter of royal grace, but the Crown Lands Act of 1851 transferred management to the government, and they are now managed as fully public facilities by the Royal Parks Agency.[4]

The most important of the royal parks make up a 768-acre (311-ha) complex consisting of St. James's Park (acquired by Henry VIII in 1532), Green Park (acquired by Charles II in 1668), Hyde Park (acquired by Henry VIII in 1536), and Kensington Gardens (acquired by William III and Mary II in 1689). The 487-acre (193-ha) Regent's Park (appropriated by Henry VIII between 1535 and 1539) was leased to the Dukes of Portland as a hunting ground until 1811. These parks underwent major transformations long before they were opened to the general public. In the eighteenth and nineteenth centuries, individuals who paid a fee were permitted to pasture their cows in St. James's Park.[5] Its lake had been marshland that was drained at the start of the seventeenth century, then turned into a Le Nôtre–inspired long, narrow, rectangular canal. In 1826–27 the architect and developer John Nash (1732–1835) remade it into a picturesque lake surrounded by naturalistic plant-

Regent's Park, London, 2007. Sir John Nash designed this park to be the centerpiece of a major real estate venture.

Regent's Park, London, 2007. Today the park provides recreational opportunities for residents of all ages.

ings and meandering walks that enhanced the value of Carlton House Terrace, the residential complex he was developing on royal property on the north side of the park. At the time of this redesign St. James's Park was effectively opened to public use, and soon enough it boasted new concession structures, bandstands, chairs, and benches. Today the lakeside in St. James Park is dotted with people enjoying the park benches or taking an afternoon stroll. Like its counterpart in Regent's Park, the lake has become a favorite spot for feeding ducks.

The lake that Nash created in Regent's Park had never been a long, narrow canal like that of St. James's, and it was therefore much easier to turn into a meandering, picturesque waterway large enough to accommodate a rowboat concession after the park was opened to the public. And unlike St. James's Park, little previous landscaping existed to affect the design of Regent's Park. Four times the size of St. James's, Regent's Park can accommodate broad meadows that make wonderful places for informal ball games, with even enough room for a major zoo.

The lease on what would become Regent's Park was due to expire in 1811. The Prince Regent, later King George IV, saw this as an opportunity to increase revenues from the property and to encourage private development in that part of London. Nash was commissioned to devise a master plan for the area and later for St. James's Park. The scheme he conceived was based on remodeling both parks and connecting them with a new 2-mile (3.2-km) Regent's Street. This investment by the Crown stimulated private real estate development on properties

adjacent to both the parks and the road, including Nash-designed façades for residential terraces.

RISING DEMAND FOR PUBLIC PARKS

As city populations multiplied at the beginning of the nineteenth century, congestion increased and the number of residents living in deplorably crowded and unhealthy conditions soared. The increasingly restive urban populations generated a growing chorus of demand throughout Europe and America for governments to acquire land and create parks for public use. City dwellers were increasing faster than housing could be built for them; manufacturing was growing faster than the infrastructure that was needed to handle its waste. There were too many horse-drawn cargo and passenger vehicles to be easily accommodated by existing traffic arteries. Living conditions were so congested and sanitary practices so primitive that epidemic diseases had become a serious threat.

Contemporary accounts provide grim portrayals of urban life. Charles Dickens described London's slums in an 1837 sketch: "Wretched houses

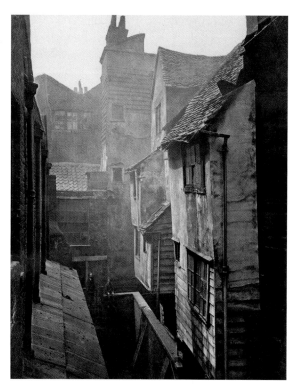

London, 1877. The city's slums were captured in this photograph of buildings in St. Bartholomew's Churchyard.

with broken windows patched with rags and paper; every room let out to a different family, and in many instances to two or even three . . . filth everywhere—a gutter before the houses, and a drain behind—clothes drying, and slops emptying from the windows; . . . men and women, in every variety of scanty and dirty apparel, lounging, scolding, drinking, smoking, squabbling, fighting, and swearing."[6] In 1848 the French writer Henri Lecouturier left a vivid record of the conditions in Paris: "The greatest number of the streets of this marvelous Paris are dirty passages, always damp with pestilent water. . . . A pale and sickly multitude crosses there without respite, the foot in soggy gutters, the nose constantly breathing infection, and the eye hit at each street corner with the most repulsive filth."[7] And fifty-four years later, in 1902, the journalist and photographer Jacob Riis recorded his impressions of New York's slums: "Like nothing I ever saw before, or hope ever to see again . . . rotten structures that harbored the very dregs of humanity . . . pierced by a maze of foul alleys, in the depths of which skulked the tramp and the outcast thief."[8]

One of the earliest responses to such conditions came from the British Parliament, which in 1833 appointed the Select Committee for Public Walks to "consider the best means of securing Open Spaces in the vicinity of populous towns as Public Walks and Places of Exercise, calculated to promote the Health and Comfort of the Inhabitants."[9] Their report recommended public parks as a means of improving public health, reducing antisocial behavior, and offering a place for leisure activities: "It is of the first

importance to [the] health [of the working classes] on their day of rest to enjoy fresh air, and to be able (exempt from the dust and dirt of the public thoroughfares) to walk out in decent comfort with their families; if deprived of any such resource, it is probable that their only escape from the narrow courts and alleys (in which so many of the humble classes reside) will be drinking-shops, where, in short-lived excitement, . . . they waste the means of their families, and too often destroy their health."[10]

Today, when urban conditions in much of the developed world have been significantly improved, it easy to underestimate how large a role public concern played in developing a constituency for public parks. When the clamor for parks arose, few people expected these conditions to disappear in their lifetimes, but they were insistent that government provide a way for people to escape such a deplorable environment. Public parks acquired and designed for recreational purposes could provide that escape. The earliest of them emerged in Great Britain in the 1840s, and they were soon followed by ambitious projects in Paris and New York, and before long throughout Europe and the Americas.

THE EARLIEST PUBLIC PARKS
IN GREAT BRITAIN

Before the Royal Parks in central London were entirely opened to the public, intense demand for additional recreation facilities forced the creation of the first such facility developed by England's national government: Victoria Park. London's existing green spaces, owned either by the Crown or by private estates, were all concentrated in wealthy sections of the city's West End. The East End, with its widespread poverty, air pollution, and inadequate sanitation, had no open public space. So dire was the situation that more than thirty thousand East End residents signed a petition to the Queen in 1840 demanding a public park.

Parliament responded by enacting a law that instructed the government to sell York House and use the proceeds to acquire property on which to create an East End park, named in honor of Queen Victoria. His Majesty's Commissioners of Woods

New York City, 1890. Jacob Riis's photojournalism depicted the city's squalid and decaying tenements as "Dens of Death."

London, 2007. Victoria Park provided residents of London's East End with recreational opportunities, but initially it failed to draw real estate development to the surrounding neighborhoods.

and Forests quickly acquired 290 acres (117 ha), 193 acres (78 ha) for the park and the rest for resale to developers in order to cover much of the park's cost. But virtually none of the sites found buyers, because well-to-do residents and prosperous businesses wanted to be in the West End. It took more than a century for that to start changing.

Victoria Park was designed by James Pennethorne (1801–1871), who had learned his trade working with John Nash. His original design of 1841 included an elaborate entry sequence with a large public square and formal entryway. Investment in the park itself was minimal, however: open lawns, clumps of trees, and roadways that provided access and circulation. By the time construction finally started in 1844, Pennethorne had simplified the design and added a central drive and two lakes. We can't know for certain that Victoria Park improved the health of the working-class residents who lived in surrounding neighborhoods or diverted them from antisocial activity, but it seems likely that it did. And the park certainly provided a popular place of recreation at no cost to a population that had little money to pay for much more than the necessities of life—and it still does.

In 1839, while British public officials were still considering how to provide recreation facilities and before the establishment of Victoria Park, Joseph Strutt (1765–1844), a wealthy resident of Derby,

decided to donate an 11-acre (4.5-ha) public park to his town. He hired the Scottish botanist, landscape architect, and writer on landscape design John Claudius Loudon (1783–1843) to design a landscape that would display a wide array of trees and shrubs that were arranged and described for visitors to the park.

Strutt had more than an arboretum in mind. He wanted the park to "offer the inhabitants of the town the opportunity of enjoying, with their families, exercise, and recreation in the fresh air, in public walks and grounds devoted to that purpose."[11] Loudon devised an ingenious design for the public use of a relatively small site. He created a series of linear walks that zigzagged back on one another, similar to the approach now used for many golf courses. To keep strollers from realizing how close they were to the perimeter and to fellow strollers on nearby paths, Loudon lined the paths with berms that were planted with labeled specimen trees and shrubs that helped to maintain privacy.[12]

The opening of the Derby Arboretum was a grand three-day celebration for 1,500 invited guests on the first day, 9,000 on the second, and another 6,000 on the third—an astonishingly large number given that the town's population was only 35,000. Yet in its day-to-day operations the Derby Arboretum was not freely open to the public; it was available five days a week to subscribers who paid an annual fee,

Derby, 2007. The design of the Derby Arboretum provides contiguous, parallel walks that are designed to function independently of one another.

or to visitors who paid an entrance fee (half-price for children).[13]

Birkenhead, a suburban town located directly across the Mersey River from the booming industrial city of Liverpool, was the first city authorized by the British Parliament to acquire land for a park designed specifically for recreation and legally open to the public at no charge. The town's leaders wanted to exploit potential growth made possible by the opening of steam ferry service with Liverpool in 1820. In 1833 they persuaded Parliament to enact a law establishing the Birkenhead Improvement Commission to plan the town's expansion. At the time Birkenhead was one-tenth the size of Derby and less than one-fiftieth the size of Liverpool.[14]

But Birkenhead was growing rapidly, and the commission pressed for public action to create a park. It argued that the more organized the town's response to growth and the better it provided for the welfare of the population, "the greater the amount of health and happiness."[15] The importance of parks to health, ethi-

cal conduct, and civil social intercourse may have been the enunciated public policy rationale, but the desire for orderly real estate development and the tax revenues that came with it may have been even more important. The commission achieved its objective in 1843, when Parliament authorized it to purchase land for a park.

The commissioners chose Sir Joseph Paxton (1803–1865) to design the park. Paxton had received his training as a gardener at Chiswick and in 1832 became chief gardener for the Chatsworth

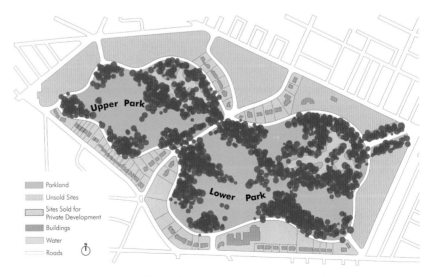

Parkland
Unsold Sites
Sites Sold for Private Development
Buildings
Water
Roads

Birkenhead Development Plan. This park was designed to spur real estate development in the suburbs of Liverpool. Many of the lots encircling the park were sold for residential development; unsold lots were added to the park or used for other public purposes.

Birkenhead, 2008. The section of this park devoted to Goth Rock and the Lower Lake provide the rough, irregular, "sublime" landscape that is a stark contrast to the open meadows of the rest of the park.

estate, where he experimented with glass greenhouses. After Birkenhead, Paxton created parks for Liverpool and other cities, but he is best remembered today for designing the Crystal Palace for the Great Exhibition of 1851 in London. The commission purchased a 226-acre (91-ha) site, which Paxton thought was "not a very good situation for a park as the land is generally poor."[16] His solution was to create an Upper Park that was separated by a through street from the Lower Park. He excavated small meandering lakes in each of them, using the fill for tree-covered berms that concealed each lake from the flat meadowland that occupied most of the site. Visitors coming to the Upper Lake from the north and west had to pass through awe-inducing piles of boulders darkened by a thick tree canopy. As one walks through the trees surrounding the Lower Lake, views of the lake open up, often enliv-

ened by exotic bridges and pavilions. Trees also conceal the view of the open meadows and lakes at the points of entry to the park, the most important of which includes a large and elaborate columned gateway arch.

While Paxton's design was interesting as a combination of the softer picturesque landscape aesthetic made popular by Capability Brown with the darker, rougher notion of the picturesque in the style of the designer Humphry Repton (discussed in greater detail in chapter 6), the park's relationship to the surrounding community is of more central importance. Paxton's plan subdivided 101 acres (41 ha) of the site into 212 building lots, some for single-family villas and some for attached residences, like the "terrace" housing that surrounded London's Regent's Park but much smaller. As at Regent's Park, a circumferential roadway separated the park from residential property, whose occupants had the illusion that the park across the street was their personal estate garden.

As had been the plan for Victoria Park, the commission intended to pay for the cost of acquiring and creating the park by selling building lots, whose value would have increased because of their proximity to the park. It placed a restriction on the houses that could be built on those lots; they had to have a minimum rental value of £70 per year, thereby determining the value of the land, the quality of the houses, and the minimum amount of tax revenue that could be expected. The commission held two auctions, but by 1846 only half the lots had been sold, mostly for villas. Eventually, property that could not be sold was added to the park.

Birkenhead, 2008. The circumferential roadway provides access to both the park and the houses built around it.

Birkenhead was a less-than-successful real estate development vehicle, and its design had little impact on future parks, but it had enormous influence as the first property acquired by a local government and designed for public recreation that was universally accessible at no charge. It attracted visitors from around the world, and as a result civic leaders now had to recognize and satisfy the demand for similar facilities throughout Europe and America.

HAUSSMANN'S PARIS

Birkenhead Park, Derby Arboretum, and even Victoria Park were limited, incremental investments that provided facilities for the growing populations in those areas. The French government, under the reign of Emperor Napoleon III, took a much more radical approach: it embarked on a massive program to accommodate more than one million new residents within the city of Paris and provide them with a much-improved quality of life. The man responsible for that program was Baron Georges-Eugène Haussmann (1809–1891), who transformed an overcrowded, poorly functioning medieval city into an expanding modern industrial metropolis by eliminating health hazards and other impediments to urbanization and simultaneously creating entirely new streets, squares, parks, and open spaces that became the framework around which private development thrived. Haussmann demonstrated how to use public open space, especially parks, as the central feature of a vast urban redevelopment effort, using parks to provide major incentives for the urbanization of Paris, structure its development, relieve congestion throughout the city, and make available recreation opportunities for a population that would otherwise be without them.

Since the late eighteenth century France has been divided into administrative districts known as departments. After graduating from law school, Haussmann worked for fifteen years in these departments, either as subprefect or prefect (the equivalent of a state governor). In 1853 Napoleon III appointed him prefect of the Seine, the department that managed Paris. Over the next seventeen years, he transformed the city. His high-handed methods were controversial from the start and eventually led to the termination of his prefecture in 1870. Robert Moses (1889–1981), New York City's no less controversial parks commissioner

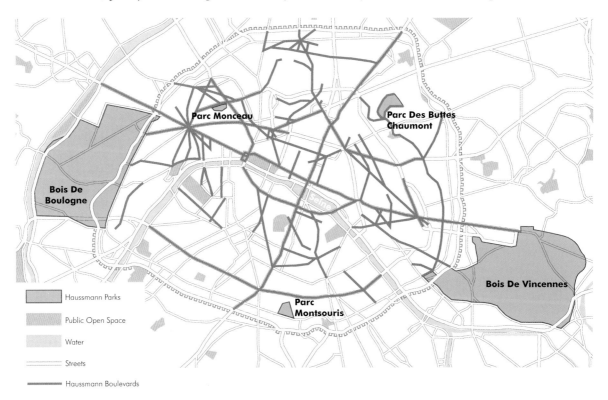

Haussmann's Park System, Paris. The complex of tree-lined boulevards connecting local squares and large parks has provided the framework for development for the past century and a half.

Paris, 2008. The framework of boulevards that Haussmann initiated created a public realm that altered the character of daily life throughout Paris.

during the middle of the twentieth century, understood better than many observers what Haussmann accomplished. He wrote that when Haussmann began his work Paris was "a medieval city to which a sophisticated modern population was struggling to accommodate itself" and that "Haussmann's great merit lay in the fact that he was both able and willing to grasp the entire problem. . . . It was Haussmann's task to open up, interconnect and extend [and provide] modern thoroughfares properly graded, sewered, lighted and planted, of adequate width to accommodate traffic requirements of the ever-growing capital."[17]

Market demand for residential and commercial property climbed in tandem with the city's population, which soared from 1.05 million in 1851 to 1.99 million in 1876.[18] Haussmann reasoned that public investment in infrastructure would increase the value of nearby private property. He used that public investment to reshape Paris by creating an entirely new public realm, which he acquired and financed using two techniques to capture a portion of the induced increase in property values: excess property condemnation and tax increment financing.[19]

Haussmann's approach consisted of four elements: transforming two huge Crown properties into large regional parks; establishing three substantial district parks; creating twenty-four "squares" that became neighborhood parks;[20] and connecting a network of tree-lined boulevards with these facilities. The Bois de Boulogne (2,090 acres [846 ha]) on the western side of the city and the Bois de Vincennes (2,458 acres [995 ha]) on its eastern

side provide the broadest range of recreation opportunities—everything from a walk in the woods to a day at the races. The three district parks, the Parc Monceau (20.3 acres [8.2 ha]), the Parc des Buttes-Chaumont (62 acres [25 ha]), and the Parc Montsouris (37 acres [15 ha]), supply recreation facilities that were almost nonexistent before Haussmann began his work and are now considered an essential part of city life. Each of the squares, which range in size from 0.25 to 6.5 acres (0.1–2.6 ha), has taken on the character of the surrounding neighborhood and provides places to sit, walk, and play that are tailored to the desires of the people who live, work, and do business in surrounding buildings. While the boulevards were meant to provide easy access to all these facilities, they also became recreation destinations in their own right, where people go window shopping, stroll, meet friends, or linger in a café sipping wine and watching the world go by.

The two large regional parks—the Bois de Boulogne and the Bois de Vincennes—contain many

Bois de Vincennes, Paris, 2008. The Route Dauphine is one of the park's many axial roadways, vestigial remnants that are of little use to contemporary Parisians.

long, straight, tree-lined promenades similar to those in London's Green Park and Hyde Park. In London they were initially planted in the seventeenth and eighteenth centuries and are still happily used today for access to these busy public parks. When the Bois de Boulogne and the Bois de Vincennes were converted into public parks, however, the similarly long, straight, tree-lined routes that crisscrossed them proved to be less user-friendly than those of the royal hunting preserves in London. Green and Hyde Parks were in the center of the city, and their tree-lined allées became busy pedestrian corridors providing shortcuts to popular greensward destinations. In contrast, the two large Bois in Paris were on the far eastern and western ends of town, and some of their tree-lined allées became busy vehicular thoroughfares to the city's central commercial districts. Others are pedestrian routes that provide few opportunities for park users to enjoy different views of the park. In the two London parks, most of the remaining space has been kept open and consistently altered to make it more people-friendly, but in the Bois much of the territory between the diagonal roadways is thickly forested with underbrush that provides a wonderful haven for small animals but leaves no room for people. In other ways, however, both the Bois de Boulogne

Lac Daumesnil, Bois de Vincennes, Paris, 2008. Haussmann and Alphand made improvements to the park that have become popular recreational destinations for Parisians.

and the Bois de Vincennes emulate their London counterparts. They have popular playing fields and flower gardens that have been continually adjusted to meet the changing demands of the city's population. Their picturesque, English-inspired lakes, created at the behest of Napoleon III, are as popular as those in London's Royal Parks. And they include one facility that does not exist in the London parks: horse-racing tracks.

Haussmann also demonstrated that government policies can improve an area by eliminating deleterious conditions that restrict growth. When he began his work, one of the reasons the northeast sections of Paris were uninviting territory for development

Bois de Boulogne, Paris, 2008. At the suggestion of Napoleon III, large sections of the park were transformed into landscapes inspired by the parks and gardens of England.

Paris, 2006. The raw walls of the quarry at Buttes-Chaumont were relandscaped and given a dramatic lake setting that is popular with twenty-first-century Parisians.

was the existence of a fetid, vermin-infested night-soil dump and abandoned gypsum and limestone quarry known as Les Buttes-Chaumont. Haussmann worked with Jean-Charles-Adolphe Alphand (1817–1891), the city's street engineer, to transform this unsightly gash in a hillside into a 62-acre (25-ha) park that became a major neighborhood asset. They used the exposed rock as a dramatic landscape feature, adding artificial rockwork to make it still more dramatic. At the bottom of the cliff they created a lake, fed by two artificial streams whose water came from city canals. One of the streams took the form of gurgling cascades of water spraying off boulders that were placed there for the purpose. At the top of the cliff, a suspension bridge leads to a romantic version of the Temple of Vesta at Hadrian's Villa in Tivoli, outside Rome. But these dramatic, man-made features are only a part of the reason for the park's success. Its designers were able to create a landscaped hillside with paths, descending from rue Botzaris to the lake below. Far more important, its lovely grass-covered slopes became favorite spots for sunbathing, picnicking, or tossing a ball around.

By the time the Parc des Buttes-Chaumont opened in 1867, it had cost 6.4 million francs.[21] The Bois de Boulogne, which was thirty-four times as large, had cost only 3.5 million (after recouping 10.9 million from the sale of excess property along the perimeter that had become far more valuable because of the park's creation).[22] But because the Parc des Buttes-Chaumont was located in a section of Paris largely inhabited by working-class residents who could not afford new construction, it did not attract developers and had nothing like the impact of the Bois de Boulogne. It did, however, provide a remarkable resource for a population that had few other recreation opportunities.

In redeveloping the 9th and 10th arrondissements (city districts), Haussmann created a net-

Paris, 2006. During the summertime, neighborhood residents picnic and sunbathe on the slopes of the Parc des Buttes-Chaumont.

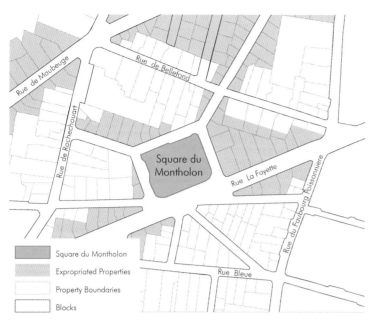

Paris. Haussmann had to acquire entire properties in order to create streets like the rue La Fayette. He sold the unneeded portions of the lots to real estate developers and kept some for small neighborhood parks like the Square du Montholon.

Map labels: Rue de Maubeuge, Rue de Bellefond, Rue de Rochechouart, Square du Montholon, Rue La Fayette, Rue du Faubourg Poissonniere, Rue Bleue

Legend: Square du Montholon / Expropriated Properties / Property Boundaries / Blocks

work of streets and squares providing access to two railroad stations (the Gare du Nord and the Gare de L'Est), the shopping district emerging along what is now called the Boulevard Haussmann, the Opera, and the Canal St. Martin. Building wide, straight streets, like rue La Fayette, required cutting through a crazy quilt of narrow roads, dark alleys, and old, often decrepit properties. Haussmann and his colleagues understood that the area needed more than a street network to become a desirable neighborhood, so wherever possible they used some of the excess property to create small neighborhood parks. And to avoid a traffic nightmare where rue La Fayette crossed other streets, they seized the opportunity (as did Robert Moses in New York a century later) to create small parks at these intersections. At the Square de Montholon, for example, delivery vehicles, public transport, private carriages, and horses from six streets terminated at a new park, and from there traffic was neatly sorted out and directed around the square.

Creating a new street inevitably involved acquiring more land than was actually needed. For rue La Fayette, for example, the entire property within the right-of-way had to be taken, resulting in the acquisition of land beyond what was necessary for the street itself. Once these properties had been acquired, the city demolished existing buildings,

installed sewers and water mains, paved the street, planted trees, and installed street lights. In the process, Haussmann ended up with excess property that included development sites facing the new streets and squares. Because they faced newly created open space and tree-lined arteries, these sites now sold for more than the city had paid for them, and the profits covered part of the cost of creating the new district.

The sale of excess property was not enough to cover the cost of creating the street, but this increase in value of all the property on either side of the right-of-way helped to make up the difference. Each property in the district paid more in taxes; sites facing the new park were worth still more and paid even higher taxes. Within a few years the additional taxes would more than cover the cost of land acquisition and public improvements. Haussmann was able to promise bankers that this annual increase in taxes would provide an income stream that would cover debt service on the bonds that financed the area's redevelopment and new infrastructure.

The Square de Montholon is just over an acre (0.4 ha) in size, yet it is a very actively used park. During most of the day it is filled with elderly people sitting on benches, parents supervising children in the playground, and people walking their dogs or just strolling. Since it is located in a mixed-use district, at lunchtime it is overflowing with young adults taking a break from their jobs to eat lunch, smoke a cigarette, read a book, or engage in conversation.

Paris, 2007. In the late afternoon, grandparents and parents watch small children enjoying the playground in the Square du Montholon.

Paris, 2008. At lunchtime the Square du Montholon is filled with workers and students enjoying conversations, sandwiches, and a smoke in the park.

Like so many of the twenty-four squares Haussmann added to the city, this small park contributes to the quality of life in the neighborhood.

Haussmann demonstrated that government could play a major role in developing sections of a city by eliminating blighting influences on property development and creating desirable destinations that made that property more attractive for private development. It is a strategy that subsequent city planners found useful ever since.

NEW YORK CITY'S CENTRAL PARK

The emergence of these first public parks specifically acquired and designed for recreational purposes was big news in the mid-nineteenth century. In 1850 a twenty-eight-year-old American journalist who visited the recently opened Birkenhead Park reported in astonishment that "this magnificent pleasure-ground is entirely, unreservedly, and forever the people's own. The poorest British peasant is as free to enjoy it in all its parts as the British Queen."[23]

Birkenhead Park may have been news, but its establishment was not surprising. And just as in Europe, the demand for public parks was growing in the United Sates. In 1851 Savannah set aside 10 acres (4 ha) for Forsyth Park (the park was later doubled in size, but it is still tiny in comparison with the 843 acres [341 ha] of Central Park). William Cullen Bry-

ant publicly advocated a large public park for New York City in the *Evening Post* in 1844. He was not alone. It became a campaign issue in the mayoral election of 1850, which was won by Ambrose Kingsland. As mayor, Kingsland used rhetoric reminiscent of England's Select Committee for Public Walks to advocate for new parks: "There are thousands who pass the day of rest among the idle and dissolute in porter-houses or in places more objectionable, who would rejoice in being enabled to breathe pure air in such a [park], while they ride and drive through its avenues free from . . . noise, dust, and confusion."[24]

The city's leaders decided that the best way to attract real estate development in underbuilt sections of the city was to invest in a single huge site, one that was more than four times the size of Victoria Park in London and nearly eight times the size of Birkenhead Park: the future Central Park. Before deciding on its development, the city's Board of Park Commissioners needed somebody to take care of the property. In September 1857 it hired Frederick Law Olmsted, the very same journalist who had written in amazement about the free public park in Birkenhead, as superintendent of the several hundred laborers already at work on the site. He reported to the park's engineer-in-chief, Egbert Veile (1825–1902), who had completed a survey of the property and proposed a development plan that Olmsted thought was inadequate. In October 1857, when the new park's board of commissioners announced a design competition for Central

Park, architect Calvert Vaux approached Olmsted and suggested that they collaborate on a plan, which they submitted in April. The "Greensward" design by Olmsted and Vaux was selected out of the thirty-three submissions received.

When they entered the competition, neither man had designed a public park. Vaux, though a practicing architect, had little experience with landscape design. Olmsted had even less. When he had applied for and obtained the job of superintendent of Central Park, he had exaggerated his qualifications by writing that he had spent "ten years . . . in the direction and superintendence of agricultural laborers and gardeners in the vicinity of New York," and that he had visited the large parks of Europe, where he gave "special attention to police details and the employment of labor."[25]

Both undoubtedly knew about Birkenhead and Derby. Reformers from all over the world had been visiting these parks to learn what a public park was and how it was managed and maintained. Olmsted had been to Birkenhead in 1850, and he visited Derby in 1859, after the development of Central Park was already under way. We do not know whether Vaux had seen these parks before coming to America. We do know that when the American landscape designer Andrew Jackson Downing (1815–1852) hired Vaux in 1850, they sailed together to America from Liverpool, and they may well have taken the ferry to visit nearby Birkenhead.[26] Olmsted was certainly impressed by the open, public character of Birkenhead Park, but very little else about it seems to have influenced the design of Central Park. The circumferential roadway is inside Central Park, where it acts as a recreational artery providing views of the scenery, very different from the roadway encircling Birkenhead Park, which separates the private residential development from the park, providing access to the general public and glimpses of what parkgoers would experience as they went through the park.

Olmsted and Vaux were more influenced by eighteenth-century English and seventeenth-cen-

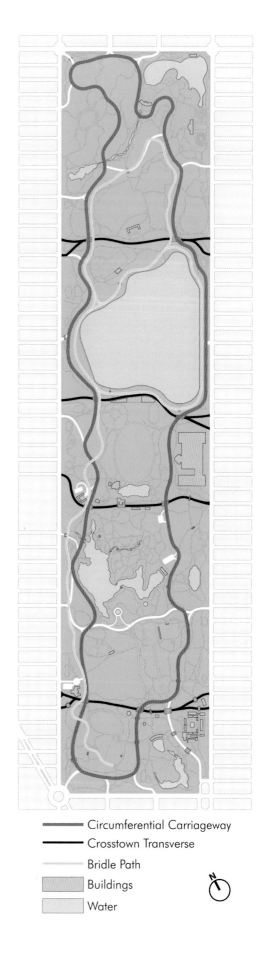

New York City. Olmsted and Vaux devised four carefully separated circulation systems for Central Park: a circumferential carriageway, four crosstown transverses, a bridle path, and plenty of pedestrian walks.

Circumferential Carriageway
Crosstown Transverse
Bridle Path
Buildings
Water

N

New York City, 1894 and 2009. Gondola rides and recreational rowing have been favorite activities for thousands of people since Central Park opened.

tury French garden design aesthetics, but the main difference between Central Park and the estate gardens and royal properties that were converted for public use is fundamental. The paved areas in those European gardens were conceived to meet the owner's objectives. From its inception Central Park was designed to be used by tens of thousands of people. Its paved areas follow what Olmsted and Vaux thought would be the routes most visitors would likely follow on a walk or ride—what we call today *desire lines*. The waterways in the earliest European parks were intended as scenery for the pleasure of those who wandered through grounds that were essentially designed to look like a traditional garden, whether English or French in character. The four meandering waterways in Central Park can certainly be thought of as scenery, but they were also specifically designed for fishing, boating, and ice-skating by large numbers of people. On the largest of these lakes, which covers 20 acres (8 ha), visitors can rent rowboats and experience the park in a very different manner.

Central Park was admired in Europe, but in the United States it played a more vital role in the emergence of the public park. Civic leaders who had been demanding the creation of public parks in Philadelphia, Chicago, St. Louis, and virtually everywhere else argued that they needed something at least as good as Central Park if they were to compete for businesses seeking new locations and for the millions of people migrating around the country. That effort has continued for more than one hundred and fifty years, and as a result nearly 10 percent of the area of most U.S. cities is now devoted to parks.[27]

Minneapolis, 2009. Residents travel from all over the city to enjoy the many different recreational activities offered at Lake Harriet Park.

TWO

KEY ROLES

Over the past two centuries public parks have become an important part of the complex, modern metropolitan infrastructure that supports the physical, social, and mental health of an entire region. They accommodate various habitats and ecosystems, help to improve air and water quality and maintain habitable temperatures, and provide a framework around which metropolitan development takes place. Public parks are not preserved portions of the natural environment that have always been there; they are human artifacts that are explicitly created for recreational purposes. But they serve many less obvious purposes as well, and they affect the very character of daily urban life. These functions include enhancing personal well-being, incubating a civil society, sustaining a livable environment, and providing a framework for urbanization.

IMPROVING PERSONAL WELL-BEING AND PUBLIC HEALTH

Frederick Law Olmsted believed that well-being depends on enjoying two very different characteristics of public parks: the refreshing and tranquilizing effect of immersion in nature, and easily available opportunities for recreational exercise—what we now sometimes call passive and active recreation. On the benefits of passive recreation, Olmsted observed that "if we had no relief from [the town] at all during our waking hours, we should all be conscious of suffering from it. It is upon our opportunities of relief from it, therefore, that not only our comfort in town life, but our ability to maintain a temperate, good-natured, and healthy state of mind depends."[1]

Olmsted was the earliest park designer to articulate the restorative effect of natural scenery, but these ideas had been generally accepted for centuries. Royal families throughout Europe regularly opened their estate gardens for the enjoyment of selected guests. For average citizens, however, there were few opportunities for relaxation or exercise. Most people worked more than sixty hours per week, with only Sundays free. The typical household consisted of five or six people living in a cramped dwelling, often shared with other families. They spent most of their waking hours at physically demanding jobs, and they had few choices to occupy what little leisure time they had.

By the middle of the nineteenth century, early forms of baseball, football, and other games were popular, but organized sports were just beginning to appear. In 1870, when Olmsted and Vaux designed 372-acre (151-ha) Washington Park in Chicago, they included for the first time in any American park 100 acres (40 ha) of flat ground specifically set aside

St. James's Park, London, 1783 and 2007. *The Mall in St. James's Park,* by Thomas Gainsborough, depicts upper-classes Londoners mingling in the natural setting provided by this Crown property. Now that the park is open to the public free of charge, it is used for recreational purposes by people of every age, income, and class.

for sports. They believed that this ground should not serve a single function. It had to be usable for all "athletic sports, such as baseball, football . . . and others which are liable to come again much more in fashion."[2] Today, when ball fields proliferate, this does not seem unusual, but it was an innovation at that time. More amazingly, when Olmsted and Vaux designed Washington Park, they explicitly

set aside parkland for people who had not yet been born and forms of exercise and activities that were not yet widely popular or would not be invented—or imported to the United States—until well into the next century. They would have been pleased, but not surprised, to find during a Saturday morning in July 2008 that the flat ground in Washington Park was filled with South Asian–Americans in white uniforms playing cricket.

Different forms of exercise come into and go out of fashion; the challenge is to design a park that can be adapted to whatever activities might be in style at any particular time. In 1924, when Houston acquired 1,466 acres (593 ha) on the outskirts of the city in order to create Memorial Park, jogging was not a popular form of exercise. Eighty-five years later, on a typical Saturday, residents from all over Houston drive to the park to join the crowds on the 2.88-mile (4.63-km) Seymour Lieberman Exercise Trail. Memorial Park accommodates 3.65 million joggers annually, plus 75,000 softball players, 64,000 golfers, 46,000 off-road cyclists, and tens of thousands of others engaged in every form of exercise.[3]

Early parks advocates in England and the United States believed that the presence of a park would promote exercise and thus help people avoid disease. And since many city dwellers were no longer engaged in physical activities such as farming and hunting, it became a common belief that they needed an outlet for their accumulated tensions and so required a place for physical exercise. Consequently, during the 1820s physical education became part of the curriculum of many universities, and gymnastic societies, patterned after German *turnvereins* (gymnastic clubs), were founded in most big cities.

American reformers, who were among the most vociferous advocates of public parks, were also determined to provide facilities specifically designed to counteract the worst conditions of slum life. Jacob Riis (1849–1914), the Danish-born writer, photographer, and muckraking journalist, made parks a major component in his arsenal of weapons to battle the slum. He was twenty-two when he came to the United States, where he reported on slum conditions for the *New York Tribune* and *New York Evening Sun.* Riis published fifteen books, and the most famous of them, *How the Other Half Lives,* is still required reading in urban affairs courses.

Chicago, 2008. Washington Park was the first park in the United States to include fields of flexible design that can accommodate any competitive sport.

Like most reformers of the period, Riis believed that living conditions determined people's behavior, good or bad: "The child is a creature of environment, of opportunity, as children are everywhere. And the environment here has been bad."[4] He vividly described the problems children faced because of the absence of a safety valve for their exuberant energy: "In a Cherry Street hallway I came across this sign in letters a foot long: 'No ballplaying, dancing, card playing.' ... Out in the street the policeman saw to it that the ball playing at least was stopped, and as for dancing, that, of course, was bound to collect a crowd, the most heinous offence known to him

Memorial Park, Houston, 2007. The Seymour Lieberman Exercise Trail has become one of the most popular recreation destinations in the city.

as a preserver of the peace."[5] Jane Addams, who in 1889 cofounded Chicago's Hull House, one of the first settlement houses in the United States, wrote that "to fail to provide for the recreation of youth, is not only to deprive all of them of their natural form of expression, but is certain to subject some of them to the overwhelming temptation of illicit and soul-destroying pleasures."[6]

Municipal playgrounds as we know them today did not yet exist. In 1872 Brookline, Massachusetts, probably became the first city to vote funds for the establishment of playgrounds. With the passage of the Small Parks Act in 1887 by the New York State legislature, the provision of places of exercise became an explicitly legitimate function of government. The act established that the taking property for the purpose of creating places for exercise and play was public use, thus empowering government to acquire property for the creation of small parks.

Boston followed suit, commissioning the Olmsted firm to design five small park-playgrounds during the 1890s. Between 1903 and 1905 the South Park Commission in Chicago hired the architectural firm D. H. Burnham & Co., along with Olmsted Brothers, to create ten small parks with playground equipment, wading pools, and field houses. By 1960 New York City had 777 playgrounds. Ultimately

Manhattan, c. 1889. When Jacob Riis photographed Mulberry Bend on the Lower East Side, it was one of the city's most notorious slums.

these neighborhood facilities became so widespread that their existence was taken for granted. With the proliferation of playgrounds, efforts shifted to improving their design. Until the 1960s playground equipment meant swings, slides, sandboxes, seesaws, and jungle gyms, but soon the trend became brightly colored structures made of sturdy but user-friendly materials formed into unusual shapes that encouraged adventure but reduced the chances that children might hurt themselves while playing.

Exercise in playgrounds probably improved the health of the children and young adults who used them. Numerous studies have tracked the decline of disease and increase in life expectancy between 1880 and 1950, but it is difficult to prove that in places where public parks were created, parks were the most important factor in improving the health

Bronx, New York City, 2000. The playground at Pelham Park is typical of the swings, slides, and seesaws that Robert Moses, the city's parks commissioner, installed in the hundreds of playgrounds he added to neighborhoods throughout the boroughs.

of neighborhood residents. Settlement houses established in slum neighborhoods also provided day care services for children of working mothers, healthy food from a community kitchen, and medical care from visiting nurses. Surely the decline in poverty and the increase in available leisure time had a major effect. Nevertheless, it seems common sense that parks contributed to the improvement in public health, if only because of their positive effect on air and water quality.

While the problems of nineteenth-century slums are largely behind us, a new generation of health problems has arisen. The U.S. Department of Health and Human Services reports that 300,000 people die each year in the United States from health conditions that are related to diet and an inactive lifestyle. Dr. Eve E. Slater, formerly U.S. assistant secretary for health, notes that "a sedentary lifestyle contributes to serious chronic health conditions, such as cardiovascular disease, type 2 diabetes, certain cancers, and overweight and obesity." Her views are echoed by Dr. Woodie Kessel, formerly assistant U.S. surgeon general, who explains that physical activity is of key importance because of the "benefits that being active provides for preventing a range of diseases, reducing the severity of suffering, and promoting health."[7]

For these reasons, Kessel and others maintain that parks have become a necessary part of twenty-first-century life, whether in suburbs or cities. As Kessel notes, parks "not only provide a place to throw a ball, toss a Frisbee, ride on a swing, chase a butterfly, and be physically active, but they also provide a haven, a refuge, a healthy environment to play with our children, our families, and friends . . . preventing a range of diseases, reducing the severity of suffering, and promoting health. Another added benefit is that [parks] are special places to improve our mental health as well."[8]

Obviously, the public today agrees with this emphasis on the importance of physical exercise, at least in theory. Private health clubs and gyms have become a major business in the United States; according to the International Health, Racquet and Sportsclub Association, between 1990 and 2006 the number of health club members in the United States rose from 20 million to 41 million.[9] Outdoors, people can be seen cycling, skating, and jogging every-

San Francisco, 2000. Contemporary playground equipment offers a wide range of adventures for small children.

where—in parks, on bike baths, and in facilities like the popular Katy Trail in Dallas.

But again, proving that physical health is improved by the presence of parkland is another matter. We know that exercise improves health, and exercise can certainly take place in parks. But it does not follow that public parks make people healthier. Public health advocates have a much tougher problem. Many variables other than the quantity or quality of parkland, such as diet, access to medical services, and so forth, may be the cause of changes in public health.

A 2008 quantitative study of the impact of parks on physical health examined children with attention deficit hyperactivity disorder (ADHD). Researchers found that although they were unable to identify the specific park characteristics (such as greenness, open space, or lack of buildings) that

were responsible, "children who walked for 20 minutes through a park had an improvement in attention vs. those who took a walk through a less 'green' area—a neighborhood or downtown area."[10]

Yet even without such quantitative evidence it seems obvious that public parks have a beneficial

Dallas, 2006. The Katy Trail is one of many contemporary recreational facilities that offer opportunities for jogging, inline skating, and bicycling.

impact on public health. Certainly the nineteenth-century reformers combating overcrowded slums were convinced that this was true. In the twenty-first century, when there is much concern about diseases that result from a sedentary lifestyle, public health advocates also believe that parks have an important role to play.

INCUBATING A CIVIL SOCIETY

Well designed and managed public parks are among the very few places where people of every class, race, and income come together, in Olmsted's words, "with a common purpose, not at all intellectual, competitive with none, disposing to jealousy and spiritual or intellectual pride toward none, each individual adding by his mere presence to the pleasure of all others."[11] Parks play a vital role as social mixing valves for an ever-increasing number and variety of people. Each set of users can enjoy the park even as an always-changing combination of other users enjoy it every bit as much.

Central Park worked exactly that way when it was opened to the public in the early 1860s. Olmsted predicted that as the population increased, the park would become ever more popular and play an ever more important part in people's lives. On a typical Sunday in May 1872, when 942,000 people lived in Manhattan, he reported that over 70,000 people entered Central Park.[12] He wrote that they were "but a small fraction of those who must be expected to visit thereafter," and he was right.[13] In May 2007, when Manhattan's population had grown to 1.62 million, the count on a typical Sunday was 200,000 people, 20 to 25 percent of whom were from outside the New York metropolitan area.[14]

People make friends in parks. An American women who lived in Paris for many years told me that when she first arrived she started going to the local park with her young daughter, and within a few days she had made friends with another family who brought their equally young son to play there. She quickly discovered that she always could find someone in the park to sit with. Within weeks, these parents with young children had become an increasing circle of her friends. But parents are not the only

Central Park, New York City, 2006. Thousands of people find ways of sharing the park with others who have come there for quite different reasons.

people who make friends in the park. Teenagers go to parks to join a pick-up baseball team, adults bring their pets to the dog walk, chess-players seek partners at the outdoor tables—in fact, it happens to almost everybody. People feel comfortable mixing with others who are in the park for similar reasons.

People want to feel safe and comfortable when they go to a park. This is easy when they are in the presence of others like themselves. But successful public parks also make people feel comfortable with those whose age, income, class, or ethnicity are different from their own and who have come to the park for reasons that may also differ from theirs. Prospect Park in Brooklyn provides a particularly vivid illustration of this mixing-valve function. On a typical winter Saturday night during the first decade of the twenty-first century, large numbers of Orthodox Sephardic Jewish and Caribbean-American boys and girls will be skating in the park's well-lighted rink. During the day, Chinese-American families will be taking photographs and shooting videos of wedding parties in popular sections of the park as Russian-Americans pass by on their walks.

This was not true in 1980. People did not feel safe when they went to Prospect Park, as was the case with many other parks during that time as well,

Paris, 2007. The Square du Temple provides parents with a place to gather and chat, and for small children to form friendships.

as park users began to avoid increasingly ill-maintained parks that gradually began to be occupied by people who engaged in antisocial behavior. Between the late 1950s and the early 1980s many people began to lose confidence in the role that public parks play as incubators of a civil society. Community bonds were dissolving throughout the United States. Thoughtful commentators will long debate the cause of this change, but there can be no doubt that it was accompanied by a major decrease in spending on parks, an alarming deterioration in their physical condition, and a sharp decline in park utilization.

Parks cannot perform their role as social mixing valves when they are abandoned by the very people they are intended to bring together. The vacuum left behind is often filled by people whom park users think of as dangerous intruders. Only when condi-

tions improve enough to attract visitors back does antisocial behavior decline. When Tupper Thomas became Prospect Park's administrator in 1980, she understood that there were not enough people in the park to provide surveillance, and she began a series of efforts to make people feel sufficiently comfortable to come there. New York City police stepped up their presence, and they assigned the park a special detail of their auxiliary police force composed of Brooklyn volunteers. This made people feel more comfortable in the park. Thomas scheduled regular events, many of which have become traditions that attract large numbers of people—fishing contests, kite flying competitions, fireworks on New Year's Eve, a children's carnival on Halloween—and provided assistance to people planning their own events. These events were covered in articles in local news-

Brooklyn, New York, 2006. Regularly scheduled events in Prospect Park convinced residents in surrounding neighborhoods that the park was a safe place for family outings.

papers that helped spread the message that the park was now safe. The people who attended these events or saw the auxiliary police patrolling the park told their friends the same thing.

The existence of a place like Prospect Park that brings large numbers of people together for common activities probably makes for a more civil society and, by extension, a reduction in crime. But how can we be sure that park utilization is the critical variable? What value do we place on a more civil society, and what is the dollar savings from the reduction in crime? These are difficult questions, but part of the answer can be found by comparing the amount of crime before and after a significant increase in the number of people who use a park.

The link between parks and crime reduction was made even by the earliest parks advocates, who believed that recreation would divert citizens from engaging in criminal activity. One of the first sites selected for park development under New York's Small Parks Act in 1887 was an infamous Lower East Side slum known as Mulberry Bend, which Jacob Riis had covered as a reporter. Calvert Vaux was hired to design a park that met the needs of the poor, immigrant population who continued to live around the new park.

After the site had been cleared and what is now known as Columbus Park created, thousands of children and adults flocked to it. Riis described the park's effectiveness in reducing crime and delinquency: "I do not believe that there was a week in all the twenty years I had to do with [Mulberry Bend] as a police reporter, in which I was not called to record there a stabbing or shooting affair, some act of violence. It is not five years since the Bend became a park, and the police reporter has not had business there during that time; not once has a shot been fired or a knife been drawn.[15]

Between 1980 and 2009, as New York itself rebounded from the fiscal crisis of the 1970s, hundreds of millions of public and private dollars were spent to restore Central Park. Better conditions were accompanied by dramatically increased park utilization. The decrease in antisocial activities was even more dramatic. The police precinct responsible for the park reported 1,006 felonies during 1982, including 709 robberies and 9 murders; in 2003 it reported only 93 felonies, including 34 robberies and no murders.[16] While it is true that crime for the entire city was declining—in 2003 it was 36 percent of what it had been in 1982—in Central Park that decline was even sharper: it dropped to 11 percent of what it had been in 1982. Prospect Park experienced the same decline in crime in response to a substantial increase in park utilization. Between 1980 and 2000, park attendance increased by over 400 percent;

Manhattan, 2008. The Mulberry Bend slum that Jacob Riis described as one of the city's most dangerous was torn down and replaced by Columbus Park, now a popular playground for Chinatown residents.

major crime decreased at the same rate and is now in single digits.[17]

Can there be any more convincing demonstration of the contribution to a civil society made by well-maintained, well-managed parks?

SUSTAINING A LIVABLE ENVIRONMENT

Most people have an instinctive understanding that the air is fresher and cooler in a public park than on city streets (especially traffic-congested streets), that park waterways are cleaner and the wildlife is healthier. By extension, they also believe that the greater the amount of parkland in a community, the more likely that regional air and water quality will be better, the air temperature will be more pleasant, and local wildlife will be healthier. In the nineteenth century, Olmsted explicitly addressed the important role that parks play in sustaining a livable environment: "Air is disinfected by sunlight and foliage. Foliage also acts mechanically to purify the air by screening it. Opportunity and inducement to escape at frequent intervals from the confined and vitiated air of the commercial quarters, and to supply the lungs with air screened and purified by trees, and recently acted upon by sunlight, together with the opportunity and inducement to escape from conditions requiring vigilance, wariness, and activity toward other men—if these could be supplied economically, our problems would be solved."[18]

In our own day, some scientists have counted the increase in species within a habitat, measured changes in ambient temperature over time, analyzed the chemical contents of the air, and determined the cleanliness of water. Unfortunately, few issue reports that demonstrate statistically the beneficial effect of new parkland. But the truth of the matter is that land that is set aside in the form of public parks plays a particularly important role in the urban ecological system. Such parks do improve air quality, retain and filter storm water and vehicular runoff, prevent erosion, mitigate the heat island effect and lower ambient temperature by providing shade; they muffle noise, block harsh winds, sequester carbon, produce oxygen, and provide a habitat for a variety of animals.

Just imagine what the quality of the environment would be like if the acreage—26 percent—of present-day New York City that is now parkland had been developed as manufacturing and office buildings, streets and rail yards, tenements and high-rise apartment houses.[19] The city would be similar to the huge megalopolises of the developing world, such as Lima, Mumbai, and Johannesburg, where most of the land is built up, squatter settlements and shantytowns extend for miles, and little parkland exists. When large amounts of industrial waste are released into the air there is not enough plant life to reduce pollution, and it affects the health of local residents and lowers their life expectancy. Moreover, that pollution spreads outside the area of its origin and reduces air quality, particularly in certain areas of the United States that also happen to be grossly undersupplied with parkland.

The relationship between parks and air quality is easy to explain. Through the process of photosynthesis, plant life converts sunlight into chemical energy, consuming carbon dioxide and producing oxygen. Human beings breathe the oxygen and release carbon dioxide. A livable environment depends on the balance between these processes. Foliage further cleans the air we breathe by filtering particulate matter. Thus, the greater the amount of land that is devoted to plant life—including public parks—the easier it is to sustain human life.

The impact of parks on water quality also is easy to understand. The rain that falls in a park is absorbed into the ground, where it feeds plant life and recharges aquifers. Rain that falls on city streets and other impervious surfaces runs off, picking up oils, heavy metals, and other pollutants and carrying them along until it flows into a sewer, which then must transport it, often a great distance, to a wastewater treatment facility. In a park, by contrast, most of the pollutants are filtered out as the water passes through the earth; others are consumed by bacteria, leaving carbon dioxide and water as byproducts. Thus parkland helps to maintain the water table, improve water quality, and reduce pollution.

The role public parks play in filtering storm water is particularly important. In areas devoid of parkland, storm water runs to street gutters and through sewer grates into city sewers. Where storm sewers are not separate from sanitary sewers, this runoff mixes with chemicals leached from roofs and

Fenway, Boston, 1973. This nineteenth-century park transformed an environmental hazard into a recreation facility that also filters polluted runoff and improves neighborhood air quality.

site is a key element in its contribution to a region's environmental health. There is nothing inherently dangerous about a floodplain that absorbs water from melting snow or rain showers, but problems arise when people build in the flood pain. Occasionally, an especially severe flood will cause a waterway to spread far beyond its usual spring runoff boundaries. That is what happened in Boulder, Colorado, in 1894, when the debris-filled waters of Boulder Creek overflowed, submerging much of the town and destroying public and private property.[21]

In 1910 the City Improvement Association of Boulder commissioned the Olmsted firm to prepare a plan for the town. Residents expected the plan to propose transforming Boulder Creek into a conventional park. But Charles Eliot (1859–1897) and Frederick Law Olmsted Jr. argued that it would be "foolishness" to do so, since a "highly polished and exquisite park with costly flowers and other decorations . . . would be ruined by flooding." Instead, they recommended respecting the results of centuries of flooding by creating a park that consisted of open fields with a few shrubs and "tough old trees" that could handle the annual runoff and still provide areas for visitors to play, fish, picnic, and stroll.[22]

Although the park Olmsted and Eliot recommended was an inexpensive way to transform a sustainable environment into a simple, practical public park, their proposal was ignored. Hundreds of houses and commercial buildings were erected within the Boulder Creek floodplain and, as could be expected, flooding continued and they sustained millions of dollars of damage. In 1983 Spencer W. Havlick, a newly elected city councilman, resurrected the Olmsted firm's plan by asking the Boulder Department of City Planning to respond to the 1910 proposal by preparing one for a park along Boulder Creek. The City Council funded the new version of the park, which now includes playing fields, picnic grounds, fish pools, kayaking areas, bird-watching sites, and a 7-mile (11.3-km) trail connecting every-

pavement and with wastewater and sewage from industrial and commercial enterprises as well as residential buildings. During periods of good weather, this toxic brew flows into treatment plants that remove pollutants and dispose of it in waterways that, as a result, are safe for swimming and fishing.

In New York City, the outflows from combined sewers go into twenty-six wastewater treatment plants (fourteen in the city itself) that treat the city's sewage. Although these outflows are far cleaner than what once entered the area's waterways, they still dump large amounts of nitrogen, phosphorus, and fecal coliform bacteria. In places where the outflows are flushed by tides, the water is fairly clean, but places not sufficiently flushed by tides remain polluted. During periods of heavy rain, when the combined flow exceeds treatment plant capacity, raw sewage spills into the city's waterways—some 27 billion gallons (102 billion liters) of overflow annually.[20] Parkland, which diverts this runoff to open land where it can be filtered through the earth as groundwater, reduces the load at treatment plants and increases plant efficiency during periods of light rain. Where there is enough parkland, it absorbs enough runoff even during heavy storms to significantly diminish the amount of untreated waste entering city waterways, resulting in cleaner water in nearby streams, rivers, bays, and harbors.

A livable environment involves more than just clean air and water. A park's appropriateness to its

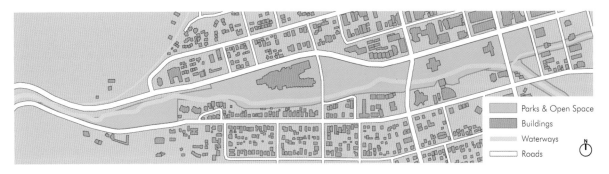

Boulder, Colorado, 2009. It took more than seven decades for the city government to implement a recommendation by Charles Eliot and Frederick Law Olmsted Jr. that Boulder Creek be made into a public park.

thing. Creating the trail required purchasing additional property and easements on property in the backyards of the private houses and commercial buildings on the edge of the creek, which was already publicly owned. That paved trail is actively used by inline skaters, bikers, joggers, and local residents on their way to a destination elsewhere in town or just taking a lunchtime break.

An area's environmental sustainability is also affected by the wildlife it supports. Wildlife may be more visible in farmland or low-density exurbs than in suburban or urban areas, but it also is abundant throughout settled areas. Homeowners who live in these more populated places are eager to tell stories about the raccoons that open garbage cans in their backyards. A few years ago newspapers, magazines,

Boulder, Colorado, 2000. Boulder Creek has been transformed into a recreational resource that also provides important environmental benefits.

and television stations were mesmerized by peregrine falcons that made their nest on a Manhattan apartment building. Indeed, a wide range of birds, insects, fish, and animals live in metropolitan areas. Parks provide an essential habitat for this wildlife. Brooklyn's Prospect Park, for example, is a welcoming habitat for red-tailed hawks, great egrets, coots, and more than two hundred other species of birds.[23]

The survival of wildlife depends on the existence of large enough core habitats and connective corridors for themselves and the flora and fauna that make up their ecosystems, and local governments in places as different as suburban Collierville, Tennessee, and urban Paris have been investing in narrow and sometimes tiny patches of green that can extend wildlife foraging and migratory territory. Two of the most extensive programs of this sort are Chicago's effort to live up to its city motto, *Urbs in Horto* (Latin for "City in a Garden"), and New York City's GreenStreets Program. Emphasizing *Urbs in Horto* originated with Richard M. Daley, whose long tenure as Chicago's mayor began in 1989. His interest in greening the city has been ascribed to his childhood admiration of the city's elm trees and a desire to replace the once-remarkable tree cover that was lost to Dutch elm and other diseases. Daley's initial commitment to that goal evolved during his mayoralty to include encouraging "green" construction, investing in public parks, restoring wetlands, generating renewable energy, and initiating a variety of programs to improve the environment.

Finding enough property for even small slivers of green space in already built-out cities is not easy, but Chicago has done so in creative ways. Many of the city's investments in environmental improvement have not required purchasing property. Rather, the city makes use of property that is already publicly owned: streets and sidewalks. Between 1996 and 2006, it invested in more than 70 miles (112 km) of planters in the medians of city streets and 300,000 new street trees.[24] The medians were planted with a variety of trees, shrubs, grasses, and flowers. Not only are the streets more attractive, they are now also safer places to drive, bicycle, and walk. One of the more innovative additions are planter benches: where sidewalks are wide enough, the city has placed concrete benches that entirely enclose a planter filled with seasonal flowers and plants. These benches pro-

vide a welcome resting place for tired tourists, workers, and residents.

By 2008 Chicago's proliferation of flower beds, street trees, planted medians, and planter benches had become noted by visitors and the subject of newspaper and magazine articles. The added greenery absorbs rainwater and carbon dioxide. It filters the air and traps dust and particulate matter, reduces noise, lowers the ambient temperature during summer months, and provides an attractive habitat for birds and small animals that control insect infestation.

Even when parkland is abundant—as in New York City, where 26 percent of its territory is already devoted to parks—appropriating the funds to pay for development, maintenance, or even reclamation can be difficult. Yet the New York City Department of Parks and Recreation and its commissioner, Henry Stern, found a way to do just that when the city initiated its GreenStreets Program in 1996. The parks department identified nearly three thousand tiny patches of land, primarily traffic islands and small city-owned lots that were inappropriate for development. Most were paved with asphalt or concrete, creating harsh heat islands that increased the release of gases and particulates into the air.

As of 2008, the department had reclaimed 2,296 of these sites, transforming them into island gardens that average 2,200 square feet (204 m^3) in size, and landscaped them with trees, shrubs, and groundcover that require a low level of maintenance and have a high tolerance for urban environmental stresses such as drought, soil compaction, and pollution. All these gardens absorb rainwater, and the new cluster plantings create microclimates that reduce ambient air temperatures by as much as two to four degrees and provide cleaner air by filtering particulates and absorbing gaseous pollutants. They also serve as wildlife habitats that offer valuable food, such as berries, and as links to larger habitat areas in public parks and other open spaces. These small parks have become important places for passive recreation, while simultaneously ameliorating the environment. The twelve-year cost of the GreenStreets Program was a mere $46 million.[25] By comparison, by 2010 New York City will have spent $3 billion to complete a 50 percent

Chicago, 2008. Landscaped median strips and planter boxes filled with flowers not only make city streets more attractive, they reduce noise, lower the ambient temperature during summer months, and provide an attractive habitat for birds and small animals.

Manhattan, 1999 and 2000. The New York City parks department's GreenStreets Program transformed this traffic island at Claremont Ave. and 116th St. into a neighborhood asset.

increase in the capacity of Newtown Creek Wastewater Treatment Plant, the largest of its sewage treatment facilities.[26]

Cities also have a long history of using parks as part of the process of cleaning and restoring polluted sites. During the nineteenth century, Boston decontaminated large areas of swamp, often filled with garbage, in the Back Bay and the Fens, turning sections of each into desirable parks around which private developers created attractive residential neighborhoods. In the second part of the twentieth century, the environmental movement shone the spotlight on "brownfields," land that had been contaminated by concentrations of hazardous waste or pollution but could be successfully reused once cleaned up. Contaminated waterfront districts became relatively easy targets for conversion to parkland because many of their sites had become obsolete and often had been entirely abandoned.

Crissy Field in San Francisco is one of the most successful examples of brownfield cleanup, and a dramatic example of how parkland can improve the environment. A surplus Army air base along a stretch of the city's waterfront included substantial amounts of polluted ground and acres of impervious pavement from which polluted runoff was flowing into San Francisco Bay. The project converted the abandoned base into grassy parkland, a public

beach, a bay-front promenade, and other amenities, in the process removing all the contaminated material from the site, restoring a tidal wetland, and creating a park. Twenty acres (8 ha) were dredged and replanted to simulate the original tidal wetland environment. The park is now home to various species of fish, birds, and other wildlife and helps to improve air and water quality in a once contaminated section of San Francisco.

The process began in 1994, when the former Presidio army base was transferred to the National Park Service's Golden Gate National Recreation Area. Part of the base, known as Crissy Field, had been used as a military airfield between 1921 and 1974. The $32 million plan for turning it into a public park was prepared by the landscape architecture firm Hargreaves Associates. While it retained many of the airfield's historic structures, the plan called for the removal of 87,000 tons of hazardous substances and contaminated soil and the transformation of

San Francisco, c. 1994 and 2000. After decades of use as a military facility, Crissy Field had become a contaminated property abandoned by the federal government. By transforming Crissy Field into a public park, San Francisco has gained a recreation facility that also improves air and water quality and a revived habitat that welcomes the wildlife once displaced from the site.

what had been asphalt paving, roads, buildings, and eroded beachfront into 28 acres (11 ha) of grassy field, 20 acres (8 ha) of tidal marsh, 22 acres (9 ha) of visitor amenities, and 30 acres (12 ha) of improved promenade and beach.

The most essential part of the plan was the re-creation of a tidal salt marsh, which had been filled in for the Panama Pacific International Exposition in 1915, before the site became a military installation. It is again being flushed naturally by twice-daily San Francisco Bay tides, by fresh water coming from the Presidio's Tennessee Hollow, and by clean rainwater runoff. More than 100,000 native plants of 110 species were planted throughout the site. As a result of the restoration, Crissy Field has become the home of 17 fish species, 135 bird species, and other wildlife that had been absent for decades.[27]

Today thousands of people go to Crissy Field to take a scenic walk along the beach, sit on the sand, enjoy the wildflowers growing in the dunes, photograph the Golden Gate Bridge, cycle next to San Francisco Bay, play volleyball, go boating or windsurfing, or just hang out. It is one of the city's most popular public parks.

PROVIDING A FRAMEWORK FOR DEVELOPMENT

Olmsted and Vaux believed that parks had a "much greater influence upon the progress of a city in its general structure than any other ordinary public work."[28] They thought it important to consider "the character of the demand" and satisfy it by providing "ease of access" to convenient, attractive destinations that could be used by "assemblages of citizens."[29] For developers to invest there, those destinations had to be combined into a system of well-designed parks and parkways that would continue to attract people to the area. Olmsted drew on this concept of a framework when he devised the Emerald Necklace of parks and parkways around which Boston grew and took shape (see chapter 8). Once I understood the effectiveness of this strategy, I began to refer to it as a *public realm framework,* and I have emphasized it above all else in my own work as an urban planner.

A community's public realm comprises its streets and squares, its transportation systems and public buildings, and its parks—in essence, it is a city's living room. Here its citizens encounter one another, move around, shop, do business, play, or just wander. Thus, the public realm is the fundamental element in any community—it is the skeleton around which everything else grows—and therefore provides the most leverage for capturing and guiding private investment in the public interest.

While the use of parks as a framework for urbanization was integral to the creation and success of Paris in the nineteenth century and of Minneapolis in the twentieth century, that is not the standard practice in planning today. It is far more common for today's planners to impose land use, density, and design restrictions on private property, yet it is the extensive park, parkway, and landscaped boulevard systems of Paris and Minneapolis that establish the quality of life of their neighborhoods. Consequently, few people pay much attention to the quality of the buildings that line their exceptional public realms. (Chapter 8 is devoted to the role of parks in shaping urbanization.)

The 33-acre (13-ha) property that would become Loring Park in Minneapolis was, like Central Park at its inception, originally on the outskirts of town—but just beyond the city's downtown. When the first 30 acres (12 ha) were purchased in 1883, Minneapolis was growing very quickly. Its 1880 population had been 47,000; by 1900 it would be 203,000.[30] The Board of Park Commissioners had grasped what Olmsted called "the character of the demand" and selected an easily accessible site. It contained a small lake with a floating bog, a pond, and marshland. At that time the bog and marshland were not considered attractive landscape features and the lake and pond were judged too small for active recreational use. So the floating bog was removed, the two small bodies of water connected and dredged, and the banks extended to create Loring Lake. The parkland that surrounded it was relandscaped. It became an ideal place for people taking an afternoon walk around the lake, lying under one of the shade tress, or reading on one of the park benches.

People wanted to live around the new park. When the park board added 3 acres (1.2 ha), it discovered that property in the area, which had been

Loring Park, Minneapolis, 1891 and 1996. The increase in property values around this park during the nineteenth, twentieth, and twenty-first centuries has been so significant that it has generated continuing real estate activity in the surrounding area.

purchased in 1883 for $4,904 per acre, cost $48,096 per acre in 1902.[31] The park had created a public realm framework around which developers wanted to build, and they were willing to pay high prices for property surrounding it. Many of the nineteenth- and early twentieth-century structures have been replaced, in some cases more than once. Today the park is encircled by properties that have greatly appreciated in value—just as Frederick Law Olmsted would have predicted.

Paris, 2002. The park islands on either side of avenue Foch added enormous value to the properties that faced them.

London, 2007. Fitzroy Square was an investment made at the end of the eighteenth century by the Duke of Southampton as a means of increasing revenues from leaseholds on surrounding property.

THREE

QUANTIFYING VALUE

By now readers should be well aware of the key roles played by public parks. In chapter 2 I cited a few studies relevant to the impact of parks on air and water quality, on the physical health of park users, and on the rates of antisocial activity in nearby communities; these lend support to the role public parks play in maintaining a sustainable environment, a healthy population, and a civil society. An even more convincing value indicator is the dollar increase in the value of real estate surrounding parks and the accompanying increases in tax revenues from these properties. In this chapter I will further quantify the benefits of parks and try to show how parks can play a major role in twenty-first-century metropolitan planning.

Establishing the dollar value of a park is difficult. In 2005 a property appraiser estimated the "real estate value" of Central Park to be about $528 billion.[1] I do not know whether New Yorkers in 2005 could have raised that much money, but in the words of Joseph Duveen, they would have been "getting it cheap." Even more difficult is establishing a dollar value for the increase in property values around parks. Buildings near parks are often in better condition than those in the rest of the neighborhood and, as a result, people believe that parks do increase property values. But the notion that parks and open space add value to surrounding properties is an

intuitive understanding that goes back hundreds of years. The kings of France created the Places Royales in order to spark development in the surrounding areas. For centuries the families that owned the great estates of London have collected increasingly valuable rents from property around the more than four hundred squares they created.

These wealthy English property owners found that they were able to maximize value by creating open space that was available to the occupants of their property. They leased blocks and lots surrounding fenced-in and landscaped squares to developers. When the leases expired, the sites and any buildings on them legally reverted to the owners, although they often renegotiated and extended the leases before they were scheduled to expire. Some squares that were originally restricted to residents are now open to the public, and the uses that surround them may no longer be solely residential. But virtually everywhere, the properties around these squares have increased in value far beyond even the most optimistic expectations. In fact, they are among the most treasured assets of their surrounding neighborhoods in London, Bath, and Edinburgh.

Rents were cheap for the first wave of tenants in these developments because construction was still ongoing. But the market heated up as development was completed, and the newly built residences became increasingly desirable to a growing number of potential tenants. Landowners could choose one of two ways to create the value-adding open space and roads that stimulated development: they could lease the entire site and require that the developer add these amenities, or they could create the amenities themselves before involving developers. The latter was more of a risk but could bring a greater, faster return.

In the second half of the nineteenth century, American cities adopted a similar approach to developing public parks. In the early 1880s, park advocates in Minneapolis argued that land should be acquired for a comprehensive system of parks that would ultimately boost the total value of the city's real estate. It was an investment that paid off handsomely in soaring real estate tax revenues from surrounding properties.

One study attempted to quantify the increase in real estate taxes paid by the wards surrounding Central Park. The impact is dramatic. During the fifteen years following the development of the park, taxes paid to the city increased more than 900 percent.[2] While there were other variables, surely proximity to the park was responsible for some of the increase.

Manhattan, 2007. The development of the Hudson River Park on the site of the former West Side Highway began with an act of the New York State legislature in 1998.

Indeed, in 1871 Frederick Law Olmsted wrote that "the larger part of the advance which has occurred in the value of real estate adjoining the park since its design began to be understood, and which amounts to $160,000,000, has grown out of a conviction that, for persons of great wealth and of certain social habits, a family residence near the park will be more attractively situated than anywhere else on the continent."[3]

Economists have continued to try to quantify the impact on real estate values of proximity to park-

Manhattan, 2009. The opportunities for passive recreation along the Hudson River Park bring people from all over the city and have greatly increased the attractiveness of living nearby.

Manhattan, 2006. Public investment in the Hudson River Park generated new private apartment construction on sites across the street.

land. A 1974 study of land values around 1,294-acre (524-ha) Pennypack Park in northeast Philadelphia estimated that the park was responsible for 33 percent of land value within 40 feet (12 m) of the park, 9 percent within 1,000 feet (305 m), and 4 percent within 2,500 feet (762 m).[4] A 1978 study of linear greenways in three neighborhoods of Boulder, Colorado, estimated that a property's value decreased by $4.20 per square foot for each foot of space between it and the nearest greenway.[5]

Especially convincing statistics on the impact of investment in parks and open space can be found in a 2007 report titled "The Impact of Hudson River Park on Property Values," prepared jointly by the Real Estate Board of New York and the Regional Plan Association. It measured sales prices for existing condominium apartments during the years 2003–2005 along the length of the Hudson River Park, a waterside park that is still being developed between Chambers Street in lower Manhattan and 59th Street in midtown—a stretch of nearly 5 miles (8 km). At the time of the study only one stretch of the park had actually been finished. In that fifteen-block section of the park, between Clarkson Street and Gansevoort Street in Greenwich Village, there was an 80 percent increase in the sales price of 285 condominium apartments. During that same period there was only a 45 percent increase in the sales

price of 657 condos along the uncompleted portion of the park.[6]

Experts point to the high prices of residences around golf courses, along beaches, and across the street from parks as evidence that being close to open space adds value. These observations, like the studies just mentioned, usually refer to properties in areas that are in high demand, but investment in parks and open space can be as effective in restoring demand for real estate in deteriorating areas. This is as true of once-thriving commercial districts as it is for low-rent neighborhoods that are pockmarked with abandoned buildings and vacant lots.

By the 1970s conditions in Manhattan's Bryant Park were so bad that they were depressing rents in surrounding office buildings—one of the reasons property owners formed a business improvement district (BID) and agreed to pay a real-estate tax surcharge to cover the cost of improving conditions in the park. (For more on BIDs, see chapter 10). The impact was immediate. In 1996, the year after park reconstruction was completed, the *New York Times* reported that property with a view of the park was renting at a $3 per square foot ($32/m²) premium over adjacent space without views.

Asking rents in the buildings surrounding the park rose at a faster rate than those in the rest of New York City—and continued to be disproportionately

Manhattan, 2004. Once Bryant Park had been restored, office space in surrounding buildings was renting at prices substantially higher than in comparable buildings in nearby sections of midtown Manhattan.

higher even during the recession of 2008–2009. For example, at the forty-nine-story Grace Building at 1114 Avenue of the Americas, across 42nd Street from the park, vacancy rates declined sharply and asking rents increased from $35 per square foot ($377/m²) in 1990 to $75 per square foot ($807/m²) in 2002. This was a much more dramatic increase than in other areas; during the same period asking rents in the Times Square area rose from $29.50 per square foot ($318/m²) to $49 per square foot ($527/m²), in the Grand Central Terminal area from $35 ($377/m²) to $55 ($592/m²), and in the Rockefeller Center area from $42 per square foot ($452/m²) to $60 per square foot ($646/m²). Asking rents at the ten-story Beaux-Arts Building at 80 West 40th Street, south of the park, increased 225 percent, compared to 67 percent in the Times Square area and 55 percent in the Grand Central Terminal area.[7]

The value added to neighboring real estate by the restored park can be quantified. The Bryant Park BID initially contained 7.5 million square feet (697,000 m²) of taxable floor area. The tax surcharge in 2002 was $0.126 per square foot ($1.36/m²), producing $950,000 annually. Based on the general increases in asking rents in midtown Manhattan, it seems reasonable to assume that half of the $40 per square foot ($431/m²) increase in asking rents was attributable to the BID. Thus in 2002 alone Bryant Park generated $150 million in actual and potential asking rents—an excellent value for the $12.6 million in real estate tax surcharges covering the twelve years between 1990 and 2002. (As a result of the construction of One Bryant Park, the amount of space in the BID grew to 10.3 million square feet [957,000 m²] in 2009. The assessment, however, remained $950,000 per year.) Another way of calculating the added value would be to capitalize the additional

Portland, Oregon, 1974. Harbor Drive was replaced by Tom McCall Waterfront Park in the mid-1970s.

Portland, Oregon, 2007. Following the creation of McCall Park, the sites across the street became more valuable, and developers purchased them for office development.

income stream of $150 million. At a capitalization rate of 6 percent it would equal $2.5 billion; at 10 percent it would equal $1.5 billion. Even discounting 90 percent of this calculation, the results make investment in the park a very successful venture.

Many other efforts have concentrated on reclaiming property along waterfronts, and these efforts too have resulted in restoring demand and increasing property values and tax revenue. In 1974, for example, Portland, Oregon, eliminated a six-lane highway along the Willamette River in order to create Governor Tom McCall Waterfront Park. Today it is the site of several new office buildings.

Similar quantitative analysis of slum properties is harder to find. There is empirical evidence, however, in formerly run-down sections of Chicago, Philadelphia, and New York, where parklike properties called community gardens sparked a neighborhood revival. These sites did not start out as gardens. They were not even owned by the people who transformed them into gardens but had been abandoned by their owners.

During the 1960s, older cities throughout the United States began losing jobs and population—an outflow that began to be reversed in many places at the end of the twentieth century. The reasons for the outflow have been debated ever since. But it left once lovely neighborhoods with empty buildings and vacant lots. As a result of tax foreclosure, thousands of these properties had fallen into city hands. In Philadelphia, 21,400 abandoned residential structures were demolished between 1970 and 1990. As a result, 9,500 of the 23,000 city-owned properties had been turned into vacant lots.[8] New York City also had a large number of vacant city-owned lots; at best they became informal garbage dumps, and at worst they became sites for gang fights, crack dens, and overt prostitution.

This was particularly evident in Loisaida, the lower Manhattan neighborhood sometimes referred to as Alphabet City because it is located on Avenues A, B, C, and D, between Houston and 14th streets. Loisaida was inhabited by a uniquely New York blend of Puerto Rican–Americans, struggling painters and sculptors, aging hippies, and older Polish and Ukrainian immigrants. Some received public assistance and others were young working people or retirees who could not afford anything better.

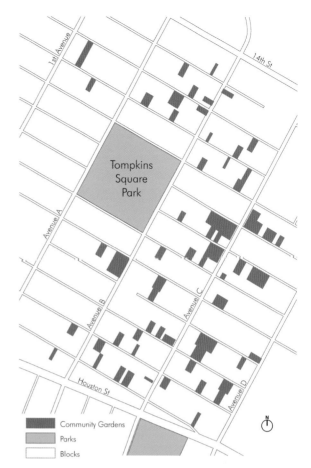

Manhattan, 2009. Abandoned properties throughout the Lower East Side were transformed by neighborhood residents into community gardens.

New York City's thousands of municipally owned residential properties are managed by the Department of Housing Preservation and Development (HPD) and vacant lots by the Department of General Services (DGS). Loisaida's vacant lots and buildings were viewed as assets by neighborhood groups and developers of low-income housing. Some city agencies also saw them as assets that could be used for public buildings. HPD thought many sites were suitable for new residential development. These city agencies had the right to prevent property from going to auction, and throughout the 1970s, 1980s, and early 1990s they kept virtually everything from going to auction.

The vacant properties had a distinctly depressant effect on surrounding buildings. Neighborhood residents thought it was criminal that the government did not do anything about the rotting garbage and antisocial activity that went on there. At first these neighbors went in illegally, cleaned out the lots, and sometimes began using them for neighborhood purposes. Informal occupancy suited neither the city government, which was subject to lawsuits, nor the neighborhood groups, which were loath to invest time and money in something that might be sold at any time. In 1978 the city's Department of Parks and Recreation established Operation Green Thumb to take over responsibility of the vacant lots, which local groups were ready to lease on a temporary basis. At the same time, HPD started making plans to sell many of the vacant properties to developers of low-rent housing, who would obtain funding from one of the federal subsidy programs.

Meanwhile, residents began taking possession of scattered vacant lots, removing the rubbish and debris and planting vegetables, flowers, and even small trees. The community gardens sprouted such colorful names as El Sol Brilliante, Brisas del Caribe, Green Oasis Community Garden, and Jardin de la Esperanza. This was by no means the first instance of citizen-sponsored gardening. It had emerged in Detroit as "Potato Patches" (1894–1917), and continued throughout the United States as "School Gardens" (1900–1920), "Garden City Plots" (1905–1910), "Liberty Gardens" (1917–1920), "Relief Gardens" (1930–1939), and "Victory Gardens" (1941–1945).[9]

The community gardens in Loisaida reflected the interests and character of the people who took care of them. But they were less like private gardens and more like tiny parks because they were used for all sorts of recreation and community activities, parties, exhibits, and even weddings. Some were only the size of a standard city lot, 25 feet (7.6 m) wide and 100 feet (30.5 m) deep. When several lots were combined, they could be as much as six lots wide—not big enough for the range of activities typical of public parks, but big enough to perform many of their roles: sustaining a livable environment, improving health and well-being, and enhancing civil society.

As more and more community gardens appeared, they provided a way of rallying residents. The gardeners developed a sense of ownership in the neighborhood, learned to respect the efforts of others, and increasingly took responsibility for activities on the block. Not only had they displaced the intruders and eliminated conditions that had a negative impact on the area, they also provided the social fabric that had disappeared when previous property owners and residents abandoned the neighborhood. All this coincided with the growth of New York City's population and the accompanying increase in housing demand.

The city government responded in 1993 by putting twenty-two Loisaida properties up for sale. The nonprofit Trust for Public Land stepped in to purchase them and thereby ensure that some of the lots permanently remained community gardens. Market conditions continued to improve, and five years later

Manhattan, 2005. The Trust for Public Land helped local residents transform this abandoned property on East 6th St. into a community garden.

the city announced that it would auction community garden sites throughout the city, since these lots could now be filled with much needed market-rent housing or with lower-rent subsidized housing. Neighborhood groups and civic organizations that favored community gardens were outraged and rallied opposition. Once again the Trust for Public Land came to the rescue. This time they were joined by the New York Restoration Project, a group founded by the actress Bette Midler. Together they raised more than $4 million, and in 1999 they purchased 114 community gardens from the city.

Loisaida today is no longer what it was when the community garden movement took hold there. New market-rate and affordable housing has been built on sites that were once abandoned. The neighborhood now includes chic restaurants and fancy boutiques, and it is very much in demand among young people. Rents for available apartments have skyrocketed. The gentrification of Loisaida, like gentrification in other once-challenged New York City neighborhoods, might well have occurred even if there had been no community gardens. The city's population grew (to a great extent because of a surge in immigration) from 7.1 million in 1980 to 8.3 million in 2007, but housing construction did not match the growth in population, and the increasing demand for residences reversed the decline of conveniently located, safe, attractive neighborhoods like Loisaida.

Would the revitalization of Loisaida have happened without community gardens? Possibly. But without some action to displace a large criminal element and provide a healthy social fabric, the process would surely have taken far longer.

Waterfront Park, Louisville, 2000. Park development requires more than conserving an existing natural environment or supplementing an existing property with grass and trees. Most great parks involve redesign, redevelopment, and replanting.

FOUR

PARK DEVELOPMENT

Effective park development depends on effective decision making, usually by many people over long periods of time. Chicagoans, for example, have been working to develop their lakeshore for generations, continuing to improve what they have already transformed into extraordinary public parkland. The landscape they have created is no accident. It is the product of decisions that reflect design principles, public policy rationales, and development and stewardship strategies that have been in play throughout the developed world since public parks emerged as fundamental components of the public realm in the nineteenth century.

Frederick Law Olmsted and Robert Moses were involved in more park development than any other individuals anywhere in the world, but the two had very different approaches to both development and decision making. As designer and sometimes construction supervisor, the Olmsted firm was responsible for landscape settings for private estates, public institutions, cemeteries, parks, parkways, playgrounds, and suburban communities throughout the nation. Although Moses advised a few cities, most of the work for which he, his staff, and his consultants were responsible was in New York State. As chairman of the Long Island State Parks Commission (1924–1963), Moses created 15 major parks and 175 miles (282 km) of parkways.[1] Between 1934

and 1960, while he was also New York City parks commissioner, he acquired 20,200 acres (8,175 ha) of parkland, built 15 huge swimming pools, created 658 playgrounds, and added 17 miles (27 km) of public beaches to the one mile (1.6 km) the city owned when he came to office.[2]

But they were similar in that neither man developed parks simply by applying formulas and calculating the correct answer. Too often, park planners apply formulas to work out how things *ought* to be—a technique commonly known as "needs analysis"—and then shake their heads in dismay when, invariably, the world doesn't behave as it should. Olmsted and Moses also shared a number of development objectives: providing easy access to any park, endowing it with a discernable, convenient circulation system, ensuring that there were popular attractions for park visitors, developing facilities that would be sustainable for generations. Both understood that park development had to be considered with an eye to what would occur over generations. There is no better advice for anyone considering park development.

The background and decision-making differences between these two planners were many, however. Olmsted, who was present at the creation of the very idea of a public park in America, managed a private consulting business with many types of clients; Moses brought the perspective of a public offi-

Buffalo, 2009. Residents from the neighborhood surrounding Cazenovia Park can erect movable goals in the front meadow for soccer, while others are already using the meadow behind the trees for an informal game of catch.

cial responsible for acquiring property, executing development plans, and administering park agencies responsible for management and maintenance. He had learned from experience that park development has to proceed with probable budget allocations, management capacity, and available personnel very much in mind. Wherever possible, Olmsted proposed parkways connecting nearby neighborhoods with the park; Moses built limited access, landscaped parkways for motorists driving to regional parks. Olmsted designed independent carriageways and pedestrian paths that allowed park users to reach desired destinations; Moses built parking lots for arriving motorists and installed durable paving materials for pedestrian use.

In an Olmsted park, the landscape itself is the attraction. The meadows in Cazenovia Park in Buffalo, New York, are shaped by groups of trees into separate places that can be used in different ways, by different people, at different times of the day. People go to the top of Burnt Knob in Iroquois Park, in Louisville, to enjoy the view. They go boating in the lakes in New York City's Central and Prospect Parks. Moses did not believe that a user-friendly landscape was enough for twentieth-century park users, so he added swimming pools, skating rinks, zoos, and other crowd-pleasers. During the 1930s, in Central Park alone he built more than twenty playgrounds to provide additional recreation opportunities for small children.[3]

Parks, then, do not just happen. Their develop-

Louisville, 2008. The landscape itself is the destination for people who come to Iroquois Park—in this case to enjoy a panoramic view of the city.

ment involves a great number of decisions about site selection, adaptation, and design. But whether newly created or adapted for recreational uses on previously developed properties, parks are a response to public demand. When that demand has surfaced, somebody must then identify and acquire sites that can be transformed into easily accessible, user-friendly places for public recreation. Thereafter, successful park development entails applying design principles and artistry to that specific site, along with the foresight to make individual park development a component of planning for an entire metropolitan area.

Manhattan Cantral Park, 2004: Using New Deal programs to finance the creation of the Great Ellipse on a site that a few years earlier had been occupied by a reservoir, Robert Moses provided ball fields that have been actively used for more than seventy years.

The history of park development includes both unfortunate and inspired responses to these issues. These varied responses reflect changing attitudes about the utility of adjacent private property, the use that occupants of those properties expect to make of what they think of as *their* park, and the demands of the neighborhoods surrounding the park. They also reflect the skills of the individuals involved in their creation. But in every case, park development and urbanization are intertwined in their responses to growth or its absence.

In this chapter we will look at the five ways urban planners and governments can use parks to shape urbanization: by responding to public demand for parkland, anticipating future demand, timing public investment in parkland to accommodate population growth, using parks to provide a framework for second growth, and seizing the opportunity to create parks whenever and wherever resources may be available.

RESPONDING TO DEMAND

When Olmsted and Vaux designed Central Park, the United States included millions of acres of untrammeled nature, but no public parks. Soon, every large city in the country wanted to do as New York had done and began acquiring land to create parks. One hundred and fifty years later, 26 percent of the territory occupied by New York City was parkland; in San Francisco the figure was 18 percent, in Boston 16 percent, and in Philadelphia 13 percent.[4]

Some people may think this is enough, but how do we determine how much parkland is enough? For most of the twentieth century, park experts believed that there should be 10 acres (4 ha) per 1,000 people. Applied to Manhattan, with its estimated population of 1,611,581 in 2006, that standard would require 16,116 acres (6,522 ha) of park—more land than the island's entire 14,870 acres (6,018 ha). The absurdity of this numbers game eludes those who believe that statistical analysis alone can provide evidence of need. Numbers do not tell the whole story.

Acquiring land and developing public parks may not be necessary where recreation opportunities already exist. Our rivers, bays, and oceans, for example, are public property. They are available for recreational swimming and boating. But these public waterways are not universally accessible; in order for the public to be able to use them, governments must adopt land use policies for shoreline properties. Two prime waterfront communities, Palm Beach, Florida, and Malibu, California, illustrate the importance of accessibility. In both places everybody is entitled to stroll along the beach, go surfing, or swim. Long stretches of Malibu, however, are lined with privately owned, multimillion-dollar bungalows that block access to the beach, restricting this majestic "public" recreation facility to beachfront property owners and their guests. In Palm Beach, a stretch of Ocean Boulevard separates its million-dollar condominiums from an equally majestic beach. Public access seems easy: anybody can use the town's streets and sidewalks to get to the beach. But meters along Ocean Boulevard restrict parking to twenty minutes, and parking on nearby streets is strictly regulated. Thus in practice the beach is restricted mainly to community use.

The no less glorious beaches of Long Island, on the other hand, were acquired by the Long Island Park and Parkway Commission and transformed into publicly owned and managed parks. Starting in 1924 the commission's chairman, Robert Moses, methodically reconstructed 6.5 miles of beachfront property into Jones Beach State Park, which became the equivalent of the country clubs and near-private beaches that served wealthy residents of Malibu and Palm Beach. Long Islanders who could afford a nominal parking fee flocked to there to swim in the ocean or in public pools, play tennis,

Malibu, 2008. The expensive bungalows of this California beach community block public access to large stretches of beachfront.

Palm Beach, 1998. Access to the beach in this Florida town is open to anybody, but parking is scarce and metered.

golf, and shuffleboard, attend concerts, and even go dancing.

Population counts and accessibility are not the only methods of trying to determine the appropriate amount of parkland for a region. Another approach is to propose a minimum distance people should travel to a park as a way of identifying locations that may have a deficit of parkland. In New York City, for example, creating a map of service districts of 0.125 miles (0.2 km) to facilities of 5 acres (2 ha) or less, 0.25 miles (0.4 km) to facilities that occupy between 5 and 20 acres (2–8 ha), 0.375 miles (0.6 km) to facilities that occupy between 20 and 50 acres (8–20 ha), and 0.5 miles (0.8 km) to parks that are larger than 50 acres (20 ha) reveals that large parts of the city appear to have a deficit of parkland (see maps). But this is deceptive. When one removes from consideration cemeteries, electric power plants, airports, and

manufacturing areas, the areas of "need" shrink. And the large areas that still appear to be unserved or underserved contain most of the city's 800,000 one-family and two-family homes—most of which have backyards. In fact, careful analysis demonstrates that only a few neighborhoods in New York City lack open space—not a surprising conclusion given the high percentage of the city's acreage that is already devoted to parkland.

ANTICIPATING FUTURE DEMAND

One of the reasons public parks exist is that people have expressed demand for them. Usually, the larger the user population, the greater the perceived demand. The eventual user population, however, will include not just the people who currently live

Long Island, New York, 2009. Anybody with a car can drive to Jones Beach State Park, pay the parking fee, and enjoy unlimited use of the ocean, the beach, the boardwalk, and a wide range of recreational facilities.

New York City, 2001. Many houses in the city have backyards, and most residents live within reasonable walking distance of city parks. Map A illustrates the location of the city's parks. Map B shows areas that are easily accessible to public parks. Map C adds land devoted to airports, cemeteries, and utility plants, and areas zoned for industrial activities. Map D adds the territory occupied by one- and two-family houses with backyards. Together they demonstrate how little of the city's residential population is without access to open space, whether in a park or backyard.

near the park, but also those who travel there and the countless generations who will use the park in the future. In some cases governments even try to shape a park's development so that what emerges is appropriate to the residents and businesses that will locate in the vicinity. Governments also may establish parks in order to attract economic activity to a neglected part of a city or suburb or to direct existing market activity to new locations. In all instances,

of course, for their policies to be effective there must be market activity that can be stimulated.

When the kings of France wanted to direct market demand to property outside the already urbanized section of Paris, for example, they created a *Place Royale,* a square or plaza often anchored by a royal statue. Henri IV created the Place des Vosges (1605), now a small neighborhood park, to attract real estate development to the 3rd and 4th arrondisse-

Place des Vosges, Paris, 2006. The kings of France created public squares, called Places Royales, to jump-start development in unpopulated or underpopulated sections of the city.

ments. Louis IV encouraged development north of the Tuileries Garden with the Place Vendome (1702) and on the border between the 1st and 2nd arrondissements with the Place des Victoires (1685). Each of these public actions was successful because Paris was a growing city throughout the seventeenth and eighteenth centuries. Development sites were continually being sought by an increasing number of businesses and households. The Places Royales were enough of an inducement to attract them to property in the surrounding arrondissements.

Population growth was extremely rapid in nineteenth-century America. At midcentury New York had a population of 516,000; by 1860 it had grown to 814,000. Much smaller Louisville, Kentucky, had a population of 124,000 in 1880, and by 1900 it had climbed as well, to 205,000. Rather than crowd even more people into existing neighborhoods, civic leaders in these and other cities sought to channel market demand to open land on the outskirts of town. New York in the mid-nineteenth century and Louisville at the end of the nineteenth century believed that a public park, or a system of parks, would provide exactly the right attraction, and both cities hired Frederick Law Olmsted to design them.

When New York City first proposed building a large public park, it had only 77 acres (31 ha) of public open space: seven public squares and a 25-acre (10.1-ha) public green at the Battery. In 1851 the state legislature designated 154-acre (62 ha) Jones Wood,

extending along the East River north of 65th Street, as the site for the new park. Three years later the city's Special Committee on Parks decided to drop Jones Wood, in part because the site included waterfront property that might be used for building additional piers along the East River, piers that might enhance the city's mercantile economy. Instead they selected the current site of Central Park, on largely open land 3.5 miles (5.6 km) beyond the northern edge of what was then settled territory. The area was five times the size of Jones Wood. The board selected the site because it was more centrally located, and on "grounds almost entirely useless for building purposes, owing to the very uneven and rocky sur-

Manhattan, 1854. Most of Manhattan, before the creation of Central Park, was largely unsettled.

Southern Parkway, Louisville, 2008. Olmsted believed that the park experience began when one left the house to follow a parkway to a large park.

face."[5] It included 135 acres (55 ha) that were already publicly owned and used as a reservoir.[6] One reason the board's decision was so successful was that the city's population was mushrooming in response to the flood of immigrants landing in New York harbor. A second was that its central location allowed the park to serve the maximum number of people on Manhattan Island. But the most important proved to be Olmsted and Vaux's imaginative design.

Louisville began a more significant program of investment in public parks in 1891, when its Board of Park Commissioners engaged the Olmsted firm to create a park system for the city. The firm continued working in Louisville long after the senior Olmsted retired, eventually opening files on thirty park projects and preparing plans for twenty-three.[7] That work began with property outside the boundaries of the city that had been purchased two years earlier. In 1889, without approval of the city council or any public vote, Louisville's mayor, Charles Jacob, purchased the first 313 acres (127 ha) of what is now 739-acre (299-ha) Iroquois Park. The site was 4 miles (6.4 km) south of the city, so Jacob also obtained a right-of-way to create Southern Parkway, a grand boulevard leading to the new park. The city treasurer reimbursed the $9,000 he had spent and transferred the site to the Board of Park Commissioners.

Iroquois Park, like Central Park, was far beyond the city's developed edge and had to be made readily accessible before developers would be attracted to its location. The Olmsted firm believed tree-lined park-

ways would provide the necessary access, enhance the park as an attractive destination, encourage real estate development along its route, and attract a large number of visitors to the park. It proposed similar parkways leading to other destinations and designed Shawnee Park and Cherokee Park. This was the same strategy that Haussmann and Napoleon III had used in creating avenue Foch in Paris and that Olmsted had used for Eastern and Ocean Parkways in Brooklyn: a grand tree-lined carriageway leading from town to the park, with park islands and service roads on either side, a key element in creating the public realm frameworks that I will discuss in chapter 8.

Southern Parkway was the first and grandest of these parkways. At 150 feet (45.7 m) in width, it was not as wide Eastern or Ocean Parkways, reflecting Louisville's smaller population and lower density. But its grandeur became apparent in later years, as the parallel pairs of oak trees that lined both sides of the parkway grew to a stately height of more than 60 feet (18.3 m). While many of these oaks perished in the tornado that hit Louisville in 1974, enough remain in place to understand the striking approach that Olmsted envisioned visitors would take to the park. The parkways that led to Cherokee and Shawnee Parks were lined with the same stately oaks, but without the continuous parallel service roads.

Real estate development enveloped these parks in New York and Louisville long ago, demonstrating the wisdom of the public officials who spent what seemed in those days huge sums on property that was then in unsettled areas. However prescient they may have been (given the huge appreciation in value since those purchases were made), their approach is not the only way to ensure that future populations will live around easily accessible public parks.

ACCOMMODATING INITIAL DEMAND

Responding effectively to public demand for parks involves timing park development to population and economic growth. Every locality faces the challenge of obtaining money to pay for park development (a topic that will be discussed further in chapter 10). If existing properties do not pay enough in real estate taxes to cover the cost of acquisition and development, the local government can issue bonds that anticipate future revenue. Another way to relate park development directly to market activity is to require real estate developers to either provide the parkland new residents and businesses demand or pay the government to develop that parkland. That is how Collierville, Tennessee, a suburb of Memphis, has been able to respond to its population's burgeoning demand.

During the 1990s Collierville began absorbing an increasing number of migrants from Memphis. Its population had grown from 7,839 in 1980 to 14,427 in 1990, and would grow to 44,000 in 2008.[8] It became clear to the town's leadership that Collierville needed additional parkland to accommodate this growing population. And, because 32 percent of new residents were recently formed families that were headed by people between the ages of 25 and 45 (more than the 28 percent typical of the rest of the United States), that parkland would have to provide space for active recreation: jogging, skating, cycling, swimming, and team sports. Rather than raise taxes on existing households, the town decided to shift the burden to new residential development.

In 1994 the mayor and board of aldermen enacted the Parkland Dedication Ordinance, which it revised in 1997. This regulation required any new residential development to dedicate 10.5 acres (4.2 ha) of public park for every 1,000 residents it would add to the town's population. Using the census-based average household size of three people, that came to

Town Owned Properties & Wolf River Corridor

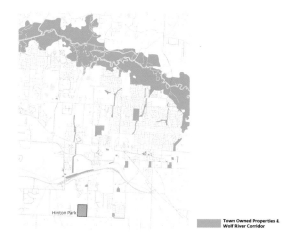

Hinton Park

Town Owned Properties & Wolf River Corridor

Collierville, Tennessee, 2008. Map of publicly owned park and open space.

Proposed Collierville Greenbelt Trail Network

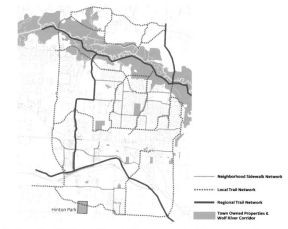

Neighborhood Sidewalk Network

Local Trail Network

Regional Trail Network

Town Owned Properties & Wolf River Corridor

Hinton Park

Collierville, 2008. Additional bike lanes, pedestrian paths, and open space proposed in the town's master plan will provide access corridors to parkland.

10.5 acres (4.2 ha) for every 333 households, or 1,374 square feet (128 m^2) of public park per residence. Each developer was required to donate the required land, an alternative payment of $40,000 per acre, or a combination of the two, under the oversight of the town's nine-member Parks, Recreation and Cultural Arts Advisory Board. The location and configuration of this parkland was determined by public officials during the subdivision approval process.

Between 1994 and 2008, the ordinance generated 85 acres (34 ha) of new parkland and over $3.2 million in payments made in lieu of donated land. As a result of careful planning by town administrator James Lewellyn and assistant town administra-

Collierville, 2006. This farmland was acquired for park development under a town ordinance that mandates 10.5 acres (4.2 ha) of public parkland for every 1,000 residents.

will be interconnected, providing residents with interesting routes for jogging, cycling, and skating, as well as alternative park destinations with the specific recreational activity they are seeking.

SHAPING SECOND GROWTH

tor Chip Peterson, acquisition has not proceeded helter-skelter, but rather in a manner that will produce an interconnected town park system. At their suggestion, in 2004 Collierville updated plans for an Overall Trail Network as part of its Greenbelt Master Plan, connecting schools and parks to a developing complex of regional and local trails and neighborhood sidewalks. Sometimes land contributions take the form of trails required in the master plan; sometimes they are small local parks. The nine local parks created during the first fourteen years of the ordinance range in size from 1 to 12 acres (0.4–4.9 ha).

Collierville's park system is evolving through both accidental increment and, where possible, by selected public acquisition financed by a $1.28 per $100 real estate tax. This is how the town acquired 110 acres (45 ha) of farmland in 2005 for the creation of Hinton Park. The largest component of the park system is the 2,800 acres (1,133 ha) of the Wolff River Wildlife Corridor, managed by the town and the Chickasaw Basin Authority. As a result of careful planning, as of 2008 Collierville owned a 695-acre (281-ha) parks system providing 88.7 acres (35.9 ha) per 1,000 residents, 12.5 miles (20.1 km) of Greenway, and 5,230 linear feet (1,594 m) of wetlands boardwalk.[9]

As the population continues to grow, so will the amount of land devoted to public parks. A large part of the financial burden of creating this additional parkland will be carried by property developers and passed on to their customers in the form of higher house prices. As the Collierville park system evolves, it will provide parkland that is easily accessible to every resident. More important, that system

Accommodating a mushrooming population within existing cities, rather than on outlying vacant land, usually requires replacing inadequate infrastructure, augmenting building stock, and creating a public realm that can handle accelerating population growth as well as the higher volume of traffic it will generate. Sometimes obstacles must be overcome in order to attract the private sector investment needed to accommodate this "second growth." In early twentieth-century San Antonio that obstacle was the river that flowed through the city, while in early twenty-first-century Atlanta the obstacle was the absence of an infrastructure of parkland that developers would be drawn to build near.

Civic leaders in San Antonio were able to capture market demand by eliminating an environmental hazard (regular flooding) and creating a public realm framework in the form of a riverfront park, the Paseo del Rio or Riverwalk. It took only two years and $430,000 to create the 1.8-mile (2.9-km) downtown portion of the Riverwalk. Only a very small portion of the city's population lives within walking

San Antonio, 1921. Until major reconstruction during the Great Depression, the San Antonio River flooded regularly, causing extensive property damage and even deaths.

distance, but nevertheless this park has proved to be a powerful force for urban transformation and has improved the quality of life in San Antonio.

Frederick Law Olmsted had described the San Antonio River in 1857 as "pure as crystal, flowing rapidly but noiselessly over pebbles and between reedy banks."[10] As it passes through San Antonio, the river bends into a horseshoe that loops through downtown. Because its banks were 15 feet (4.6 m) below street level, businesses erected buildings that fronted on the streets above and turned their backs on the river. By the start of the twentieth century, it had become a polluted eyesore cluttered with refuse. The river experienced lengthy dry periods, but at other times it flooded, and as the city grew these floods had serious consequences. Four people drowned during the flood of 1913. Fifty people died in the flood of 1921, which destroyed thirteen of the city's twenty-seven bridges. In order to lessen the danger of flooding, over the next decade sections of the river outside downtown were deepened, widened, or eliminated by creating alternative channels.

The primary flood control measure affecting the business district began in 1929 with the construction of a diversion channel connecting both ends of the horseshoe bend. This bypass provided an escape route for floodwaters. Locks were built to prevent any massive flow of water from entering the horseshoe

San Antonio, 1929. Construction of a bypass channel for the San Antonio River diverted floodwaters from the city.

during periods when the river threatened to overflow its banks.[11] Other proposals sought to control flooding by eliminating the horseshoe. Citizen groups successfully opposed plans to drain and fill the horseshoe bend, or to pave it over and rechannel the water into an underground main. Instead, many citizens wanted to transform the riverside into a park.

Robert Hugman, a local architect, was the primary leader in an effort to "restore" the river. In 1929 he had submitted a proposal that combined an evocation of the French Quarter in New Orleans with a fantasy vision of San Antonio's Spanish heritage. City leaders eventually accepted Hugman's idea, but at the time they were not able to raise the money to pay for it. Downtown property owners within half a block of the river formed the San Antonio Improvement District, and in 1938 they voted almost unanimously for a self-imposed tax of 0.5 cents per $100 of assessed value. The resulting income stream provided the debt service for a $75,000 bond issue. The city's mayor, Maury Maverick, a former congressman, persuaded the Roosevelt Administration to match it with $355,000 from the Works Prog-

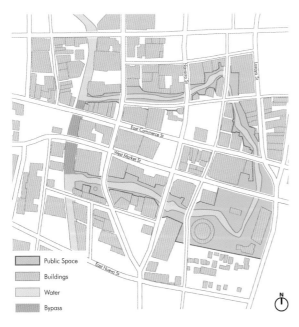

San Antonio, 2007. Government assistance helped pay for the transformation of the river from a hazard into a public park.

San Antonio, 2007. The Riverwalk has become one of the most successful tourist attractions in Texas.

ress Administration (WPA). Construction on this 21-block project finally began in March 1939 and was completed in the fall of 1941.[12]

Hugman designed the new Riverwalk. He also supervised the required temporary draining of the bend; the transplanting of shrubs and plants and the continuing care of existing trees; the planting of an additional 11,734 trees and shrubs, 1,500 banana trees, and 1,489 square yards (1,245 m²) of grass; and the construction of 17,000 feet (518 m) of walkways, 21 bridges, 31 stairways, a water pumping station, and a theater. The riverbed was deepened in some areas and filled in others in order to obtain a uniform depth of 3.5 feet (1 m), deep enough for small river boats but shallow enough to prevent drowning. The result was a charming, picturesque linear park.[13]

Initially the new park had little effect on the city, because little development was occurring anywhere in the United States during World War II. After the war, however, the factories and warehouses that once turned their backs on the river were slowly replaced by retail stores attracted by the growing number of customers who now used the park as a shortcut to various downtown destinations. These stores were followed by hotels, restaurants, and boutiques attracted by the tourists who enjoyed walking along this unique park. By the twenty-first century the Riverwalk had become San Antonio's second most visited tourist attraction, surpassed only by the Alamo.

The Riverwalk has been extended into other sections of the city. Its dominant role in the life of San Antonio, both during the day and at night, has evolved as a result of changes to private property enclosing this linear park rather than park enlargements. It has continued to provide the framework around which valuable commercial and residential buildings are built, the context for a succession of hotels, stores, and restaurants serving as tourist destinations, and the setting for a way of life that can only be found in San Antonio.

Atlanta's second growth took a very different form from San Antonio's. At the start of the twenty-first century, much of Atlanta was already developed (although at relatively low densities) when builders began to satisfy the burgeoning demand for new housing by redeveloping underutilized residential sites, empty warehouses and factories, and leftover vacant parcels outside the central business district. Much of this infill development took place within a mile or two (1.6–3.2 km) of its downtown and midtown business districts. City leaders understood that incoming residents would need additional municipal services, especially public transportation, more open space, and new recreation facilities. The city's response to second growth in this inner ring was investment in the Beltline Emerald Necklace, a system of connected urban green spaces named after Boston's famous Olmsted-designed Emerald Necklace.

Atlanta had developed around railroads, and for this reason it was uniquely situated to develop its derelict rail yards and tracks into public parks or recreation destinations. Sites for private development became available because so many companies turned to trucks to move their freight, eliminating the advantage of a location along rail lines.

Atlanta's Beltline Emerald Necklace of parks and transit, proposed in the 2004 plan prepared by my firm, Alex Garvin & Associates, for the Trust for Public Land, was approved by the Atlanta City Council in 2005. The original idea for reusing the rail belt around Atlanta was first proposed in 1999 by Ryan Gravel in a master's thesis at Georgia Tech. Alex Garvin & Associates and the Trust for Public Land suggested transforming what had been envisioned as a trail with transit service into a major addition to Atlanta's park system that will provide a public realm framework around which developers could direct the city's second growth.

The Beltline Emerald Necklace will consist of a 23-mile (37-km) Beltline Trail encircling the city and tying together forty-six neighborhoods with one another and with three subway stations in the city's existing subway system; a 20-mile (32-km) Beltline Transit system that will provide access to every major destination in Atlanta; and thirteen park jewels (four expanded parks, four new parks, and five mixed-use parks)—all well within the boundaries of the city.

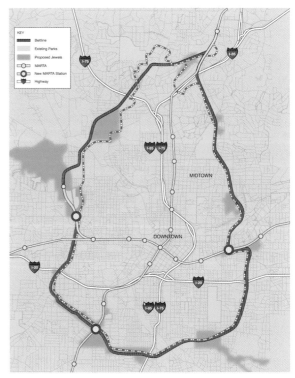

Atlanta, 2004. The plan for the Beltline Emerald Necklace provides a blueprint for the eventual transformation of the inner ring neighborhoods of the city.

This combination park and transit system is being paid for through tax increment financing that harvests twenty-five years of additional taxes collected from the increase in property value of existing and new real estate developments that benefit from the substantial municipal investment in the Beltline.

With assistance from the Trust for Public Land, the city acquired the first new park, the former Bellwood Quarry, in 2006, and the second park, Boulevard Crossing, in 2007. It is continuing to acquire railroad rights-of-way and privately owned properties that will tie together the populations and businesses located in the city's growing inner ring of suburbs. When the Beltline Emerald Necklace is completed, it will provide a public realm framework of new and expanded parks connected by transit service running along or parallel to trails for walking, jogging, skating, and cycling.

SEIZING OPPORTUNITY

Collierville's approach to creating parkland was based on standards used by the National Park and Recre-

Astoria Park, Queens, New York, 2005. Robert Moses created this park by reusing land acquired for construction of the Triborough Bridge (now the Robert F. Kennedy Bridge).

ation Association (NPRA) to determine minimum acceptable facilities for the citizens of urban and rural communities. The NPRA believes that "standards should be viewed as a guide" and "interpreted according to the particular situation to which they are applied and specific local needs." Robert Moses understood such standards were impractical, explaining that there is "no such thing as a fixed percentage of park area to population. . . . Sensible, practical people know that [it] depends upon the actual problems of the city in question."[14]

Moses believed in seizing opportunities for park development whenever and wherever they appeared—because once lost, the property was

unlikely to be available again. He did not make decisions based on formulas or theories, but rather on "the actual problems of the city in question."[15] During the Great Depression, for example, the most pressing problem was not the lack of parks, but the lack of jobs for hundreds of thousands of unemployed people—the key issue that enabled Moses to address park development by using personnel hired through New Deal employment programs.

During his first three years as New York City's parks commissioner, Moses put tens of thousands of people to work in the city's parks. He obtained $136 million from the WPA and several other federal economic recovery programs for seventeen hundred work relief projects. The army of 69,000 relief workers that he inherited when he was named commissioner in 1934 had been a major headache. Six thousand were assigned to ash-heap garbage dumps; twenty thousand were on the payroll but nobody could trace their assignments. To transform that headache into a spectacular asset, Moses announced that he needed at least five hundred technically trained landscape and construction work supervisors. He was told to use some of the relief workers as supervisors. He refused! Within a week (which

Shore Parkway, Brooklyn, New York, 2007. When the Shore Parkway was being built in the late 1930s, Moses seized the opportunity to add recreational amenities: a bicycle path, a pedestrian promenade, and benches along its entire waterside.

Flushing Meadows Corona Park, Queens, New York, 2006. The "ash heap" depicted in F. Scott Fitzgerald's novel *The Great Gatsby* was reclaimed by Robert Moses for the 1939 and 1964 World's Fairs. It became one of the city's busiest public parks.

included threatened resignations) Moses had persuaded the mayor, the Board of Estimate, and the state government to appropriate the funds he needed for tools, materials, and the five hundred technical supervisors. The following Saturday, thirteen hundred telegrams were sent to likely candidates. At two o'clock the following afternoon interviewing began. By Monday, 453 applicants had received telegrams ordering them to work that morning. Three years later they had developed 265 playgrounds, twelve Olympic swimming pools, and eight golf courses.[16]

Moses achieved stupendous results because of his opportunistic approach to the creation of public parks. Wherever the city was creating a new highway, bridge, tunnel, or housing development, Moses found a way to incorporate parkland. While building the Shore Parkway in Brooklyn, for example, he invested in a pedestrian esplanade and bicycle path between the roadway and the waterfront. He

believed that public policies provided the rationale for acquiring property for public parks, and he seized opportunities wherever they were available. In 1924, when Governor Alfred E. Smith appointed him chairman of the Long Island State Parks Authority, he began conceiving a parkway system that would provide landscaped motorways for residents of New York City and Long Island. That parkway network would provide area residents with access to public parks like Jones Beach. One of those parkways was the Grand Central Parkway, leading from the Triborough Bridge (now the Robert F. Kennedy Bridge) on the East River into Nassau County.

Construction of the Grand Central Parkway began in 1931. Moses tried to get rid of the stinking Corona garbage dump that ran along the eastern side of the parkway for about 2 miles (3.2 km) between Flushing Bay and Kew Gardens. This dump is probably the most famous pile of garbage in American literature, because F. Scott Fitzgerald included a description of it in *The Great Gatsby:* "This is a valley of ashes—a fantastic farm where ashes grow like wheat into ridges and hills and grotesque gardens; where ashes take the forms of houses and chimneys and rising smoke and, finally, with a transcendent effort, of men who move dimly and already crumbling through the powdery air."[17] At first, Moses could not find a way to eliminate this environmental hazard. Then, in the late 1930s, a group of New Yorkers who had the idea of celebrating the 150th anniversary of Washington's inaugural by sponsoring a World's Fair sought his advice. Moses persuaded them that the best possible site was the Corona garbage dump.

Moses had more in mind than just finding a site for the 1939 New York World's Fair, building it, and serving as the sole member of its board of directors. He also completed projects that public officials had spent years trying to implement. These included creating a complete drainage and sewer system for the area (including a major sewage treatment plant) building the Whitestone Bridge (connected to the Grand Central Parkway by what became the Whitestone Expressway), developing new and widened traffic arteries, and ultimately achieving his dream of permanently eliminating the Corona garbage dump—by turning the fairgrounds into 1,255-acre (508-ha) Flushing Meadows Corona Park.

Seattle, 2007. The Olympic Sculpture Park was created on a former fuel storage facility by decontaminating part of the site and building over a highway and a railroad.

FIVE

SITE SELECTION AND ADAPTATION

Robert Moses believed that parks should be developed in response to "the actual problems of the city in question," and although each city might face different problems and solve those problems in different ways, each has to confront the same questions when it plans to create a park: What specific locations are suitable for park development? Do these sites require additional investment to eliminate, alter, or add something in order to transform the space into easily accessible, user-friendly places for public recreation? And how should new parkland interact with the surrounding metropolitan region?

That a given site is available does not necessarily mean it can be made into a convenient, usable park. It may be too small, too difficult to get to or too difficult to move around in, or it may require too much expensive site work. Frederick Law Olmsted believed that the first thing to do was to investigate a proposed location in order to form "a judgment upon the capabilities and the limitations of that site," which included assessing its shape, dimensions, and topographical conditions, as well as "the number and the habits and customs of the people, which are to make use of it . . . and the convenience and pleasure of future generations."[1]

Property that is available at a low price because it is undesirable for real estate development is likely

to be just as unsuitable for park development. Many wetlands and steep slopes, for example, are as inappropriate for a public park as they are for a residential or commercial development. Occasionally a proposed site will be so unsuitable that it provokes public opposition. In 1895, when Kansas City's Board of Park Commissioners considered acquiring the first section of what is today Kessler Park, citizens objected because this steep cliff was "too rugged for a park."[2] The board went ahead and obtained the site anyway, and the city wound up with a place that could be used for hiking, but not for many other popular park activities.

Designers may well object to creating parks in problematic locations. Calvert Vaux, prior to resuming his partnership with Olmsted in 1866, persuaded the Brooklyn Park Commission to abandon some of the land intended for Prospect Park in order to acquire property that he believed had "superior landscape capabilities."[3] The commission had purchased 300 acres (121 ha) of undeveloped land divided into two unequal pieces by Flatbush Avenue, a busy thoroughfare. The park would have needed expensive bridges and underpasses so that visitors could pass safely between the two areas.[4] Instead, Vaux convinced the commission to purchase an even larger amount of land just south of the larger piece the commission already owned, and he proposed

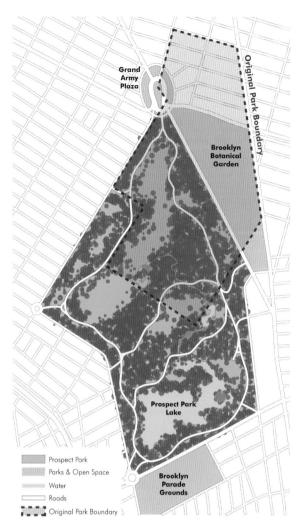

Prospect Park, Brooklyn, New York. Brooklyn leaders accepted Calvert Vaux's recommendation that the proposed park not be divided into two sections by a major traffic artery. They sold the property northeast of Flatbush Avenue, acquiring instead additional land that made possible the creation of one of the nation's greatest public parks.

that property at the north of the site be sold to pay for land that would eventually become the site of the Prospect Park Lake, Lookout Hill, and the Parade Ground.

In 1873 Olmsted and Vaux objected to transforming what was essentially a cliff on the western edge of Manhattan's Harlem section into a public park. They reported to the city's Department of Public Parks that the site of the proposed Morningside Park was "singularly incapable" of being used as a public park because most of it was not flat enough to be used for recreation purposes and did not have enough soil to support large trees. The rest of the site consisted of a steep cliff that would

be difficult to climb and in their opinion could "by no appropriate treatment . . . be made a safe and reputable place of resort at night."[5] Fourteen years later, Olmsted and Vaux prepared a design for a park on that site that was subsequently executed. On the flats below the cliff, they planned meadows that could be used for a variety of informal activities, and these remain effective as parkland today. But even though they applied all their talent and experience to minimizing stairs and "dark shadowy places," ensuring the park would be "well lighted at all points," and avoiding "all conditions that would give ruffians special opportunities for sudden acts of violence and for escaping observation," they still were unable to create usable, safe parkland out of the cliffs of Morningside Park.[6]

When he assessed the site that was ultimately adopted for Golden Gate Park in San Francisco, Olmsted doubted that its topography, soil, and climate would allow the broad lawns and great trees that could be found in the parks of London and New York. But even Olmsted could be mistaken about such things. Plans for the park proceeded; perhaps the species are different, but the large trees that were planted in Golden Gate Park offer as much shade as those in London or New York.

Olmsted also thought that a site adjacent to a given neighborhood might not necessarily be the best choice for a park that would meet the needs of all local users; he believed that "some parts of the site or the neighborhood of a city will nearly always be especially favorable to provisions of recreation of one class, other parts to provisions of another class."[7] It was better to plan for activities that were appropriate to that specific site, with the intention that the area would contain other parks that could better accommodate alternative activities. As he explained, "A site for a park to stand by itself and be little used except by those living near it should be a very different one from that for a park designed for more general use, and especially for a park which is to stand as one of a series."[8] For that reason he recommended considering parks within a regional context rather than as stand-alone facilities, proposing for Boston the 6-mile (9.7-km) Emerald Necklace that would provide the many different recreational opportunities sought by residents of adjacent neighborhoods somewhere along

Morningside Park, New York City, 2008. Olmsted and Vaux did not believe the cliff that separated Morningside Heights from the flats of Harlem below could be transformed into a park that would be safe at night.

the necklace, though not necessarily within a few minutes' walk of their residences.

PRESERVATION, ALTERATION, OR REPLACEMENT?

In places of natural beauty, creating a public park may require only minimal alterations. At Bartholomew's Cobble, a 329-acre (133-ha) preserve that rises above the Housatonic River Valley in western Massachusetts, people can explore untrammeled nature and enjoy broad vistas overlooking the surrounding landscape. But in most cases it is not enough to acquire a site and leave it as is. Parks must be convenient to get to and easy to move around in, and they must include places that people want to visit. Olmsted knew that people would travel to a park by differing means and for differing reasons, "some of them walking, others driving, others rid-

Bartholomew's Cobble, Sheffield, Massachusetts, 2008. The hiking trails and breathtaking views from this park are all it takes to attract visitors.

ing; some pursue their course alone, others seek company, some keep to the main thoroughfares, others seek secluded parts."[9] He recommended creating places that were flexible enough to be used for whatever activities people wanted; thus park destinations would have to be adapted accordingly. Those who come by car will need parking facilities; those arriving on foot or by public transportation should find convenient points of entry. If park users are not to damage the landscape, paths, trails, and roads will be needed to lead them to their destinations. Few sites can be turned into usable parks without expenditures for earthwork, construction, and plantings.

After three decades of professional practice, Olmsted had developed an unparalleled skill at transforming sites into successful parks. In each of his parks we can see how the characteristics of the site influenced his approach to park development. Some, like Iroquois Park in Louisville, involved little more than providing public access and circulation systems. Shawnee and Cherokee Parks, the other two facilities he designed for Louisville, involved more extensive alteration. New York City's Central Park, on the other hand, required complete reconstruction.

The prime attractions of the site that became Iroquois Park were its natural, heavily forested

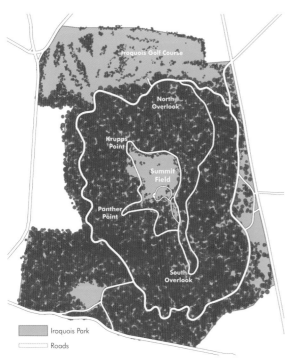

Iroquois Park, Louisville, 2008. A roadway and some minor land-scaping were all that Olmsted thought necessary to turn this site into a successful public park.

Shawnee Park, Louisville, 2008. Olmsted designed a circumferential roadway to provide public access to flexible playing fields on the park's open meadows.

slopes and the view from the top of the Burnt Knob promontory. Olmsted saw his prime tasks as preserving and exposing visitors to the awesome woodland and providing access to the view from Burnt Knob without destroying the natural landscape. He achieved this by introducing pedestrian walkways and carriage drives, one of which climbed the hill, encircled the top, and descended by a different route.

Olmsted needed to make a number of alterations for 316-acre (128-ha) Shawnee Park, which opened in 1892. This broad, tranquil meadowland, which he cleared of all obstructions, was located on the eastern edge of the Ohio River. The park sloped up from the river to the flat meadow, and around the meadow he designed a circumferential road that provides access to every section of the park, shaded by the great spreading boughs of the trees that line it on either side. Where the road ran along the Ohio, the wide openings between tree trunks provided welcome openings for the breeze and for views of the river. Unfortunately, the park has since fallen into disrepair, with overgrown weeds and unkempt shrubs and trees blocking both the view and the river breezes that were the once lovely, distinguishing characteristics of a well-used public park.

The design of 409-acre (166-ha) Cherokee Park, which also opened in 1892, posed different problems. It was essentially a valley formed by Beargrass

Beargrass Creek, Cherokee Park, Louisville, 2008. Wading in this natural waterway has delighted children and adults for more than a century.

Creek. Olmsted believed that with fewer but more significant adjustments than he proposed for Shawnee Park, the sloping hills, open fields, and shady groves of trees could become a pastoral landscape. His design eliminated overly prominent natural features that interfered with the purity of this picturesque landscape and added a substantial number of native trees and shrubs that would enhance it. The planting was intended to enclose each section of the park so that each had its own identity.

As at Iroquois and Shawnee Parks, Olmsted added pedestrian walks and a dramatic circuit drive that allows visitors to enjoy both the winding valley and the tree-covered slopes. Because of the way he placed trees and shrubs, one wanders from section to section of the park experiencing quite different landscapes: grass-covered hillsides with magnificent trees standing singly and in open groups; rolling greenswards (some of which are now used for golf); and dark, mysterious woods and limestone outcroppings lining the shallow waters of Beargrass Creek. The cumulative experience of passing through these places truly gives one a "sense of enlarged freedom."[10]

When Olmsted designed Iroquois, Cherokee, and Shawnee Parks, he was at the peak of his career, able to tap the vast experience he had amassed designing parks throughout the nation. Perhaps his relative inexperience had led him and Vaux to propose the virtual replacement of the existing landscape for Central Park thirty-four years earlier.

The more likely reason, however, was that the land in its raw state was inappropriate for use as a public park. Olmsted had become particularly aware of the character of the site during the five months he spent as superintendent of the park, before submitting the design. He described the whole site as "rugged, in parts excessively so," pointing out that "there is scarcely an acre of level, or slope unbroken by ledges."[11]

Transforming this 843-acre (341-ha), rectangular property, 0.5 miles (0.8 km) wide and 2.5 miles (4 km) long, into a functionally sustainable public park required extraordinary amounts of "time, labor,

Central Park, Manhattan, 1858, 1862, and 2007. Olmsted and Vaux decided to transform the rough topography of the southeastern corner of Central Park into a lake. By 1862 it had been excavated. For a century and a half it has been one of the most admired sections of the park.

and expense" and earthworks on a scale comparable to those of the most elaborate French estate landscapes of the seventeenth century. Olmsted calculated that 4,825,000 cubic yards (3,698,000 m³) of earth and stone were moved in creating the park, "or nearly ten millions of ordinary one-horse cartloads, which, in single file, would make a procession thirty thousand . . . miles in length."[12] Natural drainage patterns were replaced by underground conduits. During the first five years of construction, thousands of laborers were assigned to work on the park. Often their only qualification for construction work was political patronage. Using primitive tools and 166 tons of gunpowder, they "cut through more than 300,000 cubic yards of gneiss rock veined with granite . . . crushed 35,000 cubic yards of rock into paving stones," used "6 million bricks, 35,000 barrels of cement, 65,000 cubic yards of gravel, 19,000 cubic yards of sand, . . . 40,000 cubic yards of manure," and planted 270,000 trees and shrubs.[13] After the park was completed, Olmsted wrote that "it would have been difficult to find another body of land [in Manhattan] . . . which possessed less of what we have seen to be the most desirable characteristics of a park, or upon which more time, labor and expense would be required to establish them."[14]

Because Robert Moses, as New York City's parks commissioner, was dealing with development within an already built-out city of 7 million people, he had to consider a far broader range of public concerns than Olmsted faced when he was creating parks for New York or Lousiville. In New York Moses was not developing open land far from the settled sections of the city. At Orchard Beach in the Bronx, for example, he had to deal with an occupied city-owned site already used for recreational purposes; in particular, he had to relocate site occupants, a move that was certainly controversial.

A section of Pelham Bay Park in the Bronx, which had been New York City's largest public park since it was created in 1888, opened onto Long Island Sound. Although this stretch of waterfront was called a beach, there was no beach at high tide, and public access was impeded by unauthorized tent colonies and ramshackle bungalows and campsites allegedly dispensed as patronage by the Bronx County Democratic machine. During his first month in office, Moses decided that this public parkland should be universally accessible and this much-needed recreation resource made available to the millions of people who lived in northern Manhattan and the Bronx.

There was opposition from the start. "On an inspection trip," Moses later recalled, "I narrowly escaped bricks thrown by enraged squatters and was rescued by a mounted policeman."[15] Outraged leaseholders petitioned Mayor Fiorello La Guardia, but within five months Moses succeeded in canceling all leases, forcing the occupants to move, and leveling the site.

Orchard Beach, Bronx, New York, 1999. During the summer tens of thousands of residents of northern Manhattan and the Bronx come by bus to enjoy this entirely man-made public beach.

The $8 million redevelopment plan, prepared by landscape designer Gilmore Clarke, called for 115 acres (47 ha) of landfill, part incinerated trash and part white sand obtained from Rockaway Inlet in Queens. When Orchard Beach reopened for the summer of 1936, the parks department had a public park that included a 1.2-mile (1.9-km) beach more than 200 feet (61 m) across, bathhouses, a boardwalk, playgrounds, twenty-six handball, volleyball, tennis, and basketball courts, picnic grounds, and an enormous parking lot. On summer weekends it is used by tens of thousands of people, most of whom do not come by car. They take the bus from virtually every Bronx neighborhood and from Washington Heights in Manhattan.[16]

Moses's experience with Orchard Beach underscores that site adaptation does not stop after a park is initially opened to the public. It is an ongoing process that must accommodate the changes in demand that accompany the evolution of surrounding communities. The ongoing improvements to Stanley Park in Vancouver, Canada, illustrate this particularly well. This 1,000-acre (405-ha) park was created to provide city dwellers with an opportunity to immerse themselves in the beauty and sublimity of nature. It was set aside as parkland to protect it from the pressures of real estate development and leased to the city for $1 per year by the Canadian government in 1887. The following year, when it was officially opened to the public by Lord Stanley, governor general of Canada, in whose honor it was named, he dedicated it in Olmstedian language

Stanley Park, Vancouver, 1999. Many of the majestic trees in this apparently natural landscape were planted after the first-growth trees had been cleared by logging companies or downed by storms.

"to the use and enjoyment of peoples of all colors, creeds, and customs, for all time."[17]

Large sections of the site had been cleared by logging companies before the park was created. Other parts were deforested at various times by fierce wind and snowstorms. Thus while this majestic forest preserve, containing over half a million trees, appears to be completely natural, it consists primarily of planted and self-seeded second and third growths of cedar, hemlock, fir, and spruce, some as tall as 250 feet (76 m).

Stanley Park has been managed since 1888 by

Stanley Park, Vancouver, 1999. This circumferential roadway is a popular jogging and cycling trail that also provides access to the forested sections of the park.

the Vancouver Board of Parks and Recreation, an elected board that now manages 180 parks throughout the province. During that time it has made major changes to the park, adding 125 miles (201 km) of trails and roads to provide access to the forest, as well as facilities for cricket, lawn bowling, tennis, soccer, baseball, Frisbee, and golf; provided sites for the Royal Vancouver Yacht Club and Vancouver Rowing Club; opened a children's zoo, a miniature train, an aquarium, and several restaurants; created rhododendron, perennial, and rose gardens; and installed totem poles and a Japanese Monument.

As Olmsted understood so well, when large crowds are attracted to a natural landscape the problem becomes permitting visitors to enjoy a natural wonder while simultaneously retaining the sublime character of untrammeled nature. To solve this problem, the Vancouver Board of Parks and Recreation invested in a seawall and pedestrian artery encircling the natural peninsula that became Stanley Park. The seawall provides access to the forest while simultaneously diverting substantial numbers of park users away from the wilderness and toward enjoyment of the views across surrounding waterways. This 5.5-mile (8.9-km) seawall path was begun in 1914 and completed in 1980. Since then, it has been used annually by 2.5 million pedestrians, joggers, cyclists, and inline skaters. The path system also has been extended and now provides a recreation facility that stretches some 14 miles (22.5 km), from downtown Vancouver, around the park, and past miles of public beach, encircling much of the city.[18]

ADAPTIVE REUSE

During the latter part of the twentieth century, many properties that had been used for industrial production and shipping became available as a result of widespread deindustrialization. These large, run-down properties without obvious users represented a problem. Park advocates identified many of these sites as desirable for reuse as public parks, but their transformation often required decontamination, a redevelopment plan, appropriate reworking of their relationship with the surrounding area, and a public or private entity prepared to operate the new park.

As we have seen, creating a park on virgin territory is not always easy, but adapting a site that has previously been altered for human use is more complex, and it almost always involves more issues than starting from scratch. Accumulations of unhealthy or even poisonous waste may need to be removed, and decisions must be made as to whether planting, artwork, structures, or other remnants of previous activities should be retained, including land uses that are not yet obsolete. These decisions can be difficult, particularly when a site is in an area that is already built up. At the same time, one major benefit of adaptive reuse is that these once-active sites tend to be centrally located and easily accessible to surrounding populations.

Deciding what should remain and what should be removed is not just a matter of physical safety, functional utility, or aesthetic desires. Sites that were once actively used for some other purpose tend to be located in or near populated areas, and park designers and developers must decide what will attract those who are likely to use the park—both now and in the future—to return to these places.

Whether the site is an underutilized industrial property, an abandoned railroad, or a once-thriving waterfront, some of the same considerations come into play. In each of the examples that follow, the initial site selection depended entirely on seizing an available opportunity, but they demonstrate that there can be radically different approaches to adaptive reuse, that no standardized approach can be applied to every situation. Decisions are influenced not only by the opportunities and constraints of specific sites and the needs of their surrounding communities, but by design styles and trends of the times. Indeed, an increasing number of properties adapted for reuse as public parks now avoid clear distinctions between park and non-park activities, aiming for a seamless integration of the park with its surroundings.

INDUSTRIAL AREAS

The most obvious way to deal with abandoned or underused industrial sites is to eliminate all traces of previous and current uses, as Haussmann did in the 1860s when he transformed the abandoned quarry and dump in northeast Paris into the Parc des Buttes-Chaumont. But this approach can draw strong opposition from a number of stakeholders: preservationists, site occupants, the owners and employees of still-functioning businesses on the site, other firms that depend on the business they bring them, and citizens who object to cost of buying them out.

One of the earliest attempts to deal with this problem in the United States was in mid-nineteenth-century Philadelphia. Citizens had been seeking safe drinking water because they believed that the epidemics that had plagued the city since the end of the eighteenth century could be attributed to industrial pollution of its waterways. In 1854 the state legislature gave the city and county the power to acquire private property as public open space, and a year later it began purchasing private estates. Those properties were the initial components of what would become the 4,167-acre (1,686-ha) Fairmount Park, part of the city's eventual 9,200-acre (3,723-ha) system of sixty-three parks created by the Fairmount Park Commission, established by the Commonwealth of Pennsylvania in 1867.[19]

Benjamin Franklin had left the city £1,000 to pipe water from Wissahickon Creek, with the stipulation that the money first be invested for a hundred years. When the funds matured , the Fairmount Park Commission used some of them to pay for property acquisition in the Wissahickon Valley along the 7-mile (11.3-km) Wissahickon Creek tributary.[20] As a result more than sixty mills that were polluting its waters were put out of business and demolished. The commission was able to overcome opposition to the destruction of these industrial properties because the bulk of the electorate believed providing Philadelphia with a guaranteed supply of clean water was so obviously in the general interest that it outweighed other considerations.

As Fairmount Park and the Parc des Buttes-Chaumont demonstrate, regardless of the level of opposition, adaptive reuse of any site is not easy because the cost of acquisition and decontamination is frequently very high. But if new parkland is integral to generating additional private expenditures for residential and commercial development in the area, it is a price government agencies may be willing to pay. New taxes generated from private development in the surrounding neighborhood can

Philadelphia, 2009. An empty paper mill at the former industrial village of Rittenhouse Town is the only remnant of more than sixty mills that operated along Wissahickon Creek, within what is now Fairmount Park.

sometimes more than cover the cost of the park. as was the case as with Jamison Square Park in Portland, Oregon.

One common private market reaction to abandoned industrial lofts and warehouses has been to transform them into residential buildings. The phenomenon began in the 1960s in New York City and spread to Chicago, San Francisco, and Milwaukee, and it reached the Pearl District of Portland, Oregon, in the late 1980s. The district's transformation was already under way when civic leaders decided to clean up its northern section and set aside sites for parks and new housing on the city's traditional 200-by-200-foot (61-by-61-m) blocks.

The city believed the area would evolve in a better way if a district plan was in place. In 1997 the Portland Development Commission entered into an agreement with the Burlington Northern Railroad to redevelop its 34-acre (14-ha) yard and remove 30,000 cubic yards (23,000 m³) of contaminated soil. Two years later the commission began a master plan competition and public participation process that resulted in the adoption of a redevelopment plan by Peter Walker and Partners Landscape Architects. Two of Portland's traditional blocks were to become neighborhood parks (Jamison Square and Tanner Springs Park), while railroad property at the north end of the site was set aside for active recreation. These three new parks would become the public realm framework around which private developers would erect new residential and commercial buildings.

Creating the parks required extensive reconstruction, not only because the sites required decontamination in order to be used by large numbers of people but also because they needed attractions that would draw visitors. Peter Walker's design for Jamison Square, like the city's Keller Fountain Park, is organized around a cascade (see chapter 6). The water flowing over the large concrete blocks at the Keller Fountain makes it extremely popular with teenagers and adults. The cascade at Jamison Square, on the other hand, is only a few inches high and is meant for toddlers. It is even more popular; on nice summer days, hundreds of people are in Jamison Square—toddlers splashing in the water supervised by doting adults and siblings, families stretched out on the grass reading or picnicking, and older folks sitting on benches.

Adapting this block of a former loft district for use as a public park was a relatively straightforward process: demolish obsolete structures, eliminate any contamination, prepare a neighborhood redevelopment plan, and commission the design for a new park. It required money, political will, public support, and a redevelopment agency. Sometimes, however, even that is not enough. A more ingenious design may be necessary.

Seattle's Olympic Sculpture Park, which opened in 2007, occupies 9 acres (3.6 ha) that were particularly tough to transform into a public park, especially one that serves as an outdoor sculpture gallery. The leadership of the Seattle Art Museum and the Trust for Public Land had been looking for a site on which to display some of the museum's sculpture. They identified a property that had been used by Union Oil of California (UNOCAL) for fuel storage, which had left the soil and ground water contaminated. In the 1990s UNOCAL, working with the State of Washington Department of Ecology, removed 120,000 tons of petroleum-polluted soil and installed a groundwater recovery system. The configuration of the site was unpromising: there was a 40-foot (12-m) grade change and, worse yet, active railroad tracks and the heavily trafficked urban arterial of Elliot Avenue divided it into narrow north–south strips.

Despite the contaminated ground and the awkward configuration, the Seattle Art Museum and the Trust for Public Land believed the UNOCAL site had genuine potential. The location was superb: it was situated at a prominent spot on the edge of the business district, along a linear waterfront recreational facility that Seattle has spent decades establishing along the shore of Elliot Bay. To the south is the 1.3-mile (2.1-km) Alaska Way, with piers used for ferry service, restaurants, tourist-oriented entertainment facilities, platforms with spectacular views

Portland, 2007. The park at Jamison Square was created on the site of a former manufacturing and warehouse district.

Seattle, 2007. The Olympic Sculpture Park is part of the city's concerted effort to reclaim the waterfront for recreational uses.

of the Seattle skyline, and a major aquarium. This heavily used stretch continues north of the Sculpture Park in the form of the naturally landscaped 1.2-mile (1.9-km) long Myrtle Edwards Park and 1-mile (1.6-km) long Elliot Bay Park, which include bikeways, pedestrian trails, pocket beaches, and clusters of grass, shrubs, and trees.

Decontaminating a site of this sort is not technically difficult, but it requires money. The issue, therefore, is whether the end-user can afford the cost of acquisition and clean-up. Because the purchasers, the Trust for Public Land and the Seattle Art Museum, were nonprofit institutions, UNOCAL was accommodating. It reduced the price and held the site until they could raise the money to pay for it.

The design by architects Weiss/Manfredi made all the difference. To transform the previously unusable slivers into a successful public park, they proposed the construction of a land bridge that crossed over them, tying the slivers into a single, user-friendly facility. This elevated 2,200-foot (67-m) "invented ground plane," which looks like an enormous Z, rises from the fill-created park along Puget Sound to a platform that provides breathtaking views of downtown Seattle, Alaska Way, Myrtle Edwards and Elliot Bay Parks, and Puget Sound. From there it switches back, crossing the railroad and leading to a spot that overlooks polygonal meadows that display sculpture. Then it switches

back over Elliot Avenue, leading past an amphitheater to a visitors' pavilion.

The result is even more than a remediated brownfield, a sculpture display, and a repaired shoreline. It is an amazing public park where residents from surrounding neighborhoods walk their dogs and sit on benches enjoying the view, downtown office workers pass through while jogging along Puget Sound, children play among the sculptures, and tourists mix

Duisburg, Germany, 2008. The Landschaftspark adapted remnants of the Ruhr Valley's industrial past as components of a new public park.

with art lovers who have come to see a remarkable collection of twentieth- and twenty-first-century sculptures.

While all traces of previous land uses have been removed from Olympic Sculpture Park, they are apparent everywhere in the Landschaftspark in Duisburg, Germany. The creators of this 570-acre (231-ha) park took a radically different approach to the industrial landscape: doing relatively little to the site. Rusting relics of an industrial past were augmented with a few recreational attractions created within the remnants of coking facilities and ironworks and connected by pedestrian and bike paths (often along routes once traveled by railcars). The rest was left to voluntary vegetation. The park's creators avoided spending money on acquisition and decontamination except where absolutely necessary. In some areas, companies that were still operating were left in place; in others, where remediation of abandoned sites was costly and not essential for the park's operation, sites were fenced off to prevent public use.

This concept was the product of a design competition operated by the Internationale Bauausstellung Emscher Park (International Building Exhibition Emscher Park, or IBA), which in 1989 selected five teams of landscape architects to make proposals for the site. The IBA had been established to revive Emscher Park, a 43-mile (70-km) corridor within the Ruhr Valley. The valley had been an important part

of Germany's economic base since the eighteenth century. It began with coal mining and iron and steel production. One of the most successful ventures was the Thyssen coal mine, coking plant, and ironworks in Duisburg. Coal was mined at the site from 1899 and to 1959. The ironworks opened in 1903 and produced a total of 37 million tons of iron before they were closed in 1985.[21] Like the rest of the Ruhr, the complex began to decline in the 1960s and left behind an industrial landscape of strip mines, ore storage bunkers, rail corridors, iron and steel works, gasometers, and high chimneys.

The area's importance and population also declined during the last quarter of the twentieth century. Nevertheless, Duisburg at the beginning of the twenty-first century had the largest inland harbor in the world and was still the eleventh-largest city in Germany, with a population of just under half a million people.[22] While its economy was switching to energy production, environmental technologies, and modern service industries, it was still plagued by declining industrial relics that dominated the landscape and had left a legacy of pollution.

Between 1989 and 1999, the IBA spent the equivalent of $2.7 billion on more than a hundred projects for the Ruhr Valley—everything from sewage treatment plants to art projects, cutting-edge housing developments to highways.[23] Karl Ganser, managing director of the IBA, believed that contaminated relics of the industrial past could successfully coexist with a healthy economy and population. The design for the Landschaftspark by landscape architect Peter Latz has proven that he was correct.

The park is divided into three sorts of areas: places that continue to be used as before, places that are left for later development, and places that are intended for recreation. All three are connected by a series of paths that are popular for biking and strolling. Because they are not set apart from one another or from the rest of the city, it is impossible to tell where the park begins and the surrounding city ends.

The Landschaftspark looks like no other park anywhere. The rusting furnaces, rail connections, smokestacks, and all the components of the Thyssen steel mill are still there. The Emscher River, which had been used as an open sewer, was rerouted to an underground pipe and clean water was redi-

Landschaftspark, Duisburg, 2008. People enjoy wandering among the ruins of the area's industrial heritage.

Landschaftspark, Duisburg, 2008. These old storage bunkers are now used for climbing.

the Piazza Metallica, with an outdoor restaurant, an information and souvenir center, and a small café.

Some people think of the Landschaftspark's industrial relics as romantic ruins or follies, like those the British aristocracy once built on their country estates. Others think of them as nostalgic souvenirs of the time when the Ruhr Valley was the industrial powerhouse of Europe. But the Landschaftspark is no single-function industrial preserve. The ruins have become an integral part of an entirely new kind of public park: a successful mixed-use, multipurpose facility. By 2008, it was attracting more than half a million visitors per year. It has become popular with older couples who like to stroll among the ruins, bikers who enjoy cycling without having to worry about motor vehicles, and tourists (especially architects and landscape architects) avidly taking photographs and enjoying a snack at the café.

Nevertheless, it is hard to predict how Landschaftspark will fare in the coming years. Because of deindustrialization, the number of residents in nearby communities has been decreasing. Moreover, the main sections of the park are fairly distant from nearby neighborhoods, and it seems unlikely that the Landschaftspark will be as heavily used as parks in densely populated cities like London, Paris, and New York.

And while there is money for property management, it is barely enough to maintain the structures that are open to the public, and little is left for the structures that remain fenced off. Except in the scattered areas that contain recreational attractions or carefully planted isolated gardens, and along desire lines trampled by visitors, volunteer vegetation has taken over. The resulting scruffy appearance of the landscape is central to the park's aesthetic, but a century from now, will the park still attract residents from the surrounding area? Will its deteriorating buildings stand in the wind, like the ghostly mining towns of the American West, or be engulfed by nature, like Angkor Wat? Or will they have become a major tourist destination, like Pompeii?

rected to flow in the original channel built over the pipe. Where possible, areas of contaminated soil have been left in place to be remediated by filtering water through plants with masses of roots that remove toxic substances. In other places highly toxic soil has been sequestered in existing bunkers. Some sites have been closed to the public until funds for remediation can be obtained.

After a large gas storage tank was drained and decontaminated, the lower part of the tank was filled with water and turned into a deep-water indoor diving facility. A collection of old storage bunkers is now used for climbing; other bunkers were turned into formal gardens. Some locations became favorite spots for BMX bicycling, skateboarding, and walking. The most unexpected attraction is a farm dating back to 1644, which once supplied food for workers at the nearby mill. Now it has become a site for teaching about agriculture and ecology, and it also offers pony rides for children and food and drink at a small café and beer garden. At the heart of everything is

RAILROADS

The idea of combining rail service with parkland goes back to the nineteenth century. Olmsted's park plan for the Muddy River section of Boston's Emer-

Boston, 2005. Olmsted designed the Muddy River section of the Emerald Necklace to run parallel to what is now the MBTA rail track, which is hidden behind a parallel berm.

ald Necklace, near Longwood Avenue in Brookline, included a berm separating the tracks of the Boston & Albany Railroad from the park. As a result, park users are barely aware of passing commuter trains while strolling along the river. In Atlanta, the Olmsted firm included a trolley line in the wider linear park running along Ponce de Leon Avenue in the Druid Hills community.

The use of railroad property as parkland has become much more common during the late twentieth and early twenty-first centuries. Along defunct transportation corridors, old railroad rights-of-way and derelict rail yards have become opportunities for the creation of linear parks tying together once-separated neighborhoods. The rail system of the United States in 2008 was less than half its 1916 size, and it is still decreasing: more than 2,000 miles (3,219 km) of track are abandoned annually. Passenger service is a fraction of what it was before the creation of the interstate highway system.[24] Railroad companies everywhere have concentrated traffic on a few main lines, making enormous amounts of land available for reuse.

Olmsted's combination of rail and park was a partial inspiration for my own firm's proposal for the Beltline Emerald Necklace in Atlanta. But contemporary reuses of railroads can vary tremendously in rationale, approach, and design. Cedar Lake Park Trail in Minneapolis combined parkland with a greatly diminished but still functioning railroad; the Southwest Corridor Park in Boston replaced an elevated rail line; both the Promenade Plantée in Paris and the High Line in Manhattan were created on out-of-service, elevated rail rights-of-way, but the resulting parks are entirely different.

Many rail–park combinations begin as attempts to prevent some other proposed railroad reuse. For example, in 1986 community leaders in Minneapolis formed what would become the Cedar Lake Park Association. Their purpose was to stop the Burlington Northern Railroad from selling an unneeded site, which included both rail routes and a rail yard, to a developer who wanted to build a residential community there. After considerable effort, they raised $533,000 privately and persuaded the Minnesota legislature to approve a $1.06 million bond issue that would enable the group to purchase 48 acres (19 ha) and turn it over to the Minneapolis Park and Recreation Board. The $1.87 million cost of development came from the federal Intermodal Surface Transportation Efficiency Act, the Minneapolis and Minnesota governments, and the Hedberg Family Foundation.[25]

People in Minneapolis thought it was possible to integrate a functioning rail line with recreational activities when they acquired these rail yards. The result was the 3.5-mile (5.6-km) Cedar Lake Park Trail, which varies in width from 20 to 1,600 feet (6–488 m) and was opened in stages between 1995 and 1997. It extends from the intersection of I-94 and I-394 at the northern end of downtown Minneapolis to the park system's chain of major parks and Highway 100. The design, by the landscape firms Jones & Jones, Richard Haag Associates, and Balmori Associates, combines three serpentine asphalt trails (two one-way paths for cyclists and inline skaters, one path for walkers and runners) and a functioning rail line. These are surrounded by wide swales, shallow pools, meadows, and low prairie ridges planted with native grasses, wildflowers, shrubs, and trees that make up the bulk of its parkland.

The year Cedar Lake Park Trail opened, it was used by an average of seven hundred cyclists per day, three-quarters of whom were commuting to and from work. As the Minneapolis trail system has grown in popularity, the trail's popularity has

Minneapolis, 2009. Cedar Lake Park Trail coexists with a functioning rail line. The designers created two separate pathways for cyclists and skaters, and another for jogging and walking.

increased with it. In 2008 Minneapolis had 82 miles (132 km) of protected (off-street) bicycle paths. It has been named the second-ranking bicycling city in the nation by the League of American Bicyclists.[26]

Boston's Southwest Corridor Park is another example of opposition to proposed changes in land use eventually leading to the creation of a public park, with the city ultimately deciding to use property intended for transportation purposes as the site of a new park. The initial project was conceived in 1948 as part of a highway master plan for the city: a new Southwest Expressway that would connect

Boston, 2006. The Southwest Corridor Park was built over an underground subway line that replaced an old elevated rail line.

what were to become Interstate 95 and Route 128. But in 1972, in response to citizen opposition to further highway construction, Massachusetts governor Francis Sargent declared a moratorium on new highways within the Route 128 ring road around Boston, and the Southwest Expressway was never built.

The Massachusetts Bay Transportation Authority (MBTA) was already planning to demolish the Orange Line elevated subway that ran along Washington Street. Once property that had been acquired for the stalled highway project was no longer required for that purpose, the MBTA reconceived it as the combined right-of-way for its new Orange Line subway and the tracks of Amtrak's Northeast Railroad corridor. These transit lines had to be below grade, with city streets in the form of bridges crossing above. At grade, between the streets, the city created 52 acres (21 ha) of linear park. Surplus property on either side of the right-of-way was used for new housing development, Roxbury Community College, and other facilities serving the neighborhoods along the corridor.

The Southwest Corridor Park, which opened in stages in the late 1980s, includes not only plantings of trees, shrubs, flowers, and grass, but also playgrounds, tennis courts, dog walks, and a continuous pedestrian way that is separate from the bikeway that also runs the entire length of the park. The park has been so popular that it attracted real estate developers who erected apartment buildings and row houses on available privately owned sites on the blocks bounding the park.

A more opportunistic approach to abandoned railroad rights-of-way is to acquire them and adapt them for use as public parks before another user comes forward. That is how the Promenade Plantée in Paris came to be. A railroad line connecting the Bastille with the eastern suburbs of Paris was established in 1859. It went out of service in 1969. The corridor had become a weed-infested blight on surrounding property by 1989, when the city government embarked on its transformation into a public park. The design of this 2.8-mile (4.5-km) long park, by landscape architect Jacques Vergely and architect Philippe Mathieux, begins at its western end on top of a viaduct that runs parallel to avenue Daumesnil for almost a mile (0.6 km) before it reaches the 3.5-acre (1.4-ha) Jardin de Reuilly, a former railroad freight yard that was transformed into a neighborhood park. From there it continues at grade along the Allée Vivaldi, which runs through a complex of modern buildings, passes through a tunnel, emerges below grade, continues for just over a mile (0.6 km), and ends near the Bois de Vincennes.

The arcades below the western end of the Promenade Plantée have been transformed into the Viaduct des Arts, which provides studios and shops opening onto avenue Daumesnil for interior design-

Paris, 2006. The Promenade Plantée was created over the site of an abandoned railroad.

New York City, 2009. The High Line project transformed the abandoned hulk of an elevated freight railroad into a popular recreational facility.

ers, furniture makers, artists, musical instrument makers, and retailers. While the Promenade ranges from 35 to 60 feet (10–18 m) in width, it feels far more spacious because the buildings on avenue Daumesnil are another 90 feet (27 m) away, and neighboring buildings elsewhere are often set back as well.

The Promenade Plantée required creating an environment that could support trees, shrubs, and flowers on top of the viaduct section. It looks quite different from Cedar Lake Park Trail, which was designed to look like a native landscape threading through low-density areas on the outskirts of the city. Like Boston's Southwest Corridor Park, the Promenade Plantée is thoroughly integrated into the high-density neighborhoods it passes through. Nobody would think of the Promenade Plantée, or even the Jardin de Reuilly, as anything but a late twentieth-century human artifact. Despite these various differences, all three parks are heavily used and provide relief from the noise and confusion of the surrounding city, paths for strolling and jogging, and opportunities to enjoy nature.

The High Line, a park built on an elevated former freight railway on the lower west side of Manhattan, also provides an oasis of nature among city chaos. The site's transformation into a linear park is

the result of an opportunistic, adaptive reuse strategy similar to the one that created the Promenade Plantée. The process by which it was created and the park itself, however, could not be more different. The 13-mile (20.9-km) railroad, built as a way of eliminating 105 at-grade street crossings that were dangerous and disrupted traffic, ran one story

New York City, 2009. The design of the High Line includes carefully planted beds of flowers and grasses that are designed to look like native vegetation.

above grade through the middle of blocks south of 30th Street, in a cut under the streets north to 60th Street, through a rail yard to 72nd Street, and under an expansion of Riverside Park north to 125th Street. It was in operation from 1934 to 1980.

Once the railway was defunct, nearby property owners complained that it was a dangerous blight on surrounding neighborhoods. They succeeded in having a portion of it, south of the Gansevoort meat market, torn down. In 1999 Joshua David and Robert Hammond founded the nonprofit organization Friends of the High Line to fight for the transformation of the portion south of 30th Street into an elevated linear park. They obtained City Council approval in 2002. Three years later the city took possession, and the first section of the park opened in 2009.

The design team, led by James Corner, founder and director of the landscape firm field operations (the landscape architects for the project), included Diller Scofidio + Renfro (architects) and Piet Oudolf (horticulture). The team produced a planted promenade very different from the one in Paris. While it varies in width from as little as 40 feet to as much as 100 feet (12–30 m), most sections are 50 feet (15 m) wide, too narrow for extended areas like those of the Promenade Plantée that can be used by groups for a variety of recreational activities. Thus the High Line functions primarily as a promenade with benches. But it appears far more open, because every 200 feet (60 m) below the promenade is a 60-foot (18-m) perpendicular opening for another east–west street, each providing expansive views of the Hudson River and the surrounding neighborhoods. One opening cuts diagonally across the 100-foot (30-m) width of Tenth Avenue at 17th Street, where an amphitheater provides seating with a view of the traffic below and the skyline beyond. Rather than the more traditional English-, Italian-, or French-inspired plantings, the High Line design is naturalistic, with wildflowers, grasses, and trees that are common in New York City. When a 0.5-mile (0.3-km) section of the High Line opened in the summer of 2009, it attracted thousands of visitors daily.

WATERFRONTS

Plenty of centrally located sites can be transformed into public parks, particularly along city waterfronts.

The opportunity to adapt these areas often presents itself when contiguous land uses become obsolete. After the introduction of railroads, for example, some canals were no longer as attractive for shipping cargo and eventually went out of service. Similarly, the introduction of container shipping led to the creation of enormous container ports and eliminated the competitive advantage of warehouses and factories near traditional piers. The old piers, as well as nearby buildings, fell into disuse.

Approaches to retrofitting waterfront property vary. The water's edge can be transformed into public parkland, leaving privately owned buildings to be converted to new uses or replaced whenever their owners desire. Alternatively, privately owned industrial property can be acquired and remade into a public park. Where the opportunity exists, selected properties can become part of a comprehensive redevelopment scheme for a significant portion of the waterfront.

There is no one correct way to accomplish this. When the federal government created the Chesapeake & Ohio Canal National Historic Park, in the Georgetown area of Washington, D.C., it chose a waterway that was already publicly owned. In contrast, the leadership of Detroit adopted a piecemeal approach by acquiring individual underutilized and abandoned privately owned properties along the Detroit River with the intention of creating a 5.5-mile (9-km) linear waterfront park. Yet another approach was taken by the state of Kentucky, which created a quasi-public agency to acquire property along the Ohio River in Louisville with the goal of replacing a whole district with a public park.

The Chesapeake & Ohio (C & O) Canal became available for use as a park when it went out of service as a canal after a major flood in 1924. The first leg of this 185-mile (298-km) canal had been opened in 1830. When it was completed in 1850, the canal and its 74 locks, 11 aqueducts, 7 dams, and 190 culverts extended from Georgetown in Washington, D.C., to Cumberland, Maryland.[27] At the time the C & O began operations, factories and warehouses were located nearby because of the speed and low cost of shipping goods up and down the canal. Eventually, business activity along the canal began to decline when companies found it more attractive to be located along a railroad. When trucks started

C & O Canal, Georgetown, Washington, D.C., 1981 (top) and 2009. Once the canal went out of service, the industries that occupied the warehouses and factories lining its shore had no reason for remaining. Over three decades these buildings were converted into residences and office buildings, often with cafés and small shops opening onto the park. One of the horse-drawn barges that once moved freight along the canal is now used for tourist rides. After several decades of investment in real estate along the canal, it has become a popular attraction for tourists.

to replace rail as the favored method for moving freight, the utility of sites along the canal declined still further, until shipping ceased altogether.

The C & O Canal was acquired by the National Park Service in 1938 and was dedicated as a public park the following year. Proposals to transform the right-of-way into a scenic automobile parkway were opposed by Georgetown residents who did not want increased traffic in their neighborhood and by

preservationists who did not perceive the irony of favoring parkland over the canal's more historically correct role as a freight line. In 1954 Supreme Court Justice William O. Douglas dramatized the controversy by leading a well-publicized hike along the canal. Seven years later Congress passed legislation designating the C & O Canal as a National Historical Park.

It did not take long for the "new" park to attract real estate developers, who purchased nearby buildings for conversion into apartment and office buildings or for demolition and new construction. From 1968 to 1970 Canal Square became the first of many obsolete lofts and warehouses to be replaced by retail shops, offices, residential buildings, and hotels. The most important change came in 1981 with the opening of the first section of Georgetown Park, an air-conditioned shopping mall. Today the park has become such an integral part of the neighborhood that many people believe that it was always a recreational corridor.

The Washington metropolitan area has been expanding for decades, so it is not surprising that the transformation of the C & O Canal into a public park triggered real estate development along its edges. Detroit was not so fortunate. It hit its peak population of 1.85 million in 1950; in 2008 the U.S. Census Bureau estimated that Detroit's population had dropped to 919,000. The automobile industry struggled to compete with manufacturers from Asia and Europe, and the accompanying deindustrialization resulted in 5 miles (8 km) of largely abandoned waterfront. This horrified the city's leadership and galvanized park advocates into pressuring for a riverfront park created from these empty, often polluted properties.

The city responded by taking small steps. It started by acquiring waterfront property on the riverfront east of downtown to create 6.5-acre (2.6-ha) Chene Park and its 6,000-seat amphitheater in 1984 and 5.5-acre (2.2-ha) St. Aubin Park and Marina in 1989. The tent-covered amphitheater at Chene Park draws many concertgoers to its evening music events; the rest of the time the park is sparsely used by neighborhood residents, who go there to fish or to walk their dogs. The St. Aubin Park's marina has been virtually unused. At the time these parks were created the surrounding neighborhoods had lost

Detroit, 2008. The 5-mile (8-km) RiverWalk will eventually replace abandoned factories and warehouses along the Detroit River.

Over the next few years it oversaw the restoration and transformation of fifteen historic buildings into Stroh River Place, a 25-acre (10-ha) campus that includes residential buildings, offices, and restaurants. In 2001 the United Auto Workers and General Motors built an office complex for human services and union training. Omni opened a hotel along the waterfront. The 35-acre (14-ha) Harbortown residential community, with a private marina, was created in stages beginning in 1985. Twelve years later it was sold for residential and condominium conversion to a local developer who relandscaped the area and added townhouses. Despite these substantial investments, area revival was unlikely, because even at the peak of the economic boom, in 2007, real estate prices in the area remained lower than the cost of development.

most of their residents, and those that remained, as well as visitors from other parts of the city, were reluctant to travel through areas that still contained dozens of acres of abandoned industrial properties.

But these abandoned properties also presented an opportunity. Private developers began to purchase them and invest in the area. In 1979 the Stroh Companies purchased a complex of buildings surrounding the former Parke-Davis chemical works.

Another factor restricting additional investment was the lack of a comprehensive redevelopment plan. There was no way to stimulate further redevelopment unless every decaying property was removed and all remaining land decontaminated. In an effort to deal with this problem, in 2002 the city's mayor, Kwame

Detroit, 2008. Chene Park was one of the first sections of the RiverWalk to be acquired and transformed into parkland.

Detroit, 2008. The downtown section of the RiverWalk is one of the few sections of this park with plenty of nearby users.

Kilpatrick, appointed a thirty-four-member East Riverfront Study Group, which recommended comprehensive action dealing with the entire waterfront and endorsed proposals that it estimated would cost $300 million, far more than the city could afford. It also recommended implementation by a single nonprofit conservancy that could raise money from both public and private sources to acquire, clean up, and redevelop the entire riverfront. In 2003 city leaders established the Detroit RiverFront Conservancy, Inc., a nonprofit agency, to develop 5.5 miles (8.9 km) of riverfront property, from the Ambassador Bridge, west of downtown, to the area just east of the Belle Isle Bridge, more than 3 miles (4.8 km) east of downtown.

As of 2008, 2.5 miles (4 km) of East RiverWalk, three-quarters of the total, was open to the public, including additional small parks at Rivard Plaza and Gabriel Richard Park Plaza. Unfortunately, privately owned gaps make it impossible to walk the entire route without detours through still-abandoned property. While the East and West RiverWalks are still in development, the downtown portion of the RiverWalk, opened in 2007, is filled with people, including tourists, convention-goers, downtown office workers, and even some residents of the slowly emerging downtown residential community.

It may have been difficult for Detroit to assemble properties under scattered ownership, but Detroit, unlike New York, did not have to worry about highways that blocked access to the waterfront. Louisville faced both problems when it undertook its most ambitious riverfront project, the reclamation of an 85-acre (34-ha) portion of the obsolete downtown waterfront. It solved the acquisition problem through the use of eminent domain and the highway problem through an ingenious design.

During the nineteenth and first half of the twentieth century, virtually everywhere along the Ohio River the demand for waterfront recreation conflicted with railroads, motor traffic, freight depots, warehouses, and factories tied to the river's bustling steamboat and barge commerce. Olmsted-designed Shawnee Park in Louisville, which opened in 1892, was one of the city's earliest efforts to preserve the waterfront for public recreation purposes. It was followed by 54-acre (22-ha) Eva Bandman Park (1937), 17-acre (7-ha) Lannan Park (1945), and later by a string of parks along River Road on the east side of the city. Each was conceived as an independent facility because much of the property along the Ohio River was privately owned.

In 1972 Interstate Highway 64 was built along the Ohio River, cutting off public access to the waterfront. In an attempt to satisfy the demand for riverfront recreation in this now even busier transportation corridor, the city used federal redevelopment funds to create a new 7-acre (2.8-ha) park, the Riverfront Belvedere, which opened in 1973. It was built on top of a parking garage and I-64, quite high above the river, thus providing splendid views of the Ohio but no access to the water—water that seemed an uninviting prospect at the time because the Ohio, like so many waterways, was polluted and its riverfront still marred by marginal industrial uses such as scrap yards.

Demand for a different, more use-friendly waterfront culminated in 1986, when the Kentucky General Assembly created the nonprofit Waterfront Development Corporation (WDC). Its work was spearheaded by David Karem, the WDC's first board chairman, who became its first and only president/ executive director in 1987. Karem had been a member of the state legislature since 1972 and a leader in the state senate since 1980. The park could not

Louisville, c. 1980. Waterfront Park was created on a site that included a functioning highway and a brownfield that had to be decontaminated.

Louisville, 2008. The design of the Ohio River edge of the Waterfront Park restores native plant life.

have evolved as rapidly or successfully without his knowledge of state and local government, his skill at cutting through red tape, and, most importantly, his ability to charm and inspire both public and private contributors and convince them at key decision points that this massive project was in fact going to become a reality.

Interstate 64 was there to stay. Thus, the only way to regain the water's edge was to replace increasingly impoverished land devoted to scrap yards, sand and gravel companies, and derelict rail sidings. The WDC selected an 85-acre (34-ha) site under multiple ownerships, extending east of the George Rogers Clark Memorial Bridge for 1.25 miles (1.8 km). Creating a large, multiple-use public park at this location was a way of injecting new life into the eastern end of downtown Louisville. Public forums provided input for waterfront programming, and an international search for a master planner resulted in the selection of the San Francisco landscape architecture firm Hargreaves Associates to develop the Louisville Waterfront Master Plan and park design (completed in 1991). Simultaneously, the WDC began acquiring property.

The Hargreaves plan dealt with I-64 by creating

a plaza that stretches under the highway and allows large crowds to get to the waterfront on foot. Visitors coming by car enter the park at one of the long, narrow parking lots that extend into the park, separating destinations with very different opportunities for recreation. These parking fingers are matched on the river side by water fingers; two of these are marinas, one is a series of cascading fountains, and another is a summer swimming area. The formal, tree-lined sidewalk on the city side of the park is mirrored by a shoreline pedestrian walk framed by planted areas of informal native vegetation. Overall, the site of Louisville's Waterfront Park was almost entirely reconstructed, with additions of recreational fountains, play areas, and plantings new to the area.

In 1999 the first 55 acres (22 ha) of Waterfront Park opened. A 17-acre (7-ha) addition opened in 2004, followed by a portion of the last 13 acres (5 ha) in 2009. The result is a linear park framed by the Ohio River on the north and a combination of east–west streets and highways on the south. It begins on the eastern edge of downtown with a working wharf and waterfront plaza that includes a popular restaurant and the dock for the Belle of Louisville,

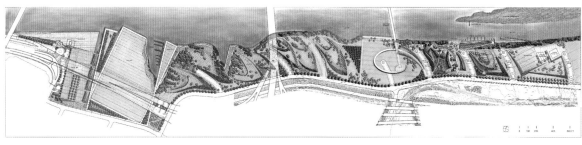

Louisville, 2009. George Hargreaves's plan for Waterfront Park

Louisville, 2008. Children enjoy swimming in some sections of Waterfront Park.

a vintage 1914 paddlewheel steamboat that offers excursions, dance cruises, and special events. The park continues as a series of spaces (in sizes and shapes reminiscent of Italian villa gardens) offering different recreation opportunities. It also includes a great lawn, used for large concerts and other events; numerous play areas; two popular playgrounds that include a waterplay area, separate sections for children of different ages, a fountain to play in, and a collection of bird sculptures by Louisville folk artist Marvin Finn; the conversion of a former railway bridge into a 1.1-mile (1.75-km) pedestrian/bicycle bridge across the Ohio (tentatively scheduled for completion in 2011); two restaurants and three concessions; a memorial to Abraham Lincoln; and many quiet areas of pastoral landscape. The WDC programs a variety of concerts and public events throughout the year. The most popular is the Waterfront Independence Festival, which has attracted as many as 170,000 visitors to celebrate the Fourth of July.

Waterfront Park is but one element of the WDC's efforts to spur downtown development. It has also sold, donated, or leased surplus property west of the park for the 13,131-seat Louisville Slugger Stadium, an 81-apartment luxury condominium, a Tex-Mex restaurant, and a boathouse for the University of Louisville rowing team. And during its first twenty-one years the WDC's efforts contributed to more than $700 million in private investment on nearby property.[28] Like the Riverwalks in Detroit and San Antonio, Waterfront Park is so centrally located that it attracts large numbers of people to what was once an abandoned and underutilized waterfront.

Brooklyn, 2006. Prospect Park is a public garden designed in the manner of a private eighteenth-century English estate for the pleasure of an entire city.

SIX

DESIGN INFLUENCES

Once a park site has been selected and acquired, designers, developers, and managers must determine what can be done with it, how best to provide access to the public, how to make sure people know their way around when they get there, and what are likely to be the destinations and activities that will bring people to the park. In chapter 5 I described different approaches to site selection and development. But park design is influenced by many other factors, including the background, aesthetics, and talents of the designers, as well as the accumulated history of landscape design and its principles. Some parks may be made to look like natural landscapes, but all parks are art. And like all artworks, they consist of places that are shaped by the imagination and skill of their creators and the cultural context within which they evolve.

Placemaking is an art that has been practiced for millennia. Architects engage in placemaking every time they design a building or organize buildings into a composition that encloses an outdoor space. Landscape designers do this when they create a garden. This placemaking tradition is a significant part of the heritage of public parks, which, in the most fundamental sense, are gardens created for the use and pleasure of large numbers of people.

Park design in Europe and the Americas is primarily based on two sources: the European gardens that emerged in sixteenth-century Italy, seventeenth-century France, and eighteenth-century England, and native landscapes that designers admired and emulated. (A third but less central source of design inspiration has been Chinese and Japanese landscape paintings and gardens.) The principles that determined the organization of sixteenth-century Italian gardens had little to do with the design of nineteenth-century public parks, but they did influence the organization of some twentieth-century European and American parks. Although these parks do not look like Italian gardens, their design is similarly based on arrangements of intimate spaces. On the other hand, English and French gardens have been influential from the very beginning and, like native landscapes, have continued to provide models for park design. In this chapter we will look at these design traditions and how they have affected the design of public parks in Europe and America since the nineteenth century.

The Italian Renaissance garden originated long before the sixteenth century, and its evolution continued for many years thereafter, just as the seventeenth-century French garden began its evolution long before André Le Nôtre was born and continued long after his death, and English eighteenth-century garden techniques predated the great landscape designers of that time and continued to be perfected

Grant Park, Chicago, 2008. Successful city parks are designed for daily use by thousands of people.

well after they had passed from the scene. The examples in this chapter may well be among the most extraordinary examples of the eras in which they were created, but they were chosen because the landscape design techniques they illustrate had such profound impact on the design of public parks.

It may be relatively easy to recognize the influence of French seventeenth-century gardens on the axial geometry of the twentieth-century Parc André Citroën in Paris, or of picturesque eighteenth-century English gardens on Brooklyn's Prospect Park and most of Olmsted's nineteenth-century parks, or of the native prairie of the American Midwest on Chicago's Humboldt Park. But the influence of garden design goes far beyond surface appearance. The Water Garden in Fort Worth looks nothing like a sixteenth-century Italian garden, but it is composed in a similar way, with a series of relatively small outdoor spaces enlivened by spectacular fountains.

In chapter 1 we saw that gardens and hunting preserves were initially created for the use and pleasure of the owners of large country estates and their guests. That emphasis on enjoying oneself and having fun carried forward into the design of public parks, but with two key differences. First, estate gardens were neither open to the public nor intended for the large crowds. Parks today are places created by public agencies for the enjoyment of large numbers of people, and while their success may be judged in

terms of their beauty as designed works of art, they must also be judged in terms of the amount of pleasure they bring to the people who use them. Second, public parks are continually evolving artifacts, not just lovely landscapes or artworks that reflect a particular aesthetic popular at the time of their creation. They also reflect the changing desires and public policy objectives of different generations—all of whom play significant roles in park development and design.

ITALIAN GARDENS

Modern garden design really began in Renaissance Italy. Like the villa gardens of ancient Rome, Renaissance gardens were designed to provide lovely settings for the recreation of a privileged few. While their designers may have wanted to emulate the classical precedents they learned about in Roman texts, those ancient gardens had long since disappeared. But many magnificent sixteenth-century Italian gardens are still in existence today, and their influence extends into the twenty-first century.

The gardens of the Villa Lante in Bagnaia and the Villa d'Este in Tivoli are vivid illustrations of a particularly Italian conception of the natural world and the way human beings interact with it: trees, shrubs, plants, flowers, and water organized

Villa Lante, Bagnaia, Italy, 2003. The Fountain of Squares is the first of several outdoor spaces that ascend this hillside site, each with its own character and landscape.

Villa Lante, 2003. The Cardinal's Table was designed to provide natural refrigeration for the food and drink served at outdoor events.

into easily understandable, geometric patterns and enhanced by works of art. Together they provide a safe, orderly setting for the daily life and enjoyment of their owners. They are compositions of outdoor rooms intended for specific human activity, and as such provide one of the principal techniques for organizing parkland—although one that rarely takes on a form today that evokes sixteenth-century Italy.

Both the Villa Lante and the Villa d'Este were built on hillsides and include lovely fountains; both organized outdoor spaces that became extensions of splendid residences. The gardens of the Villa Lante extend up the hill from the villa in the form of landscaped terraces, while those of the Villa d'Este extend down the hill from the villa. The plantings on these terraces transformed them into distinctive places, sometimes designed for specific activities but always designed to delight the eye.

The gardens of the 54-acre (22-ha) Villa Lante were developed primarily between 1566 and 1587 for Cardinal Gainfrancesco Gambara under the supervision of Giacomo Barozzi da Vignola (1507–1573) with the advice of Pirro Ligorio (1534–1583) and the hydraulic engineer Thomaso Chiruchi. The villa, in the form of two separate symmetrical structures, opens onto the lowest terrace, which is decorated with an ornamental parterre of hedges clipped into elaborate geometric patterns. They frame four geometrical pools that provide the setting for the Fountain of Four Moors, designed by the sculptor Giovanni da Bologna.[1]

Outdoor places containing sculptures, flowers, shrubs, and fountains continue up the hill on the other side of the villa, connected by a variety of

stairs ornamented with more plantings, sculptures, and fountains. The fountains are part of a gravity-powered water pressure system that animates each place in a very different manner. The long Cardinal's Table with flowing water running through the middle is unique. It was used during outdoor festivities to keep food fresh and drinks pleasantly cool.

The gardens of the 11-acre (4.5-ha) Villa d'Este, 20 miles (32 km) outside Rome, were created by Cardinal Ippolito d'Este II, assisted by Pirro Ligorio and the architect Alberto Galvani, largely between 1550 and the cardinal's death in 1572. The terraces were formed by excavating and filling the hillside to create a series of identifiable places occupying either

Villa d'Este, Tivoli, Italy, 2003. The Avenue of the Hundred Fountains is designed for one purpose: to delight visitors.

side of stairs that mount the hill to the villa. They contain sculptures, pergolas, trees, shrubs, and flowers, along with five hundred cascades, pools, water jets, and fountains. These spectacular waterworks are supplied with water flowing at 317 gallons (1,200 l) per second by an aqueduct from Mont Sant'Angelo and an underground canal from the River Arno.[2] Since its creation, the garden of the Villa d'Este has been a private amusement park for anybody lucky enough to go there. One of its most famous visitors, Franz Liszt, was inspired to create a piano portrait titled *Les Jeux d'Eaux a la Villa d'Este.*

This Italian concept of organizing space into a series of outdoor rooms scaled to human use and decorated with waterworks was carried forward into park design. Despite obvious differences in size and location and a stark contrast in appearance from villa gardens, three public parks demonstrate how these Italian sixteenth-century landscape techniques have been adapted to modern park design: the Water Gardens in Fort Worth, Freeway Park in Seattle, and the Parc de Bercy in Paris.

The Water Gardens, which opened in 1974 along with the Tarrant County Convention Center, were part of Fort Worth's effort during the late 1960s and early 1970s to create attractions that would revitalize the neglected southern end of the business district. The designer, architect Philip Johnson, created a fantasyland of fountains. Unlike the Villa Lante or the Villa D'Este, the Water Gardens were intended as a public park that is an integral part of the city, rather than a series of outdoor extensions of a private estate. But these gardens are every bit as much a series of places established to delight visitors.

Fort Worth Water Gardens, 2007. This twentieth-century park, like many sixteenth-century Italian gardens, is divided into outdoor rooms with quite different water features.

The 4-acre (1.6-ha) site of the Water Gardens is about one-third the size of the gardens at the Villa D'Este and only one-thirteenth the size of those at the Villa Lante. Unlike those wall-enclosed gardens, it has seven tree-lined entry paths that provide public access from heavily trafficked city streets to seven outdoor, ceilingless public rooms. Instead of walls, the Water Gardens are insulated from the noise and confusion of the surrounding city by built-up concrete steps covered with evergreen plantings that make it difficult to see into the park except at the entryways. Live oak trees screen out the sun, and 19,000 gallons (72,000 l) per minute of cascading water screen out the noise.

Each of the water gardens is different. One is an events plaza between the convention center and the park. A central square serves as a gathering place from which one can go to any of the other places. Piles of steps form a symbolic mountain facing the plaza that can be climbed from either side. On the other side of the mountain, the steps provide informal seating for a lawn-covered outdoor stage. The three pools are sunken. One is a pool of quiet water more than 20 feet (6 m) below grade, a secluded spot enclosed by cypress trees and centered on a shimmering water carpet. The second sunken room contains an aerated water pool with forty nozzles that spray water from below the level of the walkway surrounding the pool to the height of the walk, providing visitors with the sound of the water and a sensation of moisture without wetting them. The third sunken room is a polygonal cascade with steps that lead down through rushing water that runs over a platform as it descends a total of 38 feet (12 m) into a chasm at the bottom. Children and adults delight in the precarious process of negotiating the steps to the bottom of the cascade, where the surrounding city is invisible and the only sound is the whoosh of falling water.

The pools are enclosed by oddly shaped, wide steps that provide areas for shade trees and shrubs as well as convenient places to sit. The steps simulate "mountains" that rise above the plaza, where they also form sitting and planting areas, which Johnson explained give one "that wonderful sense of being in the Adirondacks, but small."[3] They are so small that it is hard to see any similarity with the Adirondacks, but they do provide oak-shaded shelter overlooking the park.

Fort Worth, 2009. One of seven shaded pathways into the Water Gardens.

Fort Worth, 2009. The cypress trees that enclose the Quiet Pool enhance a feeling of separation from the surrounding city.

Fort Worth, 2009. The Aerated Water Pool is an oasis cooled by evaporating water.

Fort Worth, 2009. The sound of water rushing down the Cascade creates a world away from the noises of the surrounding city.

The design of the Fort Worth Water Gardens, like the Villa D'Este and the Villa Lante, uses trees, shrubs, and constructed furnishings to create identifiable outdoor spaces. But instead of establishing a secluded private preserve, it creates public places that can simultaneously accommodate office workers eating lunch, people using the park as a shortcut to their next destination or sitting on the shaded steps reading a book, families with small children enjoying the different water features, and tourists who have come to see a truly unique attraction.

The 5-acre (2-ha) Freeway Park in Seattle would never have been created had Interstate 5 not cut a gash through the city's downtown in 1965, separating the business district from the First Hill neighborhood. In an attempt to repair the damage, Lawrence Halprin & Associates was hired to plan a park covering the highway that also would reconnect these two areas. The initial section, prepared under the direction of Angela Danadjieva, a Bulgarian-born designer on Halprin's staff, opened in 1976. It was later adjusted to accommodate the Washington State Convention and Trade Center at its north end and the Lester Piggott Memorial Corridor along it eastern edge, both also designed under Danadjieva's supervision.

Ramps on and off the highway pass through the site, as does Eighth Avenue, which flows uninterrupted through the park. They make Freeway Park quite different from ordinary small city parks with benches, trees, and flowers. Just as at the Fort Worth Water Gardens, the design creates a series of places that make the park a retreat for office workers taking a lunch break, teenagers rollerblading, and neighborhood residents walking their dogs or passing through on their way downtown. Freeway Park also uses water cascading down 30 feet (9 m) to mask the surrounding traffic noise, and the plant palette was largely restricted to species that could tolerate pollution.

Unlike the Water Garden and Freeway Park, which were entirely new landscapes dropped into the cities that surround them, the 33-acre (13-ha) Parc de Bercy emerged from the remnants of a warehouse and loft district once occupied by the wine industry. The design team, led by architect Bernard Huet, was selected in a 1987–88 competition that initially included 106 submissions. Huet chose to respect the site's flat terrain and old, nearly

Seattle, 2007. The trees and shrubs of Freeway Park reconnect sections of the city that were separated by the highway and create peaceful outdoor rooms where the public can read, eat lunch, or simply relax.

rectilinear street patterns, to retain the heavily trafficked rue Joseph Kessel, and to preserve several old buildings and more than five hundred mature trees, many of them more than a century old. As a result, some of the walkways in the park still include rails used by the trains that brought wine to the old warehouses. The remnants of the district street grid determine the shapes of many of the park's rectilinear outdoor rooms. Many of them resemble the size, scale, and shape of an Italian garden more closely than the irregular spaces of the Water Garden or Freeway Park. The Parc de Bercy, which was com-

pleted in 1995, uses water more sparingly. Its spaces are designed to accommodate recreational activities popular with residents of surrounding neighborhoods, while the Water Garden's fountains have become a tourist destination that also provides an escape for downtown workers.[4]

The Parc de Bercy is an elongated rectangle that runs parallel to the Seine at the eastern end of Paris. Rue Kessel divides the park into two unequal parts. The smaller, eastern section, called the Jardin Romantique, is itself divided by pedestrian paths and rows of trees into smaller outdoor places that easily accommodate neighborhood residents and provide them with a clear means of orientation. The narrow canal that passes under rue Kessel is a major design feature, animating outdoor spaces on both sides of the street. The stairs carry people to the high bridges that pass over its busy traffic.

The western section of the park is divided into two parts: a series of gardens and a large flat lawn named in honor of Yitzhak Rabin, the former prime minister of Israel who won the Nobel Peace Prize

Parc de Bercy, Paris, 2008. The park provides outdoor rooms of a variety of shapes and sizes, making it attractive to different people for different reasons and at different times of the day. Each section of the park has a different character and function.

in 1994. These gardens are arranged to display the canal, seasonal flowers, vegetables, grape vines, and even a collection of ninety-five varieties of roses. The Rabin Garden accommodates informal volleyball games, spontaneous picnics, skateboard competitions, a café, and even a carousel.

FRENCH GARDENS

The towering genius of André Le Nôtre (1613–1700) dominates French garden design. Le Nôtre is best known for designing the extraordinary chateau gardens at Vaux-le-Vicomte, Chantilly, and, most particularly, Versailles. These magnificent works of art did not appear out of nowhere. Just as the grounds of the Villa Lante and Villa d'Este are examples of Italian Renaissance garden design that had their roots in prior centuries, Le Nôtre's work is the outgrowth of principles of agronomy, engineering, gardening, and

land management that had long been practiced in France. Le Nôtre was introduced to these principles by his father and grandfather, who were gardeners responsible for the Jardin des Tuileries in Paris. His skills were deepened by working with major figures such as the architects Louis Le Vau and François Mansart and the painters Simon Vouet and Charles Le Brun.

Because Le Nôtre worked on the design and planning as well as the development and management of huge estates, he was able to devise techniques for laying out vast territories that extended far beyond the immediate surroundings of the sumptuous residences whose gardens he designed. In the process, he influenced regional planning in France and throughout the world.

Le Nôtre perfected the techniques of French Baroque garden design and established fundamental urban planning and park development principles that were adopted by the École des Beaux-Arts, which trained thousands of architects and influenced park design throughout the Western world, as it still does today. Those principles include axial organization and decoration, rectangular carpets of green lawn, geometric plant displays that decorate the ground plane, formal double rows of trees, geometrically clipped hedges, and strategically placed sculptures.

Le Nôtre's career took shape between 1656 and 1661, while he was working for Nicolas Fouquet, minister of finance under Louis XIV, on the extensive territory that made up the 1,124-acre (455-ha) estate of the Château de Vaux-le-Vicomte. Up to this point the great gardens of France had been fitted into the existing landscape, but Vaux-le-Vicomte was largely created from scratch. Some eighteen thousand workers leveled hills, rerouted rivers, and even removed three villages. As a result, Fouquet's estate extended in all directions as far as the eye could see. The architectural historian Vincent Scully writes that the effect is "of a vast release, not only of the human spirit, which is liberated into space, but also of some great order with the earth itself, now made visible."[5] Six thousand guests, including Louis XIV, were invited to the opening celebration, which included the premier of Molière's *Les Fâcheux* and a spectacular display of fireworks. Three weeks later Louis ordered

Diane de Poitiers' garden, Château de Chenonceau, France, 2008. The axial organization of space was a characteristic of French gardens long before André Le Nôtre became the country's premier garden designer.

Fouquet's arrest and imprisonment for financial irregularities.[6]

Like the gardens of the Villa Lante and the Villa D'Este, the properties surrounding Vaux-le-Vicomte consist of an arrangement of outdoor spaces—but the spaces are many times their size and are organized on such a vastly grander scale that they had to be connected by outdoor corridors, in this case tree-lined avenues. The estate is organized into three sections: the approach, the chateau and its surroundings, and the upper garden—all laid out on either side of an axis that stretches from northwest to southeast. The approach begins with a 2,953-foot (0.9-km) tree-lined avenue leading to the chateau, then descends into carefully manicured, geometric gardens for 0.6 miles (1 km) between the chateau to the Anqueil River, which was transformed into a canal of the same length, running perpendicular to the main axis. From there the axis extends back up to the crest of a hill that is the setting for an out-of-scale reproduction of Praxiteles' statue of Heracles, which terminates the view from the chateau, but not the estate, whose tree-lined avenues extend for another 0.9 miles (1.5 km). The entire property was surrounded by woods, giving the viewer the impression that its perfectly rational order extended to the entire world.[7]

It takes just one glance for a visitor to grasp this geometric order. Eventually, however, the visitor experiences a tension between this *coup d'oeil* (glance) and reality. There is no way of knowing the exact sizes of or distances between the pure geometric shapes that embellish the treeless, central

Vaux-le-Vicomte, France, 2008. In this view from the chateau the gardens appear to go on forever.

Vaux-le-Vicomte, France, 2008. The geometric organization of the garden places the chateau at the center of a well-defined universe.

space. What appeared three-dimensional from the chateau is rendered paper-thin by the succession of manicured rectangles of green grass laid over white gravel. As one wanders through the gardens, the clipped evergreen hedges become toy blocks, and the floral parterres become carpets in a play garden. Vaux-le-Vicomte is transformed into a world of toys laid out for the pleasure and amusement of the visitor—anything but the absolute certainty of an infinite geometric reality.

As one proceeds through the estate, this apparent geometric order becomes more and more of an illusion. The chateau is surrounded by a moat, so that it appears to float weightlessly in a pool of water. On sunny days it seems to dematerialize in the shimmering gravel that surrounds the pool. As one descends toward the canal, the chateau slowly sinks below the horizon, virtually disappearing at the water. At that point the infinite geometric order is just a memory. But after one has walked around the canal and up the hill to the statue of Heracles, the chateau reappears, and with it the possibility that Vaux-le-Vicomte is a reflection of reality rather than a clever display of pretty playthings in an amusement park for a privileged few.

Compared to the 1,977 acres (800 ha) of Versailles, Vaux-le-Vicomte itself is a toy. At Versailles, working with Le Nôtre, Charles Le Brun, and Jules Hardouin-Mansart, Louis XIV provided the public realm framework that could be extended to an entire nation. The approach to Versailles began along three tree-lined avenues of 0.6, 1.0, and 1.6 miles (1, 1.6, and 2.6 km) that led from major intersections in the

town to the chateau. The main axis continues from the window of the king's bedchamber for 0.55 miles (0.89 km) to the Grand Canal and a total of 2 miles (3.2 km) to the end of the axis. The view from the window includes dozens of sculptures, elaborate fountains, floral parterres, and full-grown trees with branches that are trimmed so the entire property is defined by green rectangular solids. Tree-lined corridors extend in all directions for nearly a mile (0.6 km) on either side of the main axis. They connect geometric opens spaces of various sizes and shapes that are settings for flowers, benches, sculptures, and smaller structures, some of which are sumptuous chateaus in their own right. From Louis's window, his control over the world seemed to continue forever.

The creation, operation, and maintenance of Versailles required massive amounts of money—which was of course supplied by the state. Versailles required a vast infrastructure to handle the supply, circulation, and drainage of water, as well

Versailles, France, 2006. The infrastructure Le Nôtre created in laying out the gardens of Versailles established land development procedures that were adopted throughout the country.

Mall, Washington, D.C., 2000. The reflecting pool is just one of many sections of the national capital that emulated the axial vistas in Le Nôtre's gardens.

as the production and distribution of all the goods and services needed by the thousands of people who lived and worked on the estate. The resulting public realm was the collaborative work of thousands of laborers, gardeners, hydraulic and structural engineers, designers, and public officials.

Le Nôtre's work provided ideas that were used by Pierre L'Enfant when he drew up a plan for the public spaces of Washington, D.C., in 1800, and by the McMillan Commission when they remodeled that plan in 1901, as well as in the parks in virtually every civic center development scheme proposed

State Capitol, St. Paul, 2009. The organization of buildings and open space of civic centers throughout the United States follows the formula Le Nôtre developed for Vaux-le-Vicomte and Versailles.

Grant Park, Chicago, 1929. Le Nôtre's axial geometry provides the inspiration for the design of the park.

during the first third of the twentieth century. In particular, Le Nôtre's work influenced the biaxial symmetry and geometric organization of the parks and gardens that provide settings for state capitols, city halls, courthouses, and corporate headquarters throughout the United States. These designs often include secondary axes that are perpendicular to the main view corridor leading to the most monumental building in the complex. However, they rarely include round points or diagonal, tree-lined corridors like those of Versailles.

In the 1909 *Plan of Chicago*, Daniel Burnham, like Le Nôtre at Versailles, used axial corridors in his design for Grant Park to form a circulation network connecting to the surrounding environment. It was Burnham's way of making Grant Park an active extension of the city. Wherever east–west streets terminated at Michigan Avenue, pedestrian axes and a view corridor were extended into the park, leading to and crossing its main axis, which extends north–south for a mile (1.6 km). The centerpiece of the park's design was to be a fountain located where the axis extending east–west from Congress Parkway crossed this main north–south axis, and here in 1927 the city erected the Charles Buckingham Memorial Fountain. This spectacular aquatic display was inspired by the Fountain of Latona at Versailles—but is twice the size.

While no grand palaces in the French style were built at either terminus of the Grant Park's main axis, the Burnham-designed Field Museum, erected in 1912, terminates the view at the southern end, just east of the axis. At the time Burnham conceived the design of Grant Park, he could not design anything to terminate the northern view because that site was occupied by rail yards. Today the yards have been replaced by office, residential, and hotel structures individually developed to take advantage of proximity to the park, but these have no relationship to Burnham's axial design.

While some large American parks include areas with axial vistas and secondary perpendicular cross-axes, they tend to be interesting grace notes within a predominantly Romantic, naturalistic design. Many others, like Lincoln Park in Chicago and Tower Grove Park in St. Louis, contain impressive floral parterres and sculpture displayed within a formal garden. But the influence of French garden design

Grant Park, Chicago, 2005. Buckingham Fountain, added to Grant Park in 1927, is reminiscent of Versailles in its design and relationship to the surrounding landscape.

tends to be most prevalent in small parks, like the upper section of Meridian Hill Park in Washington, D.C., and Mellon Square in Pittsburgh, that were easy to organize symmetrically around large rectangular lawns. Le Nôtre's influence is greatest in his country of origin, France, where it goes far deeper than the axial organization of public sites, clipped trees, and floral parterres. That influence can be seen in two late twentieth-century parks in Paris: the Parc de la Villette and the Parc André Citroën.

In the late 1970s the French government decided to replace the slaughterhouse district of La Villette in Paris with a public park. The 1982–83 design competition for this 86-acre (35-ha) site attracted 472 entries. The winning entry, by the Swiss-French-American architect Bernard Tschumi, was an essay proposing an abstract design. The park that emerged consists of five components: *linear axes* (an old canal transformed into a reflecting pool and pedestrian paths), *flat surfaces* that function like those at Vaux-le-Vicomte, *palatial buildings* (the Cité des Sciences et de l'Industrie and the Cité de la Musique—a museum and a music school—a converted metal and glass Grande Halle, and an Omnimax cinema), *avant-garde art gardens,* and twenty-five newly built, bright red *follies* intended to represent the "disjunction" of use, form, and social value.[8]

Lincoln Park, Chicago, 2008. The colors and shapes of the flower beds in the Formal Garden in this park are contemporary, but the geometry and axial organization are very much in the spirit of Le Nôtre's work in seventeenth-century France.

Meridian Hill Park, Washington, D.C., 2009. Neighborhood residents enjoy the large rectangular lawn every day, but Sunday afternoons are special: the space hosts a drum circle that draws hundreds of listeners and participants.

Parc de la Villette, Paris, 1998. The long canal segregates park users and restricts circulation among sections of the park.

The grandiose buildings, which were not designed by Tschumi, have become actively used destinations. The park itself, however, is walled off from its surroundings by the Canal Saint-Denis, railroad tracks, and the Boulevard Périphérique. The 2,723-foot (830-m) Canal de l'Ourcq divides the park into two parts and can only be crossed at either end. Tschumi's plan uses techniques derived from French formal garden design to create a park to be looked at, rather than one that can easily be used by large crowds. The extremely long axes are only accessible from a few points of entry, and thus, unlike the public realm of a French formal garden or Grant Park, the Parc de la Villette is not very convenient for visitors. Consequently, far fewer people relax on the park's flat surfaces, follow its axes, or visit its follies than come to Grant Park. By far the busiest attraction in the Park de la Villette is a small,

old-fashioned carousel that is completely inconsistent with the design of this huge park.[9]

The Parc André Citroën is a more successful example of the use of Le Nôtre's legacy in designing parks. Like the Parc de la Villette, it was the result of a city-sponsored rather than a national government initiative. It also was a redevelopment project, in this case replacement of the Citroën automobile factory, which had moved away from Paris in the 1970s. In this case, however, the city government was determined to create a "twenty-first-century park" that would serve the surrounding neighborhoods. The result was a 59-acre (24-ha) renewal project, in which 35 acres (14 ha) were devoted to a park designed by French landscape designers Gilles Clément and Alain Provost and architects Patrick Berger, Jean-François Jodry, and Jean-Paul Viguier, who won the 1985 design competition.[10]

Parc André Citroën, which officially opened in 1992, is laid out, like Vaux-le-Vicomte, in a roughly biaxial design. It includes rectangular lawns and pools of water, fountains, sculpture, small pavilions, and trees and shrubs carefully manicured into geometrical shapes. The entire park is a popular destination for joggers, while informal soccer games and picnics take place on the lawn, parents and children stroll through shady areas, and tourists line up for the popular balloon rides offered.

Some sections of Parc Citroën are heavily used

Parc André Citroën, Paris, 2008. Le Nôtre's great gardens inspired the landscaping of this late twentieth-century park.

Shelby Farms Park, Memphis, 2008. The master plan created by field operations is a free adaptation of the land management and infrastructure techniques used by Le Nôtre.

by neighborhood residents because of the recreation opportunities; others because of the diagonal walkways connecting different destinations. Its "White" and "Black" Gardens are embedded in the surrounding street network and are thus easy to get to. The White Garden, with its ping-pong tables and playground equipment, is particularly popular with children and parents who live in surrounding buildings. This is not true of the Black Garden, which is used primarily by people walking from the surrounding neighborhood to the other end of the park.

In an abstract and much less obvious way, Le Nôtre's techniques influenced the vision put forward for the transformation of Shelby Farms Park in Memphis, Tennessee, in 2008 by James Corner of field operations. The master plan for this 4,500-acre (1,821-ha) site calls for "one million trees, twelve landscapes, and one park." The twelve landscapes, while very different in appearance from the geometric spaces of Versailles, can be thought of as constellations of recreation opportunities. Like the grounds of Vaux-le-Vicomte or Chantilly, they are designed for the use and pleasure of parkgoers. And, like the gardens of Versailles, they are also organized in a way that makes drainage, water distribution, and circulation convenient and cost effective. The master plan explains it best: the scheme provides "unity,

connectivity, sense-of-place, ecosystems, identity, and inclusion" through "new circulation systems, plantings, signage, and consistent design" that will "shape the park as one."[11]

ENGLISH GARDENS

The massive earthworks, elaborate drainage and water supply systems, and complex planting schemes required to create the great seventeenth-century French gardens were just as important to the finest eighteenth-century English gardens. Their appearance could not be more different, however. Where one is rectilinear and symmetrical, the other is curvilinear and asymmetrical; where one is obviously manmade, the other appears to be natural; where one is organized to fit into a rational scheme that is instantly understandable, the other is organized to be understood only as one experiences the appearing and disappearing views from strolling through the garden.

Henry Hoare (1705–1785), "Capability" Brown, Humphry Repton, and the other creators of picturesque gardens for the country estates of the English aristocracy had a particularly significant impact on park design, particularly in the United States.[12] The principles they adhered to are wonderfully presented by the poet Alexander Pope, who designed gardens for his own estate at Twickenham. In his 1711 *Essay on Criticism* he writes:

> *First follow Nature, and your judgment frame*
> *By her just standard, which is still the same . . .*
> *Unerring Nature . . . must to all impart,*
> *At once the source, and end, and test of art,*
> *Art from that fund, each just supply provides,*
> *Works without show, and without pomp*
>   *presides . . .*
> *Those rules of old, discover'd, not devis'd,*
> *Are Nature's still, but Nature methodized,*
> *Nature, like liberty, is but restrained*
> *By the same laws which first herself ordained.*

These lines, like the eighteenth-century English garden, present a paradox. Must one "follow nature," or adhere to the "rules of old?" The answer is "nature methodized . . . restrained by the same laws which first herself ordained." In other words, a garden must appear natural, but can only seem natural if it reflects long-understood natural laws and patterns. Those rules of old were bequeathed by classical antiquity as conveyed in the paintings of the French seventeenth-century painters Claude Lorrain and Nicholas Poussin.

The aristocrats who developed the great English estate gardens traveled to Rome to see its ancient monuments, assembled often extraordinary art collections that included reproductions of famous Greek sculptures and some of the world's finest paintings by Poussin and Lorrain, and installed

Pastoral Landscape by Claude Lorrain, 1638. The gentle harmony and Arcadian imagery of Lorrain's landscapes inspired countless eighteenth- and early nineteenth-century English gardens.

Stourhead, England, 2008. The classical temple, set within an idealized landscape designed by Henry Hoare, evokes the paintings of Claude Lorrain.

Bowood, England, 2008. Capability Brown organized the waterways, lawns, woods, and fields of this estate into a graceful, idealized image of nature.

charming recollections of Greek and Roman temples at strategic locations within their gardens. Surrounding oneself with carefully cultivated, classic scenery demonstrated family culture and social status. Families who wanted to live in such surroundings frequently obtained the services of the most sought-after, fashionable scenic designer of the day: Lancelot "Capability" Brown (1716–1783).[13]

Brown learned his trade as an apprentice gardener and, beginning in 1742, spent ten years working on the gardens of Stowe. He began an independent practice when he was in his mid-thirties. By the time he died, he had established one of England's most successful landscaping firms and had been involved in creating a classic, natural look for the surroundings of more than 170 private estates, including Blenheim, Petworth, Bowood, and many others that are now open to the public.

His nickname was the result of always discussing the "capabilities" of a site with his clients. This was common at the time. In fact, he was following Pope's recommendation in the *Epistle to Richard Boyle, Earl of Burlington* (1791):

Consult the Genius of the Place in all;
That tells the Waters or to rise, or fall
Or helps the ambitious Hill the heavens to scale,
Or scoops in circling theaters the Vale
Calls in the Country, catches opening glades . . .

At virtually every estate, Brown created meandering waterways by building dams that allowed streams to flood into curvilinear lakes or by deepening them and altering their course and shape. Where possible, the flow of water was diverted to a modest cascade or flowed past a grotto that provided attractions for visitors to the garden. By gently bending the waterway, Brown created the illusion of infinite space continuing beyond one's range of vision. Irregular tree-lined coves and promontories covered with masses of foliage extended to the water's edge, adding a sense of mystery.

The earth that was scooped out of these waterways was used to create hills or to flatten a rolling meadow into gently sloping lawns that extended from the water's edge to just under the windows of the main house. The landscape's deceptively natural appearance was enhanced by planting handsome individual specimen trees as well as clumps of trees that diverted attention away from the simplicity of the sloping earthworks. Whether directing the visi-

tor's view past clusters of trees or around the bend of a waterway, Brown's intentions were the same as Pope's when he advised the Earl of Burlington:

But treat the goddess like a modest fair,
Nor over-dress, nor leave her wholly bare,
Let not each beauty everywhere be spied,
Where half the skill is decently to hide.
He gains all points, who pleasantly confounds,
Surprises, varies, and conceals the bounds.

Where the classic natural look of the landscape might be interrupted by glimpses of the world beyond, Brown planted trees that virtually enclosed the entire property, so that the resulting utopian environment extended as far as the eye could see. Like Le Nôtre's, this ideal world had been created by moving large quantities of earth, expanding and redirecting watercourses, and planting thousands of trees. Its informal appearance, however, was radically different from Le Nôtre's geometric perfection.

The aesthetics of the eighteenth-century English picturesque country estates influenced park design throughout Europe. The Englische Garten in Munich is a particularly vivid example. It included an officer's casino in the form of an English Palladian villa, broad meadows, clumps of trees, and mean-

Englische Garten, Munich, Germany, 2008. This early nineteenth-century park is an idealized version of an English eighteenth-century garden designed for active use by city residents.

dering waterways typical of an eighteenth-century estate garden.

The designs of the first public parks in the United States, including Central Park, were certainly more influenced by the apparently informal, curvilinear aesthetic of the English picturesque garden than by the specific designs of the first public parks in England. English garden design, and Capability Brown in particular, had a profound influence on Frederick Law Olmsted and thus helped set the standard for American park design for generations. Like the private estate gardens created by Brown, public parks all over America include broad meadows with carefully placed clusters of trees, meandering waterways, and plantings that screen out any glimpse of territory beyond the park. The difference is that landscape in these American parks has been altered to accommodate heavy use by large numbers of people.

When Olmsted and Vaux created their designs for New York's Central Park, Brooklyn's Prospect Park, and Chicago's Jackson and Washington Parks, they were very much aware of the style of landscape design promoted by Capability Brown and other advocates of picturesque design. In each of these parks they, like Brown, created water bodies, moved earth, and planted tens of thousands of trees and shrubs. Even so, this aesthetic was only applicable where the landscape could sustain broad rolling, grassy meadows and clusters of full-grown deciduous trees, which stood in contrast to dense, forested areas.

Olmsted and Vaux also both knew and admired the work of André Le Nôtre and were influenced by French Beaux-Arts park and garden design principles. In Central Park, the Mall, the Bethesda Fountain, and the Conservatory Lake are among the more formal sections, intended to provide an urbane contrast to the picturesque English landscape aesthetic that pervades the park. They were also influenced by the aesthetic of the picturesque landscape advocated by Humphry Repton (1752–1818), Uvedale Price (1747–1829), and Richard Payne Knight (1750–1824), who dominated the field after Brown died. Brown sought smooth green lawns, gentle curving waterways, and perfectly shaped trees. These later picturesque garden designers, on the other hand, promoted rough surfaces, deep shadows, and landscapes covered with underbrush and domi-

nated by unruly trees—an environment they called "sublime."

The landscape in each section of Central Park was altered to provide 109 acres (44 ha) of meadows and glades that have the character of a soft pastoral open space in the style of Capability Brown, but there also were 400 acres (162 ha) in the rougher, tree-covered style favored by Repton, particularly where there were rock outcroppings and large boulders.[14] The Long Meadow in Prospect Park reflects Brown's ideal, while its forested sections display the sort of landscape Repton would have advocated. The same is true of Olmsted's designs for Boston's Franklin Park, where the meadow (now a golf course) is in the style of Brown, while the "Country Park" section is Reptonian.

Brooklyn's Prospect Park provides a particularly good example of the influence of these design styles. The edges of the 526-acre (213-ha) park were heavily

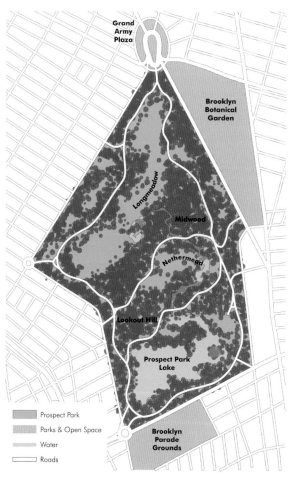

Prospect Park, Brooklyn, New York. Olmsted and Vaux's plan for this public park includes the encircling trees, meandering waterways, and broad open lawns that are typical of the private estate gardens created by Capability Brown in eighteenth-century England.

Brooklyn, 2006. A screen of trees and gently rising berms prevent the rest of Brooklyn from encroaching on Prospect Park's sweeping Long Meadow.

Brooklyn, 2006. Midwood in Prospect Park reflects the later "sublime" picturesque aesthetic of Humphry Repton's gardens.

planted with conifers (which eventually succumbed to air pollution) and understory plantings, to screen out surrounding buildings twelve months of the year and to guarantee that nobody who entered the park would get even a glimpse of the surrounding city. At the same time this provided a lovely park face for the surrounding community and made the park an integral part of the neighborhood. The lakes in Prospect and Central Parks, like the lagoons in Jackson Park, twist around bends to ensure that they "surprise, vary, and conceal the bounds."

The points of entry to Prospect Park were very carefully designed to separate pedestrians, horses, and carriages, each of which was given a circulat-

ing system that was similarly separate from the others. In fact, the land around its carriageways was built up and planted to reduce the possibility of pedestrians noticing the traffic. Vehicular circulation (for carriages in the nineteenth century, cars in the twentieth and twenty-first) was relegated to a single circumferential drive and two connecting drives that cut through the park. The result is that the landscape itself becomes the attraction, whether in the carefully designed wilderness of Midwood, or the summit of Lookout Hill, which offers views of the city and harbor beyond, or the areas for fishing or rowing in Prospect Lake, or the rolling grass of Longmeadow.

At the entry into Prospect Park, the land along either side of the path takes the form of a densely planted berm or low hill that blocks one's view of everything but the walkway. Once enveloped by this new place, one reaches a tunnel that passes under the berm. Entering the tunnel, one's eyes start adjusting to the darkness, perceiving the light at the end and the open, rolling meadow ahead. The meadow appears to be bounded by a forest but continues far into the distance, curving behind the trees, giving the impression that this place has no end—providing, as Olmsted and Vaux explained, "a sense of enlarged freedom."

The parks Olmsted and Vaux designed for Manhattan and Brooklyn energized the American parks movement. There was agitation in almost every city for comparable public facilities designed in the manner of private English picturesque gardens. One of the earliest cities to create a park of this sort was St.

Prospect Park, Brooklyn, 2006. The approach to Prospect Park's Endale Arch. The density of trees and the mass of the arch mask the tunnel . . .

. . . which opens into a spectacular view onto the Long Meadow.

Prospect Park, Brooklyn, 2006. Prospect Park's Long Meadow, "a broad stretch of slightly undulating meadow without defined edges, itself lost in a maze of shadows of scattered trees."

Louis. In 1874, after ten years of efforts that failed in either the legislature or the courts, the state of Missouri authorized a seven-person Commission to create public parks in St. Louis County.[15]

The site the commission selected for the new Forest Park was a forty-minute carriage ride from downtown St. Louis, two miles west of the city limits. To prepare the park's master plan it hired the German-born garden designer Maximilian G. Kern (c. 1830–c. 1915), who had arrived in St. Louis in 1864. The plan he devised with assistance from Julius Pitzman (1837–1923) and Henry Flad (1824–1898), engineers and surveyors for the county, called for carriage drives and pedestrian promenades, eleven artificial lakes and ponds covering 40 of the park's 1,374 acres (556 ha); numerous pavilions, kiosks, and other structures, a Hippodrome racetrack, and a wooden bandstand.[16]

Three hundred men spent two years on the preliminary work—clearing the site, tearing down the existing buildings, and removing trees. Like Prospect Park, the site was miles beyond developed sections of the city and much of it was altered to look like an eighteenth-century English garden. Unlike Prospect Park, however, Forest Park had no clear organization of spaces, no obvious pattern to the circulation system, and no pedestrian paths connecting every section of the park. It was meant for people who could afford a horse and carriage for taking drives outside the city and not for the tens of thousands who would later live around the park. Many of the spaces in between the roadways, whether primarily areas of lawn or groves of trees, were not themselves clear destinations, but they became settings for attractions that would come later.

Between 1901 and 1904 the western half of the park was used as the site for the Louisiana Purchase Exposition of 1904 and the Olympic Games of that year. Many of the buildings erected for the fair were retained to be reused for other purposes. Over time,

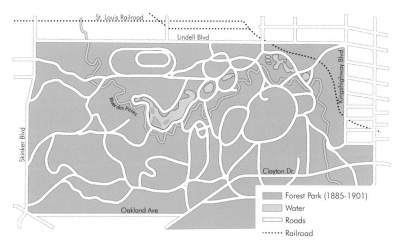

Forest Park, St. Louis, 1885–1901. Visitors to this park are confused by a tangle of roadways that lead nowhere in particular.

enough intrusions had been added to the park that the landscape was little more than a lovely backdrop to the activities that took place there. In 1915 the St. Louis Department of Parks decided to make further alterations designed for the "raising of men and women rather than grass and trees."[17] That policy continued through most of the twentieth century, making Forest Park the home of the St. Louis Zoo, the Municipal Theater, the city's art museum, the Science Center, a skating rink, a golf course, a tennis center, and numerous athletic fields, playgrounds, service structures, greenhouses, and memorials.

Like Forest Park, many parks have been designed to resemble picturesque eighteenth-century English estate gardens, and while often lovely, they are not at all Olmstedian. They may have the imagery right, but they lack well-orchestrated public access, clear circulation systems, and distinct landscape

Forest Park, St. Louis, 2003. This picturesque landscape looks like an Olmsted park, but the design does not establish destinations or offer flexible, multipurpose recreational options.

destinations that are designed as flexible settings for human recreation. Olmsted carefully modulated meadows, often moving huge amounts of earth, so they appeared to have been that way for generations. He opened views, first on one side and then on the other, always with something just around the bend to attract a visitor's attention.

The fundamental idea behind Olmsted's reinterpretation of the English picturesque garden is the creation of an image of an idealized natural world, open to anyone who seeks the restorative pleasure of green pastures beside still waters. The same approach used for large public parks can be adapted to smaller sites, transforming them into new and different places of escape. The skills required are still the ones that Alexander Pope described: to pleasantly confound by surprising, varying, and concealing the bounds.

Landscape architect Lawrence Halprin devised an original method for doing this within a series of small parks in Portland, Oregon. One of them was created on land taken as part of the South Auditorium Urban Renewal Project in 1970. This 200-foot-square (61-meter-square) site was characterized by the pervasive noise of traffic from the four streets that bounded the site and by the steep climb up the 20-foot (6-m) rise from one side to the other. It became the site of the Ira Keller Fountain.

Working with Angela Danadjieva, Halprin devised a design inspired by mountain cascades. Providing a "sense of enlarged freedom" on so small a site in a noisy urban location is not just a matter of dealing with what people see, as Olmsted and Vaux had done in Prospect Park; it also requires dealing with the ambient sound of trucks, buses, and automobiles. Consequently, Halprin and Danadjieva created something that would so fully engage visitors' consciousness that they could escape into an environment that was as different from the busy streets of Portland as the open spaces of Prospect Park were different from the residential streets of Brooklyn.

As the hill climbs, traffic is hidden on two sides by landscaped slopes that function very much like

Ira Keller Fountain, Portland, Oregon, 2007. This park attracts visitors young and old to its waterfalls, wading pools, and seating areas.

Ira Keller Fountain, Portland, Oregon, 2007. The trees and bushes screen out the activity on the streets surrounding this 1-acre (0.4-ha) park.

the berms along the approach to the Long Meadow at Prospect Park. At the top, water gathers in wading pools that recall the shallow ponds produced by glacial scouring. The water from the pools pours over concrete "cliffs," masking noise from the passing traffic that would also be distractingly visible were it not for the berms, trees, and shrubs that separate the park from its surroundings on two sides. On a typical summer day, adults sit on the cliffs sunning themselves, reading, and chatting with their neighbors. Barefoot children and adults climb the cliffs and wade in the pools. Sometimes people give impromptu performances on the concrete platforms

at the bottom of the falls. All of them enjoy the "sense of enlarged freedom" the park provides.

NATIVE LANDSCAPES

Many parks, especially in the United States, are more the result of efforts to look "natural" than to emulate the more formal designs of the past. Sometimes this is done because it seems easier to obtain, plant, and sustain native trees, shrubs, and flowers than those that originate in another part of the world. There exists a belief—not necessarily true, and often hotly debated—that native plants, having evolved within nearby topography and climate, do not usually require the same care, attention, and money needed to maintain the manicured landscapes of an Italian, French, or English style garden. Furthermore, public approval is often easier to obtain for native landscapes because they have a comfortable, familiar appearance.

Sometimes the reasons are ideological. Environmentalists believe in fostering sustainable environments. While financial sustainability is certainly one of their concerns, they often are more concerned with providing habitats that will sustain flora and fauna. As a result, they also frequently favor reestablishing native species as the most likely means of achieving this goal.

A more philosophical explanation for rejecting the formal approach to park design regards nature as an Eden inevitably degraded by any human intrusion, a concept familiar to us from such Romantic poets as William Wordsworth, who in his "Ode: Intimations of Immortality" wrote:

There was a time when meadow, grove, and
*   stream,*
The earth, and every common sight,
To me did seem
Apparelled in celestial light,
The glory and the freshness of a dream.

It is not now as it hath been of yore; —
Turn wheresoe'er I may,
By night or day,
The things which I have seen I now can see no
more.

If untrammeled nature is paradise, the obvious goal of park design ought to be its reproduction. Consequently, collecting and planting "natural" material became popular during the Victorian era in England among home gardeners seeking to reproduce the romantic tumbled appearance of the countryside. At that time, herbaceous borders that looked natural but were as carefully planted as the parterres in a seventeenth-century French garden were popularized by the work of William Robinson (1838–1935) and Gertrude Jekyll (1843–1932). Starting at the end of the nineteenth century, park designers made apparently native landscapes a central feature of the parks they created. By the start of the twenty-first century, this "native landscape" style had become a major force in park design.

Jens Jensen (1860–1951), a Danish-born landscape designer, was probably the most influential American advocate of the nativist approach to park design. He worked on Chicago's West Parks, starting out in Union Park in 1888, becoming superintendent of that park in 1895 and, in 1896, superintendent of Humboldt Park as well. He was dismissed in 1900,

Humboldt Park, Chicago, 2008. This landscape created by Jens Jensen was intended to emulate the landscape that existed before the area's urbanization.

only to be rehired as superintendent and landscape architect of all the West Side parks between 1905 and 1920. While working for the West Park Commission, Jensen began what evolved into a major, independent practice as a garden designer.

Writing about Union Park, Jensen explained that it was "the first natural garden in Chicago, and as far as [he knew], the first natural garden in any large park in the country."[18] Jensen did not start out with this approach. He began by creating formal flower beds, but he had difficulty finding plants that would flourish in Union Park and that he could afford on his limited budget. Consequently, he and his staff "went out into the woods with a team and wagon" and dug up native plants to replanted in the park. "Each plant was given room to grow as it wanted to," he reported, and these native plants established themselves so quickly and well that after a while he abandoned the formal beds altogether.[19] He later wrote that "natural selection for fitness for thousands of years" made native plants the best choice for landscape design.[20]

With the passage of time, much of Jensen's work has disappeared, but enough traces of it remain in Chicago's 207-acre (84-ha) Humboldt Park to appreciate the power of his ideas. He deepened the park's existing lagoon and used the excavated material to narrow its banks, which he planted with rushes, cattails, bluejoint grass, iris, rose mallow, arrowheads, and water lilies. The result is a modest waterway that has the appearance of the slow-moving, meandering streams so typical of local prairies. The park's large central open spaces were deliberately designed natural settings for a variety of activities, not single-purpose areas. Their edges were given a natural appearance by planting clusters of hawthorn, redbud, and other small trees along with elderberries, hazel bushes, and other shrubs typical of forest edges, binding the flat meadows together with the few large trees and making them appear to be remnants of native forest.

Jensen's prairie style, with its emphasis on flat horizontal planes and native plants, influenced several generations of midwestern landscape designers, in particular Alfred Caldwell (1903–1998). Caldwell gained practical experience as an architect while working as one of Jensen's assistants from 1924 to 1931. He maintained a lifelong friendship with his mentor and frequently sought his advice. He also worked as a landscape designer for the Chicago Park District between 1936 and 1939. In 1940 Caldwell met the architect Mies van de Rohe and the urban planner Ludwig Hilberseimer, who made him an integral part of their instructional program at the Illinois Institute of Technology, where he taught from 1945 to 1960 and again between 1981 and 1996.[21]

Like Jensen, Caldwell used native plants, groundcover, and wildflowers that he believed would help reduce the need for cultivation and maintenance and thus reduce park operating costs. He described his 1937 masterwork, the Lily Pool in Lincoln Park, as a "small elongate lagoon, made riverlike in character, [that] flows through the garden. This river, in a sense, has cut a channel through limestone, and the ledges are intermittently revealed. A waterfall at one end is the river's source. . . . The entire garden is planted as a forest. A stone walk winds through the forest near the water's edge. Wildflowers cover the ground each side."[22]

Jensen and Caldwell played an important role

in promoting native landscape design in Chicago, and the ideas behind their work had growing appeal throughout Europe and America. By the twenty-first century the emulation of native landscapes had become a popular style of landscape design. Tanner Springs Park in the Pearl District of Portland, Oregon, is a particularly good example. In 2002 the city accepted a plan for the park prepared by the German landscape architecture firm Atelier Dreiseitl/Waterscapes in collaboration with the Portland-based design firm GreenWorks. The Dreiseitl–GreenWorks concept called for restoration of a landscape that they believed resembled the area before Portland was settled. Tanner Springs Creek, which had originally drained the area, had long before been relegated to deep underground sewer pipes. The creek could not be restored, but the designers devised a drainage system that resembled predevelopment Portland. This required removing 30,000 cubic yards (23,000 m³) of contaminated fill; laying down a synthetic liner across the entire site; installing a cistern to collect runoff; bringing in enough clean soil to replace the brownfield and build up the western side of the block about 2 feet (0.6 m) above grade to provide a sufficient slope to drain runoff; and creating a simulated wetland that would cleanse the water on its way to a pond that would collect it at the bottom of the slope at the eastern end of the site.

A very small circular pond about a third of the way from the upper western end of the park is a recollection of Tanner Spring. Two meandering rivulets carry water down the gentle slope. They are buried in pipes when they cross under pedestrian paths and

Lincoln Park, Chicago, 2008. Alfred Caldwell's Lily Pool is as idealized a vision of the native prairie landscape as any of Capability Brown's garden versions of Claude Lorrain's landscape paintings.

Tanner Springs Park, Portland, Oregon, 2007. The wild grasses planted in this park are intended to reduce maintenance expenditures.

Cedar Lake Park Trail, Minneapolis, 2009. The grasses and wild flowers planted in this park can be sustained without major expenditures.

run through the grasses on their way to the pond. During weeks with no runoff, city water is pumped through the system.[23]

All the planting is native to the landscape around Portland. The upper western side of this square park includes Oregon oaks, bigleaf maple, and red alder obtained from a local tree salvage company. The middle section is filled with tall grasses that lead to sedges and rushes that further purify the water on its way to the pond, which is filled with smooth pebbles. At the eastern end of the pond is an art wall made of salvaged railroad ties.

Cedar Lake Park Trail in Minneapolis (see chapter 5) illustrates a less forced attempt to restore a native landscape. When this rail corridor was acquired for park purposes it had been untended for years and was covered with refuse, weeds, and invasive plant life. The design, by Balmori Associates, involved removing nonnative trees and shrubs, eradicating or burning nonnative vegetation, preserving native plants, and adding native prairie grasses, herbaceous plants, shrubs, and trees. The native landscape is settling in and providing an attractive setting for cycling, inline skating, and walking.

Successful native-landscape park design, whether it involves dozens of acres, as at Cedar Lake Park Trail, or a single acre, as at Tanner Springs Park, requires as radical a site reconstruction as Le Nôtre undertook on the much larger site of Vaux-le-Vicomte or by Olmsted and Vaux on New York's Central Park. The resulting appearances of the landscapes are, of course, quite different. But the aftermath is identical: ongoing interaction among citizens, park administrators, and public officials to continuously readjust the park to the changing needs of an evolving body of park users.

Chicago, 2008. The city spent one and a half centuries creating a 27-mile (43-km) park along Lake Michigan.

SEVEN

PARKS AS EVOLVING ARTIFACTS

The initial design of a public park is only the starting point of its existence. Unlike paintings or sculptures, parks are not finished artifacts that remain forever the same. Over time every park becomes the product of a living natural landscape and its interaction with the generations of people who use it. It will be different next month, next year, and still more different in the next century. Nowhere is this more evident than along the Chicago lakeshore, which—unlike the parks we've looked at so far—was neither a single, premeditated purchase nor initiated with a single design.

In 1809 the area along the lake was a prairie landscape traversed by Indian trails. A hundred years later, when the *Plan of Chicago,* the nation's first comprehensive city plan, was published, the city's population had reached almost 2.2 million. At that time large swaths of the rest of the lakeshore were devoted to garbage dumps and railroad facilities. As of 2009, the 33-mile (53-km) lakeshore contained 3,130 acres (1267 ha) of parkland, twenty-five public beaches, and nine harbors accommodating five thousand boats. All of the parkland is owned and managed by a single park agency that is responsible for 552 parks covering more than 7,300 acres (2,954 ha) throughout the city. Not only were the trees, shrubs, flowers, and grass in the lakeshore parks all planted, but the shoreline was refashioned as well. Two thou-

sand park acres (809 ha) were created with landfill, and other sections were excavated or dredged.[1]

Chicagoans' desire to use the lakeshore as a recreational resource began from the moment the city was founded. That is presumably why the city's original plan designated the downtown lakeshore as "Public Ground—Common to Remain Forever Open, Clear and Free of Any Buildings, or Other Obstruction Whatever."[2] Today, in addition to parkland, the lakeshore accommodates six museums, three theaters, four band shells, a zoo, a planetarium, two water treatment plants, the nation's largest convention center (2.67 million square feet or 248,000 m^2), a 61,500-seat stadium, and an amusement park, and it has been the site of two World's Fairs.

The reasons for the continually changing landscape, however, go beyond the impact of the activities that have taken place on the site. They include the changing demands of the people and businesses in neighboring sections of Chicago, their changing opinions about what constitutes intelligent, attractive uses for the shorefront, and the changing public policy objectives of their governments. Some the changes to the lakeshore were the result of alterations in climate, the ordinary evolution of plant life, or other natural forces. Others are a reflection of shifts in aesthetic preference. Many are the product of action by a single individual, civic organization, or government agency.

Tens of millions of people over nearly two centuries had a hand in creating the Chicago lakeshore, and tens of millions more will contribute in future years. Among them, three individuals made notable contributions in the late nineteenth and early twentieth centuries: Montgomery Ward (1843–1913), Frederick Law Olmsted, and Daniel Burnham (1846–1912).

Aaron Montgomery Ward, who established what would became one of the world's most successful mail-order retailing companies, accomplished only one thing that affected the lakeshore—but it was crucial. At his own expense, he went to court to ensure that the downtown lakeshore remained parkland that was "forever open, clear and free." For twenty years, starting in 1890, he fought construction along the shore in what became Grant Park, and he repeatedly won cases on the basis that the original plan required the downtown section of the lakeshore to be "free of any buildings." At first the court allowed only one exception: the Art Institute (1893).[3] There have been others since.

Ward's role began and ended with preservation of lakeshore for public use. Olmsted's and Burnham's impact came from their visions of a better future. They thought of themselves as artists whose medium was the built environment: for Olmsted, primarily the design and arrangement of land and plantings; for Burnham, primarily the design and arrangement of buildings.[4] Olmsted is responsible for the design of Jackson Park, one of the lakeshore's three major parks (Grant and Lincoln Parks are the others). Burnham provided a vision for the entire 33 miles (53 km).

INITIAL DEVELOPMENT

The early settlers of Chicago were attracted to the open land along the lake, but it was not where most of them established their businesses. As the railroad became more and more important to the city's economy, it, rather than Lake Michigan, became the major factor in the way the city developed. In 1852 the Illinois Central Railroad was given permission to construct a protective breakwater that would prevent the meager coastal area from eroding into Lake Michigan and granted a right-of-way for trains to come into the city on the breakwater. Initially, the water that occupied the area between the shoreline and the railroad became a popular site for recreational boating. But by the time of the Great Chicago Fire of 1871, which destroyed eighteen thousand buildings, killed three hundred people,

Chicago, 2008. Nearly two-thirds of the 3,130 acres (1,267 ha) of parkland along Chicago's lakeshore is created land that was underwater when the city was founded.

Chicago, 1892. During the nineteenth century, much of the lakeshore was used as a dump.

and left ninety thousand homeless, it had become a stagnant backwater, and debris from the fire was used to fill in the lagoon.[5]

Local restrictions prohibiting construction between Michigan Avenue and the lake were ignored throughout the nineteenth century. The undeveloped waterfront land that was referred to as Lake Park did not satisfy the demand for recreation facilities. Civic leaders and public officials during the first thirty years of Chicago's existence had advocated the creation of public open space. In 1849 one of them even proposed creating parks "all improved and connected with a wide avenue, extending along the lakeshore."[6] Small amounts of land were acquired for public use, but only in 1867 did the effort to create large public parks reach the state legislature. Two years later, the legislature established separate park commissions for North, West, and South Chicago. Each of them directed its attention to territory that was largely beyond the settled areas of the city, where transportation, commercial, and industrial firms were not seeking sites for development. By the time they were unified into the Chicago Park District in 1934, the parks the commissions created were embedded in a complex, densely settled metropolitan region.

LINCOLN PARK

The North Park Commission was responsible until 1934 for what would become Chicago's largest park:

Lincoln Park. This 1,212-acre (490-ha) facility started out as a 60-acre (24-ha) portion of cemetery property, used informally for recreation rather than burial. Careless management made the cemetery a potential health hazard. Water accumulating in newly dug graves flowed into Lake Michigan, contaminating the city's water source. In 1864 the Chicago Common Council designated the property part of a larger site set aside for a public park. Cemetery lot owners were paid for grave sites and given six months to transfer bodies to other cemeteries.[7]

The following year the park was formally named in honor of President Abraham Lincoln. A zoo was added in 1868. Thus when the North Park Commission took possession a year later, the beginnings of the park were already in place. The commission hired landscape gardener Swain Nelson (1828–1917) to prepare a development plan, which was completed in 1873. Initial work consisted of creating a number of artificial lakes, using landfill to extend the park into Lake Michigan, building a system of walks and drives, and landscaping a road along the lakeshore edge, which, because of investment in the park, was becoming a fashionable residential area.

Continual investments in improvements have made Lincoln Park an increasingly popular recreation facility. By the start of the twenty-first century, it included six bathing beaches, three marinas, a golf course, a conservatory with formal gardens, numerous works of art, and one of the nation's most admired zoos. In good weather its South Pond is filled with families enjoying the very popular paddle boats. Lincoln Park's formal garden was established around its first greenhouse in the 1870s. In 1890 the greenhouse was replaced by a glass conservatory,

Chicago, 2007. Lincoln Park is now surrounded by tall buildings, and it provides hundreds of thousands of residents and workers with a wide range of recreation opportunities.

Chicago, 2008. The Formal Garden in Lincoln Park provides a quiet refuge for park users.

which now stands at its northern end. The southern end of the garden is dominated by a sculpture of the German poet Friedrich Schiller by Ernst Rau, erected in 1886. On weekend afternoons the garden is filled with people of every age.

The park's most unusual feature is the lovely 1937 Lily Pool, designed by Alfred Caldwell. There is nothing like this secluded "native" prairie landscape anywhere else in Lincoln Park. Whether there ever was anything on the site that looked like the Lily Pool is debatable, but its charm and beauty make it a treasured part of Chicago's park system. The Lily Pool is a narrow meandering lake enclosed in long horizontal bands of cut limestone strata that resemble the walls of Frank Lloyd Wright houses of the same era. A circumferential walkway beckons visitors to pass through tall grasses and seasonal

Chicago, 2008. Alfred Caldwell designed a Lily Pool for Lincoln Park that was inspired by an idealized vision of the prairie landscaped that the city replaced.

wildflowers that dance in dappled sunlight filtered through the trees. Along the way they stop to admire the pool with its lily pads and aquatic plants, lingering to enjoy the gentle stillness of an idealized midwestern glade.

Lincoln Park's alteration has continued unabated since its creation. For example, the Couch Mausoleum (sometimes called the Couch Tomb), the last remnant of the original cemetery, has been successively ignored, hidden, and restored over the course of more than 150 years. Today the rejuvenated structure has regained its significance as a monument to Chicago's history.[8]

JACKSON PARK

Olmsted's vision for the Chicago lakeshore evolved with the growth of the city, with his experience creating parks around the United States, and with changing citizen demands for the shoreline area. His work in Chicago began in 1869, when his firm was hired by the South Park Commission. It recommended creating what are today two large parks, Jackson and Washington Parks, and a number of landscaped boulevards leading to them. The site of Jackson Park was 6 miles (9.7 km) south of downtown, and much of its 593 acres (240 ha) were either swampy, waterlogged, or under water when the property was acquired by the South Park Commission in 1870. The plan prepared by Olmsted and Vaux called for dredging parts of the site to create small lakes and lagoons, using the scooped-out mud and sand to build up the rest of the site so that it would be sufficiently above the water table to support large stretches of open meadow, clusters of

shrubs, and some large trees. The plan also called for cutting a channel from the lagoons to Lake Michigan, so the park could be used for boating by vessels coming and going to the lake. Olmsted and Vaux envisioned building a 1,000-foot (305-m)

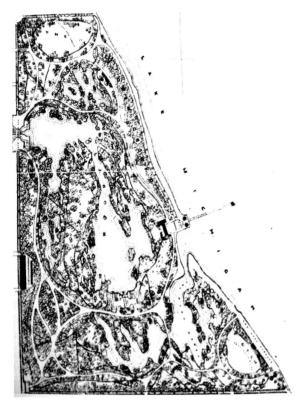

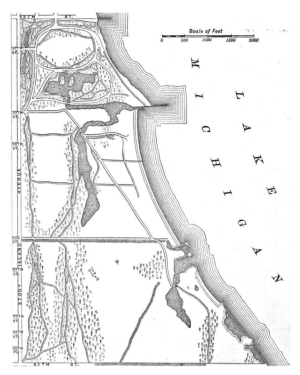

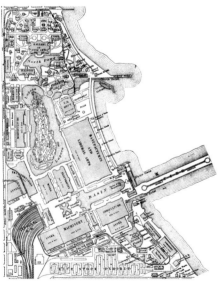

Chicago, 1871, 1890, 1893, and 1895. Olmsted and Vaux's original design was not implemented. In 1890, when the site was selected for the Chicago Fair, only the northern portion had been transformed into parkland. Olmsted's plan for the 1893 Fair created a small city with its own railroad station and water, sewer, electrical, and transit systems. After the fair closed, the site was transformed into a public park with many (but not all) of the features of the original design.

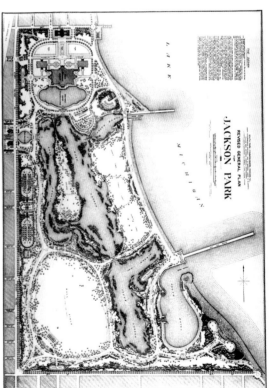

Chicago, 2008. The meadows and clusters of trees that Olmsted imagined would create a pastoral setting within Jackson Park have become the backdrop for a golf course.

pier extending into the lake and importing sand to create 1.6 miles (2.6 km) of beaches. The expensive earthworks and plantings were intended to transform what Olmsted called "a swamp without beauty" into an attractive destination. It was the lake itself, however, that he thought would provide the drama and the unifying element of the design.[9]

The Great Fire of 1871, along with increasing costs and decreasing tax revenues, prevented the South Commission from implementing much of this plan. Some of the land was dredged and a short section of beach created. Then, in 1891, Burnham and Olmsted were hired to recommend a site for the World's Columbian Exposition of 1893. They recommended the site of the unfinished Jackson Park. Olmsted and Burnham prepared a plan for an event that has legendary status. Eight thousand people worked to erect the fair's two hundred buildings and to transform the surrounding landscape; more than 27 million people visited it over six months. The landscape alone required planting more than a million aquatic plants, ferns, and herbaceous plants and a hundred thousand small willows.[10]

When the fair was over, Olmsted's firm was hired to plan and execute the site's transformation into what we now know as Jackson Park. All traces of the buildings that once occupied the fairgrounds were removed, except Burnham's Fine Arts Building, which was reconstructed in the 1930s to house

the Museum of Science and Industry. Some of the waterways created for the fair had to be reshaped, while others were finally dredged and the lagoons created. A sufficient amount of earth was brought in to accommodate broad areas of grass that could serve as playing fields. Masses of shrubbery were planted to enhance the picturesque setting. Olmsted's plan included planting large trees to animate the scenery and provide shade. Even more important, his proposed network of paved paths and scenic drives made the whole place publicly accessible.

BURNHAM'S VISION

Daniel Burnham was the founding partner of Chicago's largest late nineteenth- and early twentieth-century architecture firm. He had been responsible, together with his partner, John Wellborn Root, for designing the Rookery, the Monadnock Block, and other major buildings in Chicago. After Root's death, Burnham's firm went on to design Union Station in Washington, D.C., the Flatiron Building in New York City, Penn Station in Pittsburgh, and many other major buildings. His direct involvement with the lakeshore began when he served as director of works for the World's Columbian Exposition of 1893. Thereafter, he and his firm produced numerous plans for the lakeshore, and the most important of these appeared in the *Plan of Chicago* Burnham published in 1909.

Like Olmsted, Burnham had continually changing ideas about the lakeshore. The year following the fair, when the south lakefront consisted of wooden squatter shacks, stables, mountains of ashes and garbage, railroad sheds, and discarded freight cars, he persuaded some of the city's most important business and civic leaders to support creating a landscaped South Shore Drive connecting Jackson Park with the Loop business district.

Burnham described Lake Michigan as "living water, ever in motion, and ever changing in color and in the form of its waves. Across its surface comes the broad pathway of light made by the rising sun; it mirrors the ever-changing forms of the clouds, and it is illuminated by the glow of the evening sky."[11]

His 1896 proposals were intended to transform the lake's contaminated, ill-used shores into a great park. He recommended that the city obtain the necessary rights to shoreline properties, remove obsolete rail lines, and add enough landfill to create a sumptuous linear park that would include grassy meadows, lagoons, piers, beaches, a landscaped parkway extending to the new park, and a boat basin that would replace the downtown rail yards. The plan was well received, but no action was taken.

From 1906 to 1909 Burnham worked with the English architect-planner Edward Bennett on the *Plan of Chicago,* which is generally accepted to be the first comprehensive plan for any American city. This 164-page volume covered the historical evolution of city planning throughout the world and in Chicago in particular, described the city's economy and infrastructure, and proposed fundamental changes to the central business district, street and rail systems, parks, and lakeshore.

Burnham's thinking about the lakefront evolved greatly during the thirteen years between his 1896 proposal and the 1909 plan. By the time he and Bennett completed the *Plan of Chicago,* the proposed southern and downtown sections of this parkway had become far more ambitious than they had been in the 1896 plan. At that time, about a quarter of the lakeshore was publicly accessible and the Illinois Central Railroad tracks ran along the lakefront from downtown to Hyde Park.

Burnham now proposed a linear park extending

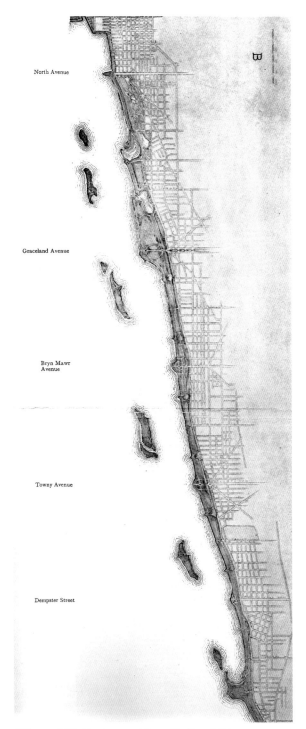

Chicago, 1909. Burnham and Bennett's *Plan of Chicago* proposed transforming the entire lakeshore into parkland.

from the South Side of Chicago all the way north to Wilmette, a total of 33 miles (53 km). He argued that "wherever possible, the outer shore should be a beach on which the waves may break; and then slopes leading down to the water should be quiet stretch of green, unvexed by the small irregular piers and the various kinds of projections which today give it an untidy appearance."[12] He proposed to achieve this with refuse from the 1 million cubic yards (764,000 m³) of spoil (mostly ashes and basement excavations) that the city annually dumped in the waters of Lake Michigan. The city adopted the plan in 1911 and spent the next half-century making Burnham's dream a reality.

By 1920 the city had approved a $20 million bond issue to pay for a portion of the proposed southern section of the linear park. The park districts began the landfill operations Burnham had suggested, eventually adding 1,200 acres (486 ha) to the 450 acres (182 ha) that existed when the *Plan of Chicago* was published.[13] Today this southern portion of the lakeshore is called Burnham Park. It was the site of the 1933–34 Century of Progress Exposition, Chicago's second World's Fair. Even more extensive landfill along the northern lakefront continued during the Depression with federal public works funding, creating a golf course, lengthy new peninsulas, harbors, and beaches.

Chicago, 1889. The lakefront provided open space, light, air, and views for the occupants of the buildings along Michigan Avenue, but not parkland.

GRANT PARK

The people who first settled in Chicago may have conceived of the downtown lakefront as public open space, but this did not yet mean a public park. The open space opposite Michigan Avenue that was named Lake Park in 1844 was largely undeveloped until it was renamed in honor of President Ulysses S. Grant in 1901. Shortly thereafter, the South Parks Commission began to expand the park with landfill and beautify it.

Grant Park was an unpromising stretch of space along Michigan Avenue. It included major rail yards and the Art Institute when Burnham and Bennett proposed widening the avenue and transforming the entire site into a "spacious and attractive public garden" that would include new locations for the Field Museum and the Crerar Library, a public library that is now operated by the University of Chicago.[14] Like other civic leaders, Burnham saw the downtown lakefront as the proper setting for major public buildings, but the rulings in Montgomery Ward's successful lawsuits stood in the way.

Finally a compromise was reached that created new parkland south of the restricted Grant Park area, where the new Field Museum, Shedd Aquarium, Adler Planetarium, and the Soldier Field stadium were built during the 1920s. These facilities brought millions of people to the park. In 1940, for example, about one million people visited the Art Institute and a similar number went to the Shedd Aquarium and Soldier Field, 1.45 million visited the Field Museum, and 3.5 million attended concerts in Grant Park.[15]

Between the building restrictions and inevitable changes in fashion and administration, the park did not take the precise form Burnham and Bennett proposed. As they explained, "Such radical changes . . . cannot possibly be realized immediately. Indeed, the aim has been to anticipate the needs of the future as well as to provide for the necessities of the present . . . Therefore it is quite possible that when particular portions of the plan shall be taken up for execution, wider knowledge, longer experience, or a change in local conditions may suggest a better solution."[16] Under Bennett's guidance after Burnham's death in 1912, Grant Park was transformed into a public garden that was very much in the spirit of what they proposed—less the buildings for a cultural center. The last section was put into place in 2004, when Millennium Park, the 24-acre (10-ha) northwestern section of the park, was completed.

Grant Park is a fundamentally a biaxially symmetrical recollection of a French Baroque garden with floral parterres, hedges clipped into geometric forms, and allées of parallel trees, centered on the

Chicago, 2006. Grant Park added so much value to the property along Michigan Avenue that virtually the entire frontage was rebuilt after it was established.

grandiloquent Buckingham Fountain. The park's formal appearance does not inhibit its active use as a recreational facility with sixteen softball fields and twelve tennis courts, as well as a heavily used recreational path running along the lake and two pleasure boat harbors. It also boasts two music shells and lawns that host rock, blues, jazz, gospel, country, and classical music festivals.

NAVY PIER

The *Plan of Chicago* called for the construction of piers flanking both sides of Grant Park, stretching for a mile and a half into the lake, to serve both recreational and commercial needs. Burnham and Bennett noted that 95 percent of freight traffic in Chicago was handled by railroads and only 5 percent by water. They did not believe this would change, but they did believe that waterborne freight should be handled at new facilities on the lakefront rather than at existing river wharves.

The north pier was the only one built. Like Grant Park, it did not take the exact shape illustrated in the *Plan of Chicago*, but the design of Municipal Pier No. 2 by Charles Sumner Frost, like that of Grant Park, was very much in the spirit of the illustrations in the

plan. As the plan recommended, it included extensive recreational facilities: promenades, beer gardens, and even a large ballroom. When the pier opened for public use in 1916, it cost $4.5 million and was the largest pier in the world, measuring 3,000 feet (914 m) long and 292 feet (89m) wide.[17] It was used by the U.S. Navy in both world wars, and it was renamed Navy Pier in 1927 in recognition of the navy veterans of World War I.[18] A decline in maritime activity coincided with the decline in the economy during the Great Depression and, more importantly, with the increasing use of cars and trucks. The use of the pier by steamships dropped precipitously, from 471,000 passengers in 1926 to 258,000 in 1931.[19] This

Chicago, 2008. Navy Pier attracts millions of tourists who enjoy everything from the carousel to the Ferris wheel.

downward trend made the pier an easy choice for reuse as a naval training station during World War II and then as a branch of the University of Illinois until 1965.

After a series of redevelopment schemes that failed to materialize, in 1989 the city and state created a Metropolitan Pier and Exposition Authority (MPEA) to manage both Navy Pier, just north of Grant Park, and the 2.6 million-square-foot (242,000-square-meter) McCormick Place Convention Center that had been built in stages starting in 1958 along the lakeshore south of the park. The city sold MPEA the pier for $10 million and the state provided a $150 million grant toward its $200 million transformation into a public entertainment park, designed by VOA Associates of Chicago.

When Navy Pier reopened in 1995, it included 19-acre (8-ha) Gateway Park; the Family Pavilion, which includes the Children's Museum, an IMAX Theater, restaurants, and shops; Crystal Gardens, a 33,000-square-foot glass-enclosed park; Pier Park, with a Ferris wheel, carousel, and skating rink; the 1,500-seat Skyline Stage theater; the 170,000-square-foot (15,800-m²) Festival Hall exposition pavilion; and 1,150 indoor parking spaces. Navy Pier had become a park people went to for fun, and it now attracts nine million visitors annually.

MILLENNIUM PARK

The last part of Grant Park to be developed was its neglected northwestern corner. This rail yard was platformed over to create a site for 24-acre (10-ha) Millennium Park, which opened in 2004. The new park includes formal gardens and plazas, a reconstructed peristyle (originally designed by Edward Bennett), the Pritzker Band Shell and BP Bridge designed by Frank Gehry, Jaume Plensa's Crown Fountain, Anish Kapoor's sculpture *Cloud Gate*, the 1,525-seat Harris Theater, restaurants, souvenir shops, Lurie Garden, and thousands of new underground garage spaces.

Millennium Park is the product of a concerted effort by hundreds of people to create something great in time for the turn of the twenty-first century. They certainly succeeded in creating something great, even if it wasn't completed in time for the mil-

Chicago, 2005. The last portion of Grant Park was completed in celebration of the millennium.

Chicago, 2008. Anish Kapoor's *Cloud Gate* has attracted thousands of people to Millennium Park since it opened in 2004.

lennial celebration. Development of the park began in 1996, when Mayor Daley persuaded the industrialist and philanthropist John Bryan to spearhead an effort that eventually raised $220 million of the project's $484 million total from private sources.[70] The project succeeded because of the vision and commitment of Chicago's city government, as well as that of many others, particularly Cindy Pritzker (who fought to obtain Frank Gehry as the designer of the Pritzker Pavilion and BP Bridge), the Crown family (who selected Jaume Plensa to design its extraordinary water feature), and architect Edward Uhlir (who was responsible for bringing the project to completion).

Since it was unveiled in 2004, the Crown Fountain in the Millennium Park section of Grant Park

Chicago, 2008. Jaume Plensa's Crown Fountain brings thousands of children and their families to Millennium Park.

has been one of the most popular places in Chicago. Designed by the Spanish sculptor Jaume Plensa for a 48-foot-by-232-foot (14.6-by-70.7-m) rectangular site on the Michigan Avenue edge of the park, it is named in honor of its donors, Lester Crown and his family. It consists of an enormous pool of water only quarter of an inch deep, bounded on two sides by rectangular glass blocks 50 feet (15 m) tall, 23 feet (7 m) wide, and 16 feet (5 m) thick. These are not ordinary blocks. They are illuminated video LED screens that operate twenty-four hours a day throughout the year. On the sides facing each another, the screens display the faces of one thousand individual residents of Chicago chosen from local schools, churches, and community groups. The faces change approximately every five minutes.[21]

From mid-spring to mid-fall, water cascades down the sides of the blocks. During that period, just before the faces change, the person depicted on the screen puckers his or her lips and for thirty seconds spouts water at anybody below. The kids wait for this magic moment while splashing around on the sheet of water. Their parents sit along the edge enjoy-

ing the show. When the water is turned off for the winter, the blocks become high-tech sculptures animated by the changing colors and images projected onto screens.

Officials had long understood what Burnham articulated so clearly: that Chicago was in continuing competition with other cities for affluent residents, tourists, corporate headquarters, and retail customers. Millennium Park proved to be well worth the huge sums spent on it. It has improved Chicago's competitive position as a tourist destination to a remarkable extent; a market study determined that the nearly four million tourists attracted to Millennium Park had increased "hotel, restaurant, shopping and entertainment sales by nearly $190 million a year" and that the park was "responsible for encouraging at least 25 percent of the 10,000 units of new housing under construction or planned in neighborhoods nearby."[22] The tax revenues generated from this tourist spending and property development on sites across the street from the park can now be used to provide services throughout the rest of the city.

Chicago, 2008. Lake Shore Drive, like many parkways, combines commuting with the pleasure of driving through a lovely landscape.

LAKE SHORE DRIVE

Lake Shore Drive, the 16-mile (25.7-km) limited-access highway that runs from Jackson Park in the south to the northern end of Lincoln Park, is the unifying element tying together the open spaces and recreational destinations along Lake Michigan. Like each of them, Lake Shore Drive did not come into being all at once. It kept changing along with the changing land of the publicly owned lakeshore and the private properties fronting the lake.

Its nineteenth-century beginnings were as an elegant frontage road for the mansions being built facing the lake, on the "Gold Coast" north of the Chicago River, and as a pleasure drive through Lincoln Park. Daniel Burnham provided the vision that transformed Lake Shore Drive into a very special place. Its final form, however, reflects the requirements of regional transportation demand.

The southern portion of what Burnham imagined as a scenic parkway opened section by section between 1917 and 1932 as new landfill was created. The historian Carl W. Condit provides a vivid description of the process: "The first step was the construction roughly parallel to the shore of a continuous cofferdam of massive stone blocks set in concrete. Behind this seawall spoil accumulated from excavations for buildings, canals, tunnels, and railroad facilities was deposited by trucks and shovels from the shore outward, while at the same time wet sand dredged from the lake bed was pumped into the outer area of the fill behind the cofferdam."[23]

What emerged was a lovely park and parkway that was very much in the spirit of what Burnham had proposed, but altered to meet the exigencies of "wider knowledge, longer experience, or a change in local conditions." By the early 1930s, new sections in Lincoln Park were engineered with the gentle curves and cloverleaf interchanges of a superhighway. The north and south portions were connected in 1937, when the double-decked Link Bridge was built over the rail yards and the Chicago River.

Lake Shore Drive has undergone continuing changes to meet regional traffic demand. Today it remains far more than a traffic artery and something less than the scenic pleasure drive that Burnham depicted in the *Plan of 1909*. But it is very much part of Chicago's extensive lakeshore. Thousands of people use it daily to reach the recreation opportunities at Navy Pier, to get to the marinas where they keep their boats, to arrive at Jackson, Grant, or Lincoln Park, to go to the beach—or just to enjoy the sweeping views of the skyline, the lake, and the remarkable strip of man-made parkland in between.

THE EVER-CHANGING LAKESHORE

Every generation of Chicagoans has valued the city's magnificent lakefront. They have spent billions of dollars over more than a century and a half developing this asset without calculating whether it provided the correct amount of space per population, whether it was located where it would best serve that population, or whether it met proper environmental standards. Approximately 43 percent of the city's parkland is located along the lakeshore. Clearly, that

Chicago, 2008. Chicagoans have the benefit of beaches right downtown.

Chicago Lakeshore, 2005. The 2,800-acre (1,133-ha) park along Lake Michigan has provided a public realm framework for the city's development.

is not the result of applying a numerical formula or locating parkland on a geographically equitable basis. Instead, the people of Chicago intentionally chose to create a great waterfront with destinations that would be beautiful as well as easy to use.

The lakeshore—with its 27 miles (43 km) of park and parkway and 7 miles (11 km) of park beaches—shapes the quality of life for the hundreds of thousands of people in twenty-first-century Chicago who live in apartments or work in offices within walking distance of the park. Except for bad weather days during the winter, the lakeshore is filled with people sitting in the sun, jogging, skating, cycling, strolling, picnicking, sailing, playing volleyball, or just enjoying the lake. From the end of May to the beginning of September, fifteen of the twenty-five

public beaches permit distance swimming at or just beyond the boat line. A designated dog-friendly area even allows pets to splash and play in the lake.

Many smaller cities, such as Pittsburgh, Portland, and Seattle, have also been at work reclaiming their waterfronts for public use to make a significant difference to their residents' quality of life. On nice days thousands of people fill these waterfronts. But none of the largest cities in the United States has an amenity comparable to Chicago's, next to its business district and so near its residences. New York City includes 18 miles (29 km) of much broader, sandy public beaches, also heavily used by millions of people every summer, but for most New Yorkers getting there requires a long bus or subway trip. Between the northern boundary of Los Angeles County and the Palos Verdes peninsula stretch almost 50 miles (80 km) of beachfront, a remarkable potential resource because 27 miles (43 km) of this coastline are in public parks. But like the beaches of New York City, these beaches are not where most people in the Los Angeles metropolitan area live, work, and shop. Among the rest of the ten largest cities in the United States, six of them (Houston, Philadelphia, Phoenix, Dallas, San Antonio, and San Jose) cannot have comparable parkland because they are not located near an ocean or major lake, and only San Diego has a comparable coastline and better beaches. But it has not yet spent the time and money to create parkland with the complexity, depth, and utility of the lakeshore parks of Chicago.

Over nearly two centuries the citizens of Chicago have transformed the barren shores of Lake Michigan into one of the most extraordinary public parks in the world. Certainly designs by towering figures like Olmsted and Burnham, as well as by far less well-known figures, played significant roles in engineering that transformation. But each of those designs was amplified by the demands of generations of Chicagoans who called for and obtained improvements to what had already been accomplished. Is there any better demonstration that great public parks are continually evolving artifacts?

Brooklyn, New York, 2008. Prospect Park, Grand Army Plaza, and Eastern Parkway provided the framework around which the Crown Heights, Prospect Heights, Park Slope neighborhoods developed.

EIGHT

PARKWAYS AND PARK SYSTEMS

Parks are continually evolving, so is every-thing around them. Frederick Law Olmsted had a profound appreciation of the interaction between parks and surrounding regions. He saw that parks provided people with a means of escape "from the cramped, confined and controlling circumstances of the streets of the town"—the "sense of enlarged freedom" I mentioned in chapter 6.[1] Olmsted believed this sensation should start when one left one's home or place of work and continue to unfold along the route, along a landscaped artery leading to the park and beyond it to an entire system of parks. Going to the park, Olmsted said, should be "a pleasing and refreshing element of daily life."[2] It should take place where "driving, riding, and walking can be conveniently pursued in association with pleasant people."[3] The residents of Chicago, Louisville, and Minneapolis travel to local parks along parkways that are themselves part of their park systems.

Olmsted also believed that "parkways, if judiciously designed, are likely to become the stems of systems of streets which will be the framework . . . of our cities of the future."[4] He was prescient: parkways proved to be a cost effective technique for shaping metropolitan regions because they increased the value of adjacent property and rendered it more attractive for development, and thus they generated the additional real estate taxes needed to pay

for their own development as well as for other government services. This is the concept I referred to earlier as a "public realm framework" for regional urbanization (see chapter 2). Olmsted used this technique most effectively in creating the Emerald Necklace, the 6-mile (10-km) string of parks that runs through Boston and neighboring Brookline.

As roadways extended beyond downtown, opening increasing amounts of land for suburbanization, so did pressure to acquire parkland. On Long Island, Robert Moses created limited access parkways and regional parks simultaneously. Minneapolis and Chicago adopted the more common approach: creating regional entities to acquire and manage parkland, while leaving the roads to transportation agencies. Boulder, Colorado, purchases land beyond the city limits as a way of providing a greater variety of park environments for its citizens, interconnecting regional parks, and preventing sprawl.

It is not clear who first suggested the appropriateness of providing tree-lined boulevards leading to public parks; the idea of a landscaped access route probably originated with the boulevards that provided grand entrances to royal gardens and forest preserves, such as the Champs-Elysées in Paris and Berlin's Unter den Linden. Applying that idea in the early days of public parks in the United States, John S. Wright, a Chicago real estate developer and early

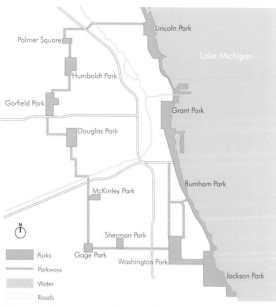

Chicago Parkway System. Beginning in the nineteenth century, the city created a parkway system connecting the lakeshore parks with inland neighborhood parks.

parks advocate, argued in 1849 that there should be public parks in every part of the city and that they should be "improved and connected with a wide avenue . . . surrounding the city with a magnificent chain of parks and parkways."[5] At that time, nothing like that existed in any city.

It took many decades and several different development entities for Chicago to realize John Wright's dream of linking local parks by encircling the city with parkways. The 29-mile- (48-km) system that emerged ranges in width from 66 feet (20 m) to 750 feet (229 m) and contains 540 acres (219 ha) of green space that connect seven neighborhood parks with the parks and parkways lining Lake Michigan.[6] It was largely created during the final decades of the nineteenth century, when market demand induced developers to seek sites further and further from the downtown Loop. They were initially attracted to locations that had nearby parks and parkways. As a result, many of the city's finest mansions were built along Drexel

Boulevard, Grand Avenue (now Martin Luther King Boulevard), and other landscaped parkways.

The use of landscaped boulevards as a city planning device, however, originated in Paris. Georges-Eugène Haussmann started his tenure as prefect of the Seine with the avenue Foch, the first landscaped boulevard specifically created to begin the park experience before a visitor arrived there. It demonstrates as well as any of Haussmann's public works how open space can be used to direct urbanization.

The idea of a grand boulevard connecting the Arc de Triomphe with the Bois de Boulogne came from Napoleon III, who had lived in London between 1837 and 1841 and again in 1846, and had gained an appreciation of the extraordinary impact on daily life achieved by the opening of the royal parks to public use. He had seen the investment in new residential development around Regent's Park and believed that investment in the Bois de Boulogne and in wider new streets connecting it with the 16th arrondissement, west of the Bois, would have the same impact on Paris. Napoleon III initially entrusted his ambitious development scheme to Jacques-Ignace Hittorff, chief architect of the city of Paris. Within days of becoming prefect of the Seine, Haussmann met with Hittorff to review

Louisville, 2008. Olmsted designed Algonquin Parkway so that the recreational experience begins when you leave your residence and travel to the park. The tree canopy provides a public realm that is so dominant that the private residences on either side are barely noticed.

Paris, 2006. Avenue Foch simultaneously provides a route from the Bois de Boulogne to the Arc de Triomphe, a neighborhood recreational facility, and a setting for luxury real estate development.

his plans. Although the proposed boulevard was to be wider than any of the new streets then proposed for the city, Haussmann did not believe an ordinary street would open the 16th arrondissement to development, much less satisfy the emperor. He is said to have angrily responded that 40 meters (131 feet) was not nearly enough—that in fact the street would have to be triple that width, 120 meters (394 feet). He also demanded greenswards of 32 meters (105 feet) on each side, 8-meter (26-foot) service roads, and a 10-meter (33-foot) setback for houses. All together this added up to 140 meters (460 feet) of space between residences, more than three times the 40 meters Hittorff had proposed.[7]

This new boulevard was named avenue de l'Impératrice, in honor of Empress Eugénie; it was renamed avenue du Bois during the Third Republic, and since 1929 it has been known as avenue Foch. It was quickly lined by some of the most sumptuous private residences in Paris. But Haussmann and Napoleon III both understood that one grand boulevard would not be enough to attract developers to what would become the city's premier residential neighborhood. Additional boulevards would have to connect the Bois with other sections of the neighborhood. Consequently, they extended the western end of avenue Victor Hugo to the Bois and connected the Bois with the Trocadero by creating the avenues Henri Martin and Georges Mandel, both of

which, like the avenue Foch, are lined with luxury residential buildings.[8]

These developments inspired Olmsted and Vaux to propose boulevards leading to Prospect Park in Brooklyn and to Jackson and Washington Parks in Chicago, and an entire parkway system for Buffalo. Because they envisioned these boulevards as the start of the park experience, they wanted to prevent the sounds and smells of the surrounding city, as well as the sight of nearby buildings, from intruding and detracting from people's enjoyment of their time in the parkway.

Olmsted and Vaux wrote that it would be difficult "to control the form of the houses" along a parkway, but that it was possible to "take care that if they build very ugly inappropriate houses, they shall not be allowed to force them disagreeably upon our attention when we desire to pass along the road upon which they stand."[9] Their solution was to require that houses be set back from property lines and that trees be planted at property lines, separating these houses from the street. Once the trees matured, people passing by on horseback or in carriages (and later in motor vehicles) or walking along the street would experience a green public realm that continued seamlessly into the park. The combination made the corridor of space enclosed within the arch of trees the dominant experience.

In broader parkways, like Eastern and Ocean Parkways in Brooklyn, the central roadway (designed

Brooklyn, New York, 2005. Ocean Parkway is divided in five linear sections: two service roads separated by park islands from the central artery that extends from Coney Island on the Atlantic Ocean to Prospect Park.

for long-distance travel) was accompanied by service roads that provided local access. The trees that flanked these service roads enclosed green corridors that, along with park islands, separated local pedestrian and vehicular traffic from the central artery. The Olmsted firm continued recommending such parkways well into the twentieth century. What the firm had in mind is best illustrated by Louisville's 26 miles (42 km) of parkways, which are still varied in planting, design, and dimension, even though many of the trees were destoyed by a tornado in 1974. (See chapter 4 for more on Louisville's parks and parkways.)

Landscape architects H. W. S. Cleveland (1814–1900), George Kessler (1862–1923), and others followed Olmsted's lead in proposing landscaped boulevard–park connections. Cleveland proposed them for Minneapolis in 1883 and for Omaha in 1889. He had been working in Chicago at the time of the Great Fire of 1871, and he believed that parkways were also "the best possible barriers against the spread of conflagrations."[10]

Kessler designed what he thought of as landscaped boulevards for Kansas City in 1893 and for Memphis in 1901. He chose to emphasize their role in spurring the construction of valuable "compact and well built-up residence sections."[11] With the exception of the carefully structured landscape of the Paseo, his Kansas City "boulevards" were tree-lined streets

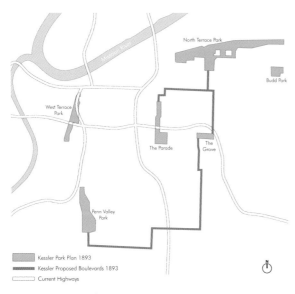

Proposed Kansas City Park System, 1893. George Kessler connected three parks with wide tree-lined streets that emulated Olmsted's work, without understanding that parkways are more than traffic arteries flanked by trees. They must be part of the recreational system.

100 feet (30.5 m) wide. The real parkways that are a true asset to the city were added later by others.[12] People did build grander homes across from them, but even those later parkways did not result in compact development. The three landscaped boulevards Kessler designed for Memphis have park islands and are flanked by large trees. Two of them connect to Overton Park. East Parkway has median islands so wide that they can be considered parkland, and it is lined with grand houses on very large lots. But, as in Kansas City, these parkways did not lead to the compact development Kessler envisioned.

With the coming of the twentieth century and the emergence of motor vehicles, an entirely new form of landscaped roadway emerged: the scenic, limited-access parkway. Grass, trees, shrubs, and even flowers were still planted, but not for the benefit of pedestrians, who were virtually eliminated; the landscaping was provided for the pleasure of motorists. Instead of park islands interrupted by cross streets, limited-access parkways were continuous, linear parks on either side of the roadway and sometimes in a median separating automobiles traveling in opposite directions. These scenic parkways were designed to move at least three times as many cars at more than double the speed of ordinary streets, but with an accident rate that was at least five times lower. This was achieved by limiting access to interchanges, including merging and diverging lanes, and providing grade-separated intersections.[13]

The earliest limited-access parkways appeared in the environs of New York City. The Bronx River Parkway, which extends from the city into Westchester, was the result of state legislation in 1907 creating a Bronx River Commission to create parkland, deal with water pollution that was killing animals in the Bronx Zoo, and simultaneously accommodate automobile traffic.[14] The Long Island Motor Parkway, which no longer exists, opened in 1908 (prior to the Bronx River Parkway). It was a private venture of William Kissam Vanderbilt II, intended to be used for automobile races that would not be interrupted by intersecting local traffic. It extended 45 miles (72 km) from Queens to Ronkonkoma on Long Island.[15]

Neither of these roads, nor most of the limited-access parkways that were built after them, were planned as park experiences culminating in a public

Northern State Parkway, Long Island, New York, 2009. The Northern State Parkway provides access for tens of thousands of people to state parks and for suburbanites to destinations throughout the New York metropolitan region.

Jones Beach State Park, Long Island, New York, 2009. Even during winter months thousands of people drive to Jones Beach to enjoy its recreational opportunities.

park. They were intended to improve motor traffic circulation by removing private automobiles (particularly Sunday and other recreational drivers) from conventional arterials where they were in conflict with local traffic and business activity. But Frederick Law Olmsted Jr. perceived the park aspect of these new arterials, which he thought of as "greatly elongated real *parks*."[16] The earliest group of parkways truly conceived in this manner was created by Robert Moses. Like Olmsted Senior's parkways, Moses's Northern State, Southern State, and Meadowbrook

Parkways, for example, provided motorists a pleasant drive on their way to park destinations that Moses was creating on Long Island, such as Jones Beach.

The new motor parkways, like their nineteenth-century antecedents, had a huge impact on the pattern of metropolitan urbanization. They may have been conceived as a way of opening up regional parks to city dwellers with cars, but they were just as easy for suburbanites to use when driving to the city to work or shop as they were for pleasure driving or a trip to a public park. The most beautiful of them— the Taconic State Parkway in the Hudson Valley of New York in particular—were artfully designed park experiences as well as access routes to regional park destinations.

As parkway fingers extended into the countryside, they opened up vast amounts of territory for suburban development. Consequently, any public

Taconic State Parkway, New York, 1976. This limited access parkway offers a recreational resource for travelers while also providing residents of the Hudson River corridor with access to large state parks.

Buffalo, 2009. A recreation facility with four carefully designed baseball fields tends to be unused during most of the week and intensely used after school and on weekends.

parks they connected now had to serve entire metropolitan regions. Many new suburban parks consisted of single-purpose recreation facilities, such as baseball fields or swimming pools, for nearby communities, rather than traditional large public parks that simultaneously accommodated many different functions and served visitors from many different parts of a city.

Robert Moses, serving as the unpaid president of the New York State Council of Parks from 1924 to 1963, summed it up: "Mass production of automobiles, shorter working hours, and an enormous increase in outdoor activities, sports, and recreation marked the end of the age in which parks could be considered exclusively municipal functions."[17] Moreover, as increasing amounts of land have been consumed for development, there has been a growing realization that the emerging landscape of parks and parkways had to do more than serve nearby suburban communities. They had to shape the character of entire metropolitan regions.

Frederick Law Olmsted understood this role long before America began its love affair with the automobile. While devising a parks plan for Buffalo in 1869, he wrote: "A park exercises a very different and much greater influence upon the progress of a city in its general structure than any other ordinary public work."[18] His understanding was the result of systematic thinking about both user demands and the appropriate ways of satisfying those demands at very different sites throughout a city. It also reflected

the influence of Haussmann, who was using parks and tree-lined boulevards as a major device for restructuring the entire city of Paris.

BOSTON

Olmsted's parks—and the tree-lined boulevards that led to them—in Brooklyn, Chicago, Louisville, and Buffalo played a part in restructuring these cities, just as Haussmann's parks and boulevards remade Paris. But it was in Boston, between 1878 and 1895, that Olmsted was able to demonstrate how a park system could shape a metropolitan region.

Olmsted's professional relationship and friendship with the architect Henry Hobson Richardson brought him to Boston with increasing frequency. He spent four summers there beginning in 1878, and in 1881 he moved his office from New York to Boston. Two years later he purchased Fairsted, a house in Brookline, which continued to be the home office of the Olmsted firm until it closed in 1963. Congress designated it a National Historic Site in 1979.[19]

Olmsted's involvement with Boston parks began in 1874, when Charles Sprague Sargent, the director of the Arnold Arboretum in Boston, wrote to him seeking his opinion about the Arboretum's potential. He told Sargent that it would be difficult to combine a facility whose single purpose was displaying trees with that of a multiple-purpose public park that also had to accommodate activities that inherently risked

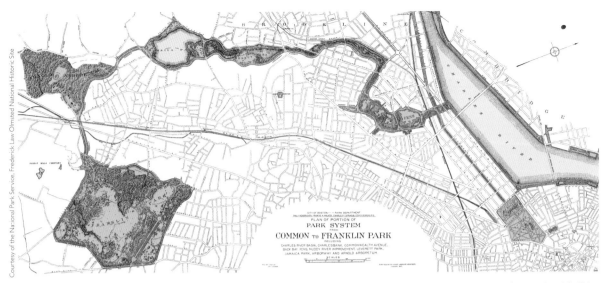

Boston, 1894. Frederick Law Olmsted designed the 6-mile (10-km) Emerald Necklace, which provides a wide variety of recreational facilities for residents of Boston and Brookline.

damaging the landscape. Olmsted eventually found a way to combine these functions and, in 1878, began preparing plans for and supervising the development of the Arboretum as a public park.[20] His work for the Arnold Arboretum was initially separate from his involvement first with the Fens, a tidal salt marsh that bounded the western end of the Back Bay, and then with a series of parks and parkways that he dubbed the Emerald Necklace.

It was Olmsted's desire to satisfy the demands of very different neighborhoods in both Boston and Brookline that resulted in a 1,100-acre (445-ha) metropolitan park system starting at the already-existing Boston Common, Public Garden, and Commonwealth Avenue Mall and extending 7 miles (11 km) through parks at the Muddy River (now Riverway Park), Leverett Pond (now Olmsted Park) and Jamaica Pond, the Arnold Arboretum, and two landscaped boulevards (Arborway and Jamaicaway) to Franklin Park.

In 1878 the recently appointed three-person Boston Park Commission asked Olmsted to judge a design competition for the 106-acre (43-ha) site of a park for the Fens. The Fens was the receiving basin for the Muddy River and Stony Brook, which carried runoff from the surrounding communities of Brookline, Dorchester, and Roxbury. From the 1820s onward, both streams carried an increasing amount of raw sewage from these communities that flowed downstream until it mixed with marsh mud, becoming an increasingly malodorous health hazard from which most animal life was long gone.

Olmsted did not believe that a competition would produce a satisfactory plan and refused to participate. He described the site as "a gulf of mud and water of such depth that the cost of filling it up and preparing it to be built upon" would be prohibitive,[21] and he condemned it as "a complicated nuisance, threatening soon to be a deadly peril to the whole city as a propagating and breeding-ground of pestilent epidemics."[22] He insisted that the project required the collaboration of an architect, a structural engineer, a sanitary engineer, a landscape designer, and a construction manager, as well as the participation of the city engineer and superintendent of sewers. Once the commissioners had carefully examined the submitted designs, they agreed

Boston, 1996. The Fens was transformed from a stagnant, polluted waterway into a cherished recreational facility.

Boston, 1879. Olmsted's plan for the Fens combined a natural drainage system and roadways connecting nearby neighborhoods with recreational facilities.

without intruding into the new park; and the pedestrian paths, grass, trees, and shrubbery of a real public park.[24]

The Fens and the Muddy River sections of the Emerald Necklace became the multidisciplinary projects that Olmsted envisioned. They dealt with tidal inflow from the Charles River, water retention and outflows from the Muddy River and Stony Brook, runoff from surrounding communities, garbage and sewer service, vehicular movement, railroad service, and all the functions of a public park. This required rechanneling the park's meandering waterway as well as major earthworks on both sides of the stream.

with Olmsted, and they accepted his offer to become the commission's "advisory landscape architect" for a period of three years.[23]

What emerged in 1880, two years after the Boston Park Commission hired Olmsted, was a plan that combined a meandering stream flowing along a newly excavated, landscaped course; an interceptor sewer that carried Muddy River waters directly into the Charles River; a 30-acre (12-ha) storage basin for storm runoff; a restored salt marsh; bridges that carried traffic from one side of Boston to the other

Olmsted was a master at multipurpose design. The complex linear park he devised is the result of the interaction of six different objectives: purchasing the most easily acquired and sometimes the least expensive properties; installing a sewer system; providing the gradual slope needed for the stream to flow naturally into the Charles River; camouflaging the MBTA transit line connecting Boston with Brookline (see chapter 5); fashioning a peripheral

Boston, 2005. Because of Olmsted's thoughtful design, residents walking through the park on either side of the Muddy River are unaware of the adjacent neighborhoods .

Boston, 2008. The path encircling Jamaica Pond has become a popular neighborhood gathering place.

edge that would allow a greater number of real estate development sites with park views than would have resulted from the most direct, straight route from Jamaica Pond to the Charles River; and wherever possible creating relatively flat open areas that could be used for recreational purposes.

The need to drain runoff from contiguous property resulted in the park's taking the form of a shallow valley with appropriate landscaping and continuous pedestrian walkways along both sides. The park itself is bounded on both sides by vehicular roadways that extend the public realm beyond the park (giving the impression of greater breadth) and provide access to neighboring communities. Wherever these roadways are high enough above the streambed, Olmsted planned bridges over the park connecting streets that ran through the neighborhoods on either side of it. As a result, pedestrians can walk for miles without interruption from traffic, and traffic can flow uninterrupted between Boston and Brookline.

Leverett and Jamaica Ponds are parts of a chain of freshwater ponds within the stream valley. They are too small to support more than minor sailing or rowing, but the 70-acres (28-ha) Jamaica Pond had been a popular spot for ice-skating long before Olmsted was engaged by Boston's board of commissioners of the Department of Parks to transform it into an effective public park. Olmsted did not believe this required extensive earthwork, but it did require acquiring 60 acres (24 ha) around the pond's periphery and some landfill to accommodate a continuous pedestrian path encircling the pond. The park is heavily used, particularly on nice Sunday afternoons.

The southern end of Jamaica Pond Park is connected to the Arnold Arboretum by a landscaped boulevard called Jamaicaway: a central roadway carrying regional traffic flanked by tree-lined park islands, which are in turn flanked by service roads bounded by tree-lined planter strips, sidewalks, and the front yards of houses that are required to be set back from the street. Where Jamaicaway reaches the Arboretum, it continues with one side lined with houses. On the opposite side is the relatively short eastern edge of the Arboretum, which can be entered only at one end and extends for about a half a mile (0.8 km) westward.

Although the Arboretum was originally open to private vehicles and horses, private cars are not permitted today. The roadways and pedestrian paths meander through its 265 acres (107 ha), always with something to be seen beyond the bend, as well as an interesting view on the right and another on the left. The 4,500 woody plants that line these routes

Boston, 2005. The parkways connecting the Jamaica Pond Park with the Arnold Arboretum and Franklin Park make driving a recreational activity.

Boston, 2008. The Arnold Arboretum combines the preservation and presentation of a wide variety of trees with opportunities for recreation.

are arranged in botanical sequence and labeled with their scientific and common names and country of origin. The Arboretum is dominated by two hills, both encircled with roadways; one has a pedestrian path leading to the top and the other a path that winds its way up to a scenic overlook at the summit.

As large as the Arnold Arboretum was, it was essentially arranged for the display of trees and, despite Olmsted's design, could not provide the variety of recreational opportunities that are usually found in parks of that size. Despite the efforts of the board of commissioners, at the time that Olmsted's designs for the Arboretum were completed Boston did not as yet possess any large park. He reported that there were 186 localities in the Boston region that owned "a body of land, great or small, or avail-

able to serve, at least for ventilating purposes." Of these, 71 were improved or being improved, 56 were public squares, commons, or gardens, 39 were burial grounds, and 47 would probably be sold.[25] Consequently, Olmsted argued, the city needed to acquire a large park that could offer what could not be found within any of these smaller spaces. He had prepared a preliminary plan for this sort of park in 1885.

In 1886 the city's Common Council authorized issuing $50 million in bonds for park development. It also decided to devote the proceeds of a bequest from Benjamin Franklin—similar to the one Philadelphia used to clean up Wissahickon Creek (see chapter 5)—to the creation of a large park. The money had been invested and was due to mature in 1891–92.[26] Boston used the funds to pay off the debt

Boston, 1994. The meadow at Franklin Park was transformed into an actively used golf course.

Boston, 1994. The wooded sections of Franklin Park are intended to provide an escape into a "country park."

on land for a large park in West Roxbury, and named it Franklin Park in his honor.

Olmsted had by then designed large parks for Manhattan, Brooklyn, Chicago, Buffalo, Montreal, and Detroit, and he believed that large parks were fundamentally different from small parks. He thought small sites were best used to provide facilities that served local communities, and he thought the best sites were those whose particular topography and dimensions made them an appropriate choice for a variety of recreational activities, especially if they also included unique natural features or were of historical significance. Rather than multiply amenities that could be provided on small sites throughout Boston, he wanted the 527 acres (213 ha) that were to become Franklin Park to be a place where city dwellers could enjoy woodlands, semiwooded areas, undulating meadows, rock outcroppings, meandering streams, ponds, a wide variety of vegetation—things found only in the country.[27]

Creating a public park on this parcel presented a number of challenges. The West Roxbury section of Boston is rocky, and site did not have much soil that could sustain the open turf needed for active sports. It contained scattered trees and had no sizable bodies of water. The budget for park development did not allow for the massive earthworks Olmsted had implemented at Central and Prospect Parks. His design overcame these difficulties while minimizing expenditures. The bulk of the money went to changes in grade, additional soil, boulder removal, tree planting, 6 miles (10 km) of vehicular roads, 15 miles (24 km) of pedestrian and bridle paths, and a small number of rustic structures. By the end of 1896, $3.34 million had been spent on land and construction, compared to the $7.75 million spent creating Prospect Park twenty-two years earlier.[28]

Olmsted's design for Franklin Park concentrated active recreation facilities in what he called an "Ante-Park," beyond which stretched a larger pastoral "Country Park." The formal entry was through the Ante-Park. It began at Peabody Circle and continued down the Greeting, a formal, tree-lined, linear promenade (similar to the Mall in Central Park). The other principal components of the Ante-Park were the Little Folks' Fair, 14 acres (5.6 ha) of playgrounds and entertainment for children; Sargent's Field, 8 acres (3.2 ha) of tennis courts and ball fields;

and the Playstead, 40 acres (16 ha) of flat ground for spectator and athletic events.[29]

Alternately, one could go from Peabody Circle to Refectory Hill for refreshments on a terrace overlooking the park, or go directly to 334-acre (135-ha) Country Park and walk or take the Circuit Drive around the park. Possible destinations within the Country Park included the heavily wooded Scarboro Hill and Schoolmaster Hill, which offered lovely views, the forested Wilderness area, and the meadows at Ellicott and Nazingdale. In these places Olmsted wanted to avoid the "urban elegance" of a small city park; he preferred "well known and long tried trees and bushes to rare ones; natives to exotics; humble field flowers to high-bred marvels; plain green leaves."[30]

During the decades that followed the opening of Franklin Park in 1889, some sections were remodeled to accommodate changes in demand. In 1910 the Greeting began to be transformed into a zoo. After a quarter of a century of operation, some of the meadowland was opened to use by golfers; then in 1922 an 18-hole golf course was installed.

The Emerald Necklace provided Boston and Brookline with a dazzling array of very different parks and a lovely setting for daily life in their heterogeneous neighborhoods. It also provided the world with a demonstration of the validity of Olmsted's ideas about park systems and their roles in shaping metropolitan development. Those ideas were carried forward by the partners in the Olmsted firm—Charles Eliot, John Charles Olmsted, and Frederick Law Olmsted Jr.—and by countless other landscape designers. Eliot devoted his talents to the expanding Boston Metropolitan and Cambridge Municipal Park Systems.[31] The Olmsted brothers contributed major work for park systems in Seattle, Portland, Denver, and Louisville.[32] While the Emerald Necklace influenced park development throughout the United States, its greatest impact was on the developing park systems of Minneapolis and Chicago.

MINNEAPOLIS

In 1883, when Minneapolis established its elected Park and Recreation Board (originally known as

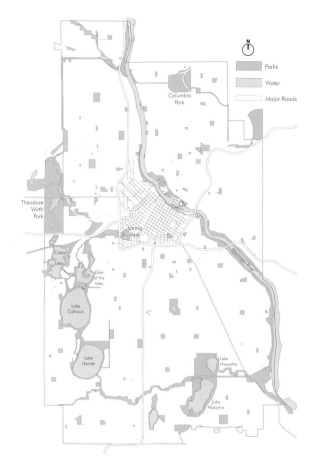

Minneapolis, 2009. This park system provides easy access to 182 park properties in every section of the city.

the Board of Park Commissioners), the city possessed only 6 acres (2.4 ha) of parkland. It enacted legislation levying an annual tax of $1 per $1,000 of assessed value on every property in the city to pay debt service on bonds that would cover the cost of

the park system. By 1945 the park tax had risen to $23 per $1,000; in 2007 it was $74 per $1,000.[33] These taxes go directly to the Park and Recreation Board and must be used solely for park purposes.

The 6,624-acre (2,681-ha) Minneapolis park system that has emerged is arguably the best located, best designed, best maintained, and best managed system in the United States. It includes 182 properties, 17 lakes and ponds, 49 recreation centers, 396 sports fields, 55 miles (89 km) of parkways, 43 miles (69 km) of pedestrian walkways, an equal length of bicycle paths, and much, much more. Nobody in Minneapolis lives more than six blocks from a park.

The board began by hiring H. W. S. Cleveland to prepare *Suggestions for a System of Parks and Parkways for the City of Minneapolis.*[34] That document established the structural elements around which the system would develop: parkland along both banks of the Mississippi River, surrounding Minnehaha Falls and Minnehaha Creek, and around the city's major lakes, all connected by a series of landscaped parkways. While Cleveland's language in arguing for this system was very different from Olmsted's, the landscape he proposed was similar.

In his reports to park commissions, whether in Boston or anywhere else, Olmsted wrote eloquent explanations of the importance of adjusting to the character of the topography and climate and servicing the demands of nearby communities, and of the roles parks play in shaping the way of life of the people who use them. Detailed proposals followed—but only after the rationale and strategy for park development had been established. Cleveland

Minneapolis, 2009. Theodore Wirth created a park by preserving a streambed lined with a generous amount of parkland and neighborhood service roads called the Minnehaha Parkway.

Minneapolis, 2009. Lake Calhoun provides a wide variety of recreational facilities to the residents of nearby neighborhoods. During the summer, sailing is particularly popular.

assumed everybody understood the need for parks. He went directly to the physical actions he was recommending and the financial aspects of his proposal. He thought that the need to acquire property was urgent, arguing for "securing the areas that are needed before they become so occupied, or acquire such value as to place them beyond reach," because "wealth cannot purchase lost opportunity."[35]

Another key figure in developing the Minneapolis park system was Theodore Wirth (1863–1949), superintendent of parks for thirty years, beginning in 1906. He had spent ten years happily performing the role of superintendent of parks in Hartford, Connecticut. When he began Minneapolis owned 31 miles (50 km) of parkway and 57 park properties covering 1,810 acres (732 ha). When he retired it had 62 miles (100 km) of parkway and 144 park properties covering 5,241 acres (2,121 ha). He supervised the acquisition of property, landscaping, and dredging that transformed the lakes into user-friendly recreation facilities. In short, he brought Olmsted's philosophy and Cleveland's development objectives to reality.

Before Wirth became superintendent, Minneapolis had concentrated on parks as passive pastoral landscapes providing relaxation and refreshment through contact with nature. Wirth believed that

"from the very beginning, recreation was really the fundamental meaning of parks."[36] Because the system's lakes included 1,497 acres (606 ha) of water, he devoted particular attention to water-based recreation. When he started his work, the lakes were undeveloped, with large areas of swampland; during periods of heavy rainfall or snow melts they flooded. Dredging and deepening some sections, filling in lowlands, regrading, and relandscaping shorelines allowed him to create unusually appropriate facilities for sailing, canoeing, kayaking, rowing, swimming, fishing, and ice-skating. The periphery, like that of Olmsted's Jamaica Pond Park, was landscaped with enough space for volleyball, tennis, basketball, and other sports.

Wirth fitted the parks for the winter sports that were appropriate in Minneapolis, and he also added golf courses, ball fields, playgrounds, and all the other recreational facilities that twentieth-century residents expected in their park system. He tried to distribute these equitably throughout the city, with the result that residents of Minneapolis have a huge variety of recreational choices. The Park and Recreation Board has used the cash flow from the park-specific real estate tax I described earlier to maintain these facilities and to renovate and update them to meet changing demand.

Minneapolis, 2009. The periphery of Lake Harriet simultaneously accommodates every sort of activity nearby residents might enjoy, while the lake itself is one of the city's most popular destinations for watersports.

The state of Minnesota extended the city's regional approach to parks in 1967 by passing legislation that created a Metropolitan Council that was required to produce a Regional Recreation Open Space Policy Plan. This was followed in 1974 by the Metropolitan Parks Act, which established a Metropolitan Parks and Open Space Commission that conssited of nine representatives of local governments, including Minneapolis and St. Paul. It was instructed to identify and establish priorities for areas that regional agencies should acquire and develop in order to "meet the outdoor recreation needs of the people of the metropolitan area." As of 2007 this larger regional system consisted of 51,785 acres (20,957 ha) of parkland and included thirty-five regional parks, ten park reserves, four special recreation features, and twenty-two regional trails.[37]

CHICAGO

By the turn of the twentieth century, Chicago was well on its way to creating a necklace of parkways connecting its inner neighborhoods with Lake Michigan. Civic leaders understood that they had to turn their attention to undeveloped property surrounding the city. Two institutions were key: the Chicago

Park District, which has been responsible for the city's parks since 1934, and the Forest Preserve District, which has been responsible for parkland in the surrounding suburbs since 1913. Both evolved over a number of years and reflect modern concerns about conservation and recreation.

The idea of a regional forest preserve began to take shape in 1903, when the Board of Commissioners of Cook County established an Outer Belt Park Commission charged with "the creation and establishment of an outer belt line of parks and boulevards, encircling the city of Chicago and embracing the Calumet and Des Plaines Rivers and the Skokie Marsh."[38] Two years later the Illinois State Legislature passed the Forest Preserve Act of 1905, which emphasized the establishment of scenic highways passing through what was then still rural Cook County.

The forest preserve idea was embodied in the regional park system Daniel Burnham illustrated in the *Plan of Chicago*. Burnham, like H. W. S. Cleveland in Minneapolis, believed it was important to begin creating that system as soon as possible: "The time to secure the lands necessary for such a system is now, while as yet the prices are moderate and the natural scenery is comparatively unspoiled. Every year of failure or neglect to act largely increases the expense and diminishes the opportunities."[39] In response to public pressure, the state legislature passed the Preserve Enabling Act of 1913, "to restore, restock, protect and preserve the natural forests and such lands together with their flora and fauna, as nearly as may be, in their natural state and condition, for the purpose of the education, pleasure, and recreation of the public." In 2007 the Forest Preserve District established by this act owned approximately 11 percent of Cook County, or 67,800 acres (27,438 ha). The preserve property is not set aside exclusively as a habitat that excludes human beings; rather it is genuine parkland, providing places for picnicking, camping, hiking, bird-watching, canoeing, sledding, horseback riding, fishing, swimming, golfing, inline skating, and countless other recreational activities.

The Forest Preserve's focus on recreation was matched by the City of Chicago. At the beginning of the twentieth century, the South Park Commission issued bonds to finance the acquisition of 671 acres (272 ha) of parkland for creation of small local parks, each approximately 10 acres (4 ha) each in size. Each of the seventeen new parks it established contained outdoor swimming pools and athletic fields as well as clubhouses for the public that contained gymnasia, reading rooms, eating facilities, and club rooms. The clubhouses were intended to provide recreation opportunities summer and winter.

The Great Depression made it difficult for the city's twenty-two park administrations (including the large South, West, and Lincoln Park Commissions) to finance further park development, and in 1934 they were consolidated into a single Chicago Park District. In 2007 the Park District had an annual budget of $85 million and managed more than 7,300 acres (2,954 ha) of parkland, 552 parks, thirty-three

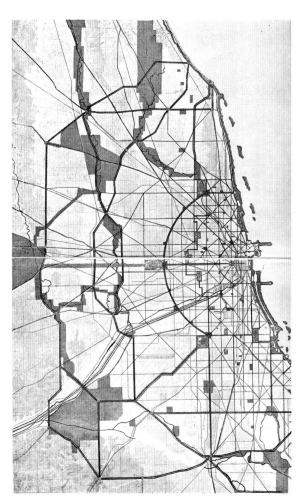

Chicago, 1909. The *Plan of Chicago* recommended creating a 50,000-acre (20,234-ha) regional park system.

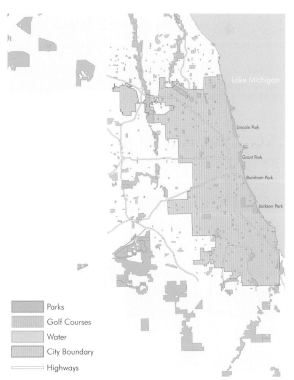

Parks
Golf Courses
Water
City Boundary
Highways

Chicago, 2009. Today, a hundred years after the *Plan of Chicago* was published, the Forest Preserve and city park system together include more than 74,000 acres (29,947 ha) of parkland.

Chicago, 2008. By the twenty-first century there were indoor recreational facilities in Sherman Park and throughout the city.

beaches, nine museums, two conservatories, sixteen historic lagoons, ten bird and wildlife gardens, and thousands of special events, sports, and entertainment programs.[40]

Burnham's vision of a metropolitan park system became a reality, providing the framework around which Chicago's urban and suburban neighborhoods have developed. But the city's twentieth-century emphasis on recreation ensured that the two large metropolitan park systems are more than just green space. As a result, the Chicago metropolitan region contains places for every conceivable recreational activity, ensuring a quality of life that is difficult for most metropolitan areas to match.

BOULDER

Some communities in America do have more parkland than Minneapolis or Chicago. For example, in 2000 there were 36,501 acres (14,771 ha) of parkland in Phoenix, including South Mountain Preserve Park—at 16,283 acres (6,589 ha), the largest city park in the United States—and North Mountain Preserve Park, the third largest.[41] But this parkland is largely desert and mountains. It does not include the quantity, quality, or variety of recreational opportunities available in metropolitan Minneapolis or Chicago. The city with the most parkland per capita is Boulder, Colorado.

The city of Boulder has a small population—91,700 in 2006, with an additional 190,600 in the rest of Boulder County[42]—but residents enjoy 304,545 acres (123,245 ha) of parkland in the county,

including 34,574 acres (13,992 ha) operated by the city's Department of Parks and Recreation, 79,482 acres (32,165 ha) of county-owned parkland, 1,373 acres (556 ha) of state-owned parkland, and 188,804 acres (76,406 ha) of federal parkland.[43] In all, 63 percent of the county's area is parkland. This extraordinary amount of parkland is the product of Boulder's setting at the foothills of the Rocky Mountains and a population determined to enjoy its pleasures.

National forest preserves had been in place for decades when civic leaders became concerned about the possible loss of easy access to the stunning natural landscapes that surrounded the city. They also began to worry about being engulfed by the residential subdivisions spreading across the landscape from Denver. In 1959, in an attempt to retard construction in the lovely foothill landscapes surrounding the city, a city charter amendment created a "blue line" beyond which the city would not supply water. Eight years later, Boulder became the first city in the nation to impose a sales tax of 0.4 percent to pay for the acquisition, management, and maintenance of open space. In

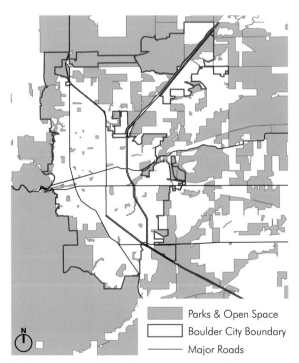

Parks & Open Space
Boulder City Boundary
Major Roads

Boulder, Colorado, 2009. City, county, state, and federal governments provide each individual citizen of Boulder County with more than 1.7 acres (0.68 ha) of publicly owned parkland.

1993 it added another 0.3 percent to the sales tax. As of 2008, when the sales tax for open space had leveled off at 1.28 percent, the tax had paid for 40,000 of the city's 46,000 acres (18,616 ha) of parkland.[44]

The system that gives each resident of Boulder County 1.7 acres (0.69 ha) of parkland may not have been the product of a plan, but it was the result of planning. Every year recently collected tax proceeds were available to purchase whatever land seemed to be most likely to be developed or would do the most to enhance the existing system. Over nearly half a century, Boulder protected streambeds, preserved the foothills of the Rocky Mountains on its west, and separated itself from surrounding subdivisions to the north, east, and south with a greenbelt of parks. The resulting park system provides hiking opportunities in mountain landscapes; prairie fields in which to wander; bicycle and jogging trails; greenways connecting athletic fields, schoolyards, picnic areas, and playgrounds; and the particularly wide variety of ecosystems possible only within such close proximity to the Rocky Mountains.

Manhattan, 2006. Even small parks like Greeley Square require constant maintenance.

NINE

STEWARDSHIP

Creating a public park is only the start—even for extraordinary parks like Brooklyn's Prospect Park, Chicago's lakeshore, or Minneapolis's interconnected park system. The development process does not stop when a park opens to the public. Parks are living landscapes, changing with the time of day and the season of the year. What is there one year may be gone the next, not just as a result of natural processes but through of human interaction with the landscape. A park may be badly or well cared for, left alone, adapted to new uses, or physically altered. But it will always be changing. Thus, making decisions about public parks requires an appreciation of the ways in which they change and, particularly, the ways in which people change them. More important, it means that parks require ongoing attention if they are to be of continuing value to surrounding communities. They cannot survive unless they are cared for, paid for, and properly managed through stewardship, financing, and governance.

Too often people assume that a new park will not need much attention during its first years of operation. But the maintenance of a park, like that of a new car or the training of a puppy, begins immediately. Spring plantings must be protected until they establish themselves. During the summer, the grass needs to be mowed. When the leaves drop in the fall, they have to be gathered and disposed of or mulched. In the winter sidewalks need to be shoveled. Because such day-to-day activities involve expense but not much glamour, park maintenance is often neglected.

Stewardship is more than just a matter of picking up the trash, pruning dead branches, or replacing flowers as the seasons change. Successful parks attract large numbers of people, and even though these crowds don't intend to cause damage, they do. Olmsted understood this. In 1872 he pointed out that Central Park had been "rendered uninviting by tobacco quid and spittle, cigar stumps, nut shells, papers, and offal of fruit and other food, which visitors cast away . . . so that a tidy woman approaching to take a seat draws back in disgust."[1] He also stated the obvious: the problem could be solved if staff picked up litter on a regular basis. As long as parks assign staff to pick up refuse, litter is not a problem, and will not be as long as money is available to pay for its removal and personnel to supervise that work.

Olmsted also saw "a great vigorous oak tree killed in two years by the trampling of the ground over its roots" and watched turf disappear "in any place where a hundred footsteps have fallen in rapid succession." The problem, he said, is to protect parkland from "the riotous actions of a mob unconscious of wrong purposes and indignant at obvious constraints upon what it regards as harmless conduct."[2] Consequently,

Manhattan, 2008. Bryant Park employs people who pick up litter to keep the park a pleasant destination for thousands of people.

"Greenhouses were falling to pieces, their girders and supports having crumbled into rust. Band stands were toppling on shaky foundations while walks and driveways were filled with ruts and mud holes. Lagoons were eating their way into the banks, and acres of land were without trees or shrubbery, fountains were out of repair, bridges had rotted until they were dangerous to cross, and the whole system bore evidence of rack and ruin."[4]

When voters approved a $2 million bond issue for refurbishment of these parks, Jensen worked hard to restore them.[5] Yet seventy-five years later the same parks were again in disrepair: "Structures and stone work . . . [had] deteriorated and thousands of shrubs and small trees [had been] cut down for security reasons . . . [The landscape] had been invaded by aggressive native and non-native plants that . . . drastically altered the intent and character of the original design"[6] Just as Jensen had, park officials in 1992 had to engage in extensive restoration.

This same cycle of investment, deterioration, and restoration is repeated all the time. Sometimes the initial design was inappropriate or inadequate, and later remodeling may be unsuccessful. Budget cuts and the resulting physical deterioration frequently stimulate citizen action and renewed funding. But all too often the cycle begins again as soon as park renovation is complete.

Every government will face periods of stringency or bad leadership. Park stewardship cannot be left to the vagaries of the moment; it must be ongoing and rely on techniques that protect parks against the effects of down cycles. How are effective management and adequate maintenance budgets achieved? Before addressing that question, it is helpful to examine the histories of three parks in New York City that have been through these cycles and emerged as very successful public facilities: Central, Prospect, and Bryant Parks.

he tried to design parks in a way that would mitigate such problems, by separating open areas intended for large numbers of people from secluded places for quiet enjoyment and by providing circulation patterns that channeled pedestrians and vehicles along paths and away from landscape features. But even in the most well-designed parks, ongoing maintenance efforts are necessary to repair damage and keep plantings and facilities in good condition.

While ill-conceived park design may cause problems, adequate funding, capable personnel, and enterprising management can often overcome even the most egregious design errors. The initial plan for Forest Park in St. Louis lacked the genius of Olmsted's work. From the beginning its amenities were augmented to meet consumer demand, with intrusions meant to add "the concept of social utility" to "the element of natural beauty."[3] But "improvements" could not prevent Forest Park from falling victim—like many other parks in other cities—to deferred maintenance, budget cuts, and poor management during the 1980s, and these conditions were not remedied for nearly two decades (see chapter 11).

Failure to invest in ordinary maintenance has dogged public parks since the earliest days. In 1905 Jens Jensen returned to work on Chicago's West Side parks, after a five-year hiatus, as overall superintendent and landscape architect. To his dismay, he found that inadequate maintenance had taken a heavy toll:

CENTRAL PARK

Central Park has been through several cycles of deterioration. Each was followed by the installation of talented managers who made necessary repairs and restoration. The reasons for deterioration were different in each case, but the solution was always

Manhattan, 1904. Throughout its history, large crowds of people in Central Park have left its lawns littered.

the same: adequate funding for maintenance combined with intelligent management.

The first period of deterioration began after Olmsted left New York in 1862 to become executive secretary of the U.S. Sanitary Commission (the precursor to the Red Cross), before construction of the park was complete. Even though it was unfinished, the park immediately became popular—it saw 4.3 million visitors in 1863 and 6.1 million the next year.[7] The surge of people surely caused damage, particularly because the park's managers were not prepared for so many visitors. But the root cause of the problem was the plundering and mismanagement of administrators who owed allegiance to William "Boss" Tweed's Democratic Party machine.

Olmsted and Vaux were recalled and appointed advisory landscape architects to the park board in 1871, and as long as they were involved the park remained in good shape. Vaux eventually became the head landscape architect for the New York City parks department and brought with him Samuel

Parsons (1844–1923), who had been his apprentice and became his partner from 1887 until Vaux's death in 1895. Parsons then became the head landscape architect for the city until he was fired for political reasons in 1911. Once he was out of the scene the park began to deteriorate once again.

For the next two decades the emphasis was on using the park for active recreation, team sports, and public events, which escalated wear and tear. Automobile traffic replaced carriages on the circumferential road; crowds and increasing pollution stressed the landscape. Robert Moses became parks commissioner in 1934, and within a few months he was using federal relief funds to put thousands of laborers to work clearing away the squatters from the site of the lower reservoir, which had been taken out of service and drained four years earlier and replaced with the Great Lawn and the Turtle Pond, unfinished landscapes that had suffered from years of deferred maintenance. He built a zoo, installed playgrounds, and converted the building that housed the sheep that grazed on the Sheep Meadow into a restaurant, Tavern on the Green.[8]

Manhattan, 1934 and 2004. When the lower reservoir in Central Park was dismantled, Robert Moses seized the opportunity to create the Great Ellipse, which provided ample sites for baseball and other active sports.

During the twenty-six years he served as parks commissioner, Moses got things done in Central Park (and in every other part of New York City). After he resigned in 1960 to work on the 1964 World's Fair in Flushing Meadows, Central Park again began to deteriorate. While the primary reason was inadequate funding, the park's skilled staff was left without effective leadership. In 1961, the year after Moses left office, the city's capital budget allocated $42.2 million ($289.5 million in 2007 dollars) to the parks department. The money had to cover improvements to the park system's 900 playgrounds, 104 swimming pools, 14 golf courses, 534 tennis courts, three zoos, seven ice fields, 890 playing fields, 36 recreation centers, 18 miles (29 km) of public beach, and almost 25,000 acres (10,117 ha) of parkland with 2 million park trees in 1,472 separate parks and playgrounds.[9] By 1979 the capital budget allocation had dropped to $19 million ($53.6 million in 2007 dollars), less than a fifth of what it had been eighteen years earlier.[10]

No wonder Central Park ended the 1970s with miles of crumbling pavement, thousands of trees with exposed roots and dead branches, playing fields whose turf had been ground into dust, hundreds of benches with missing slats, broken drinking fountains, rest rooms that had been closed for years, and missing light bulbs on lampposts that were defaced with the same graffiti that covered much of the rest of the park.

The deterioration that resulted from a decline in park spending in New York happened everywhere else as well. The millions of people who could not afford alternative means of recreation were left without usable public facilities. Government appropriations no longer covered the cost of fixing lampposts, repainting and repairing graffiti-covered benches, replacing crumbling pavement, removing dead trees, or preventing weed infestation. Residents shunned places in such poor condition, and the parks they abandoned attracted drug dealing and violent crime.

When area residents began to abandon public parks, some people assumed this was evidence of the parks' obsolescence. Those who disagreed had only one model for dealing with park deterioration: generous federal assistance in the form of public works. But neither the Nixon nor the Ford administration

was interested in reviving the WPA. They had to pay for the Vietnam War, the Cold War, and the ambitious programs initiated by the Johnson administration's War on Poverty.

New York City's parks department was by then competing for money with agencies that had not existed when Moses had been parks commissioner and were not considered government responsibilities when Olmsted and Vaux designed the park. Things became even worse in the mid-1970s, when the city nearly went bankrupt and was compelled to make huge personnel and services reductions in every agency, particularly in the Department of Parks and Recreation, which by then had lost much of the skilled staff Moses had assembled.

In 1975, during the worst period of this fiscal crisis, Elizabeth Barlow Rogers agreed to serve as the unpaid head of a task force on Central Park and to manage a summer intern program financed by the federal government.[11] A relative newcomer who had moved to New York City in 1964, she had become concerned with conditions in the city's flagship park. Rogers continued to work on a volunteer basis to improve the park until 1979, when she became the first person to fill a newly created position: Central Park administrator. Since the city was just emerging from a terrible fiscal crisis, it could make only modest increases in the budget of every city agency. Rogers understood that local government would never appropriate the money that was needed, nor have the tenacity, over decades of changing mayoralties, to maintain the level of stewardship that was required to keep Central Park in good condition. The solution she devised—a private, nonprofit conservancy that could raise money from the public—has become a model for the entire country. The Central Park Conservancy raised funds, hired a dedicated staff to augment city workers, and developed a long-term restoration plan that would ensure the park's continuing improvement.

Since 1980 the conservancy has taken primary responsibility for restoring and maintaining the park, under a contract with the city's Department of Parks and Recreation. As of 2008, it had spent $450 million on the park; at that time, the conservancy had an endowment that was valued at about $120 million. It raises between $25 and $30 million annually in private donations, has a permanent staff of 250, manages 3,000 volunteers, and provides 85 percent of Central Park's $27 million annual operating budget.[12]

Rogers began by hiring a group of young "horticulture" interns to work in parallel with city personnel, performing tasks much broader than their title might suggest. In addition to initiating horticulture projects, they made long-delayed repairs and removed graffiti. Bringing these new people into government was crucial because so many of the dedicated civil servants hired by Moses had retired, and the accumulated knowledge of how to deal with treasured portions of the park had gone with them.

The parks department provided the impetus and leadership for state-funded restoration of the Sheep Meadow and park structures such as Belvedere Castle, which had long been abandoned. Much of what Rogers advocated was not glamorous: replacing missing bench slats, fixing the water fountains, repairing the sidewalks. One of the most effective projects was hiring sculptor Kent Bloomer to design a new lamppost luminaire, which was installed throughout the park. These new lampposts provided the lighting that helped to increase security in the park. The design is so admired that it is now used all over the United States.

The first major private contribution to the Central Park Conservancy came from Yoko Ono, who donated $1 million to relandscape, maintain, and endow a 2.5-acre (1-ha) section of the park in memory of her husband, John Lennon. The site, now known as Strawberry Fields, took its name from the well-known Beatles song. This donation was followed by a similar gift for the 5-acre (2-ha) formal Conservatory Garden. In both cases, Rogers appointed one of the young recruits to be a horticultural "gardener" responsible for everything in that part of the park, not just the plants and flowers.

Rogers's most important action, however, was to develop a master renovation and management plan, published in 1985, which established a carefully staged action program to deal with the rehabilitation of every section of the park. The plan provided the basis of the conservancy's first capital campaign, established a multiyear restoration cycle, became a fund-raising vehicle, and provided the conservancy with its central role: the stewardship of Central Park.[13]

After Rogers stepped down in 1996, landscape

Manhattan, 2008. The luminaire designed by sculptor Kent Bloomer in cooperation with architect Gerald Allen in 1982 is one example of the high level of quality demanded of all additions to the park since the establishment of the Central Park Conservancy.

architect Douglas Blonsky, whom she had brought in during 1985 as director of design and construction, took her place as administrator. By that time the conservancy had dealt with the most visible and pressing park issues. Blonsky established a system of zone management inspired by the management technique Rogers had pioneered at Strawberry Fields and the Conservatory Garden. He divided the park into forty-nine zones, each assigned to a single gardener who was responsible for not just horticulture but everything in the zone and everybody who worked there, including volunteers. The zones inherited expertise, equipment, and specialized crews created by the conservancy years earlier. Each zone gardener quickly developed an intimate understanding of his or her area and built relationships with the people who used it. The combination of decentralized responsibility and central management resulted in a strong sense of staff ownership, accountability, and, most important, responsible management that was responsive to the demands of both the landscape and its users.

PROSPECT PARK

In 1980 the administration of mayor Edward Koch applied this same management structure to Prospect Park in Brooklyn by creating the job of Prospect Park administrator. Parks commissioner Gordon Davis appointed Tupper Thomas the park's first administrator. She was one of a number of Americans who answered President Kennedy's call to "ask not what your country can do for you—ask what you can do for your country" by dedicating herself to government service. Thomas, who is a native of Minneapolis, had received a small college grant to study grassroots politics in New York City, and after graduation she moved to the city. In 1967 she joined the city government, working on issues of housing and neighborhood preservation.

Like Central Park, Prospect Park was in poor condition. But its problems had been caused by years of neglect rather than heavy usage by hordes of people. Like Rogers, Thomas established a non-profit institution, the Prospect Park Alliance, to supplement city funding. Because the neighborhoods around Prospect Park did not have as large a population as those around Central Park, the large number of people with high incomes, or the nearby corporations ready to make contributions to a world-renowned park, Prospect Park could not expect to attract the substantial donations that Central Park

enjoyed. Thomas decided to augment that strategy by reaching out to the diverse ethnic communities around Brooklyn, scheduling events that would bring them to the park, and encouraging them to play a personal role in park stewardship.

One of the first projects she initiated was the restoration of the cherished carousel, which had originally been built for Coney Island and had been moved to Prospect Park in 1952. Lack of maintenance had forced it to cease operations in 1983. Working with members of the Prospect Park Alliance, Thomas obtained private donations and government grants that paid for the restoration of the carousel, which reopened in 1990.

Thomas used the same approach to restore the tennis center, the skating rink, and the pedal boats that visitors could rent to enjoy the lake. But unlike the communities around Central Park, the neighborhoods surrounding the park could not initially generate enough user revenue for these facilities to be profitable. Thomas believed that improving the quality of service would increase their popularity. Consequently, as contracts expired the Prospect Park Alliance took over their operation. Donations and grants paid for physical improvements. By the end of the first decade of the twenty-first century, Alliance-operated concessions had become sufficiently popular to generate a moderate profit.

BRYANT PARK

Tupper Thomas developed community organizing techniques that were appropriate to Brooklyn.

Brooklyn, New York, 2008. Tupper Thomas, Prospect Park's first administrator, used community organizing principles to encourage residents to use the park.

Daniel Biederman, president of the Bryant Park Corporation, took a very different approach to park stewardship. Bryant Park is one one-hundredth the size of Prospect Park and is located in the midst of midtown Manhattan's high-rise office buildings and retail stores, rather than among charming row-house neighborhoods with quite diverse populations. It occupies 6.5 acres (2.6 ha) between 40th and 42nd streets, behind the New York Public Library. The site, purchased by the city as a potter's field in 1823, became the location of the Croton Reservoir in 1842. When the reservoir was completed in 1847, the space behind it was opened to public use. A crystal palace was erected in 1853, in emulation of London's 1851 Crystal Palace exhibition; it burned down five years later. In 1884 the site, then known as Reservoir Square, was renamed in honor of writer William Cullen Bryant. Its role as a public park grew when the reservoir was replaced by the imposing main branch of the New York Public Library, which opened in 1911.[14]

One reason that Bryant Park was not particularly inviting during its early days was that a noisy elevated subway—the El—ran above its Sixth Avenue edge. By the late 1920s the park had become a hangout for homeless men. Civic leaders thought that Bryant Park should be used primarily by people who worked or shopped in the area or were visiting the library. In 1933 the Architects' Emergency Committee, which had been formed to help out-of-work colleagues, and the Sixth Avenue Association sponsored a competition for a design to revitalize Bryant Park. The winner, Lusby Simpson, envisioned a symmetrical scheme centered on a rectangular lawn, in the manner of André Le Nôtre.

Robert Moses had just been appointed New York City parks commissioner. He believed that the park could become a major midtown asset when the El was replaced by underground service, which was scheduled to occur between 1936 and 1940. He decided to implement Simpson's plan and commissioned landscape architect Gilmore Clarke to prepare a new design that was inspired by Simpson's work.

Many observers thought physical improvements would be enough to transform Bryant Park into a permanent asset. Mayor Fiorello La Guardia knew better. When he was asked at the park's reopening whether Bryant Park would again be allowed to

Manhattan, 1934 and 1943. Bryant Park was reconstructed using fill from the Sixth Avenue underground subway, which replaced the elevated line that used to run along the park. It was completely restored and remained in excellent condition until Robert Moses retired in 1960.

deteriorate, he replied, "Oh, we can keep it like this as long as we keep Moses."[15] As I noted earlier, after Moses resigned as commissioner the percentage of the city budget devoted to city parks plummeted. In 1963 the parks department had 6,071 full-time employees; by 1998 the number had declined to 1,156. Without enough enterprising management and maintenance personnel, the flaws in the park's physical design became apparent.

Security became an increasingly significant issue with the decrease in parks department personnel. The 1934 reconstruction had raised the level of the park 4 feet (1.2 m) above street level and surrounded it with walls, fences, and shrubs, making it difficult for people walking by and, more important, police patrols driving by to see into the park. Soon enough it became an attractive hangout for addicts, pushers, prostitutes, and muggers. Starting in 1973, at nine o'clock every evening police barricades were placed at all park entrances to keep unwary passersby out. The crime rate continued to rise: by 1975 the number of crimes reported reached nine hundred a year, and murders occurred in 1976 and 1977. Conventional wisdom held that the park could never be made safe and ought to be closed.

Bryant Park was in devastated physical condition. Laurie Olin, the landscape designer later hired to redesign it, reported "trees overgrown—ground beaten bare—trash overflowing the waste cans, stuffed into the long-abandoned light boxes—lights broken off and missing; pavement not repaired—hedges allowed to grow up to hide the ugly lights, themselves neglected and ugly."[16] Once again civic leaders responded. Instead of depending entirely on redesign and reconstruction, a group that included the Rockefeller Brothers, the New York Public Library, and Time, Inc., hired Daniel Biederman, a recent graduate of the Harvard Business School, and sociologist William H. "Holly" Whyte to propose actions that would make Bryant Park a successful park and a midtown asset. Whyte, who had been studying pedestrian patterns for a generation, advocated actions that would encourage people, lots and lots of people, to want to visit the park. He proposed installing attractions that would draw large numbers of midtown shoppers and office workers and removing obstacles that obscured the view of what was happening in the park at any time, day or night.

Biederman accepted Whyte's diagnosis and applied business administration techniques to the problems and their solutions. His first goal was to make the park financially sustainable. Once there was enough revenue to cover all park expenses, he concentrated on marketing and management strategies that would increase utilization. He devised a series of actions that included establishing entirely new management, making minor physical improvements, incorporating attractive four-season mixed plantings, introducing new attractions, scheduling and programming events, and carefully supervising ongoing maintenance.[17]

When these solutions were first proposed, the city's Department of Parks and Recreation was in no position to execute the program. Its annual $210,000 budget allocation for Bryant Park was barely enough to cover routine maintenance. Biederman, working with Marshall Rose, a representative of the New York Public Library, crafted a plan that could pay for everything. The Bryant Park Corporation was created to operate the park and use sustainable revenues that would pay for restoration and day-to-day management. Those revenues included concessions such as sandwich stands, cafés, and restaurants; funds from sponsors who covered the cost of movies, concerts, and other audience-attracting events; tax payments from a new business improvement district (BID) on the properties facing the park; and modest charitable donations.

The city entered into an agreement that turned over day-to day management to a newly created Bryant Park Restoration Corporation, but committed to continuing to provide $210,000 annually toward park maintenance. The corporation's board of directors consisted of the area's major property owners, including the New York Public Library, with Biederman as president. The parks department technically continues to govern the park and ensures that the public interest is protected. But the Bryant Park Corporation that Biederman established in 1984 still manages and maintains the park. Since 1998 the city has not had to spend a penny on Bryant Park because the corporation has been receiving enough revenue to cover all management and maintenance expenses.

Once the financial obstacles had been overcome, the restoration of the park could begin. Whyte had explained the physical problem: "Bryant Park is cut off from the street. . . . You can't see in. You can't see out. There are only a few entry points."[18] The remedy was the work of three firms: Hanna/Olin (overall landscape design), Hardy, Holtzman, Pfeiffer (architecture), and Lynden B. Miller Public Garden Design (planting design). When the park was closed for reconstruction in 1987, the drug dealers, prostitutes, and muggers had no choice but to clear out.

The central lawn that dominated Bryant Park was excavated to a depth of 37 feet (11 m) to reach the bedrock, which had formed the base of the reservoir that had once occupied the site. The city appropriated $17 million to create 3 acres (1.2 ha) of underground library space on two levels that contained 84 miles (135 km) of shelves, along with drainage, a roof structure, and a replanted lawn covering everything. Paving throughout the park was replaced; shrubs

Manhattan, 2005. People in Bryant Park are attracted by the chance to purchase a snack or a drink while they sit at a table and enjoy the park.

Manhattan, 2008. Thousands of people come to Bryant Park because they can arrange movable chairs in configurations that allow them to have conversations, sit in the sun, or read the paper.

and trees were pruned and planted (opening up views in and out of the park), and 300 feet (91 m) of mixed border plantings were designed and installed. New entrances with broad, welcoming stairs were constructed, and existing entrances were made more open and inviting. Lighting was installed everywhere, even on the cornices of buildings across the street.

The park reopened in stages between 1991 and 1995, and it soon became the active centerpiece of the district. The lawn and shady spots under the trees offered eight hundred tables and four thousand movable chairs so that visitors could sit where they liked—independently or in groups. Biederman conceived a series of attractions and worked with Hugh Hardy to house them

Manhattan, 2005. The café in Bryant Park generates substantial income that helps to pay for maintenance.

Manhattan, 2005. Thousands of people come to Bryant Park to play chess, take a ride on a carousel, and enjoy its many other attractions.

in architecture that seemed to grow naturally from their locations. He negotiated lucrative deals with concessionaires to operate these attractions, which included the 5,280-square-foot (490-m²) Bryant Park Grill, a 5,000-square-foot (464-m²) outdoor café, two newsstands, and four kiosks offering light fare. Rental fees from the concessionaires help to cover park maintenance expenses. Far more important, every day each of them attracts hundreds of office workers, shoppers, and tourists.

As Biederman gained experience managing the park, he added a carousel, wireless Internet access, a reading room, chess tables, and a temporary winter rink offering ice-skating free of charge. Three to seven daily events, including early evening and lunchtime concerts, bring even more people to the park. Monday night movies during the summertime attract an average audience of six thousand; the 1997 opening night film, *The Wizard of Oz,* brought twelve thousand people.

STEWARDSHIP REQUIREMENTS

In examining the histories of these three parks and many others, I have identified six requirements for effective park stewardship: an adequate and reliable stream of revenue; a multiyear management plan that deals with every section of the park; personnel that are held accountable for the conditions within the park; equitable distribution of resources; responsiveness to changing park-user demands; and, perhaps most important, entrepreneurial management.

AN ADEQUATE REVENUE STREAM

Whenever there is a government revenue shortfall (and they are inevitable), somebody will propose eliminating "unnecessary" activities and services or cutting operating budgets, and parks are the usual victims. To prevent this, citizen groups in St. Louis, Atlanta, Memphis, and other cities across the country have followed New York's example and created nonprofit conservancies to augment and even eliminate reliance on government funding. Business improvement districts, like the one created for Bryant Park, provide another funding alternative, as do dedicated taxes, like those used by Minneapolis to maintain the finest park system in the nation. (These financing methods are detailed in chapter 10.) Whatever technique is employed, there is no way to maintain a park without money.

MULTIYEAR PLANNING

Master park renovation plans are essential because it is rarely possible to raise all the money that is needed or accomplish everything at once. The Central Park Conservancy pioneered the use of master renovation plans, and they were followed by Piedmont Park in Atlanta and Shelby Farms Park in Memphis. Master plans have the added benefit of providing a vision for future action, galvanizing community support, and identifying projects that can be targets for fund-raising.

But creating a plan is only the beginning. As Dwight Eisenhower once remarked, "Plans are worthless, but planning is everything."[19] In the mid-1980s, at the time Tupper Thomas was just starting the effort to restore natural woodlands in Prospect Park, she commissioned a plan for the park's Ravine section.[20] The plan recommended restoring the original Olmsted and Vaux landscape, including its waterways. Executing these recommendations required considerable ingenuity because the parks department did not possess detailed construction documents but had to depend on old photographs.

All the waterways in Prospect Park are artificial. Water is piped into the park from underground conduits and gurgles out from a pile of boulders into a small pond, flowing from there through the Ravine into the large lake in the southern part of the park. The boulders that remained were not arranged as they were depicted in the photos. Additional boulders were donated from a construction site by a nearby hospital. Restoring the pond required draining the water, but that would have killed the fish and turtles who lived there. So volunteers were brought in to move them temporarily to the lake.

The waterways in the Ravine now look very much as they did in the nineteenth century. The turtles and fish are back. The plan had been necessary to gain support for park restoration, but the crucial element was the planning that allowed the restoration to proceed successfully. Although the project became a multiyear effort that went far beyond that initial document, enough of the plan's recommendations were implemented to show that the effort and expense would be worthwhile.

ACCOUNTABLE PERSONNEL

Good management is dependent on effective personnel—and vice versa. Robert Moses believed that "the ideal thing . . . is to have first-class men operating first-class machines, but first-class men can operate any machine and third-rate people can't make the best and most modern gadget work."[21] Even the best possible staff requires supervision and ongoing training. By dividing Central Park into zones and assigning a skilled staff member to be in charge of everything in his or her zone, Douglas Blonsky achieved a level of personnel accountability that had never before been possible.

EQUITABLE RESOURCE DISTRIBUTION

I like to say that one must start with the bones, add flesh, and leave the jewelry for last. One of the legacies of the first twenty-five years of the restoration of Central Park was action on its most pressing problems (the bones), such as crumbling pavement and broken lighting fixtures, which affected everybody. This has allowed the conservancy to proceed with

Manhattan, 2005. Capital investment in Central Park restored both the landscape and its users.

some of its most important features (the flesh), such as the Bethesda Fountain and the Sheep Meadow, which attracted everybody.[22] Afterward, work continued on remaining unrestored major landscapes, such as the Lake, the Ramble, and the North Woods. The conservancy has been replacing the rustic shelters and other architectural features designed for the park by Calvert Vaux (the jewels). The comprehensiveness of the program is important because it touches every aspect of the park: ecological systems, flora, fauna, infrastructure, utilization patterns, and public structures.

Some improvements may be particularly useful to one group of park users or to one nearby residential community. Taken together, however, they provide benefits to visitors to every part of the park on an equitable basis. That stress on equity allows the development of a broad constituency and reduces significant opposition.

RESPONSIVENESS TO CHANGING DEMANDS

Serving all park users is more than just a matter of maintaining the park and ensuring continuation of its services. Park management must also be responsive to changing user demand. Renegotiated kiosk contracts in Bryant Park have resulted in better and better service for parkgoers. The Bryant Park Corporation installed wi-fi service and later introduced

winter ice-skating, both very popular with today's park visitors.

Virtually everything Biederman added to Bryant Park and Thomas added to Prospect Park has been accepted with delight by park users because the additions have been chosen in response to the changing demands of the times. Dedicated citizens are also always looking for ways to improve their parks; interest groups regularly propose activities they believe ought to take place there; public agencies are continually seeking sites for memorials, traffic arteries, and revenue-producing facilities that they want to add to some park.

Of course, many proposed additions may not be beneficial. Some may be opposed because a particular interest group considers them to be intrusions that alter the designer's original intentions. Determining original intent can be very difficult, however. To arrive at the "correct" design for each part of the Chicago lakeshore, should we restore the barren Lake Park of 1844, Olmsted's 1870 design, his 1893 design, Burnham's 1896 design, or his 1909 design? Because they were added later, does one remove Buckingham Fountain, Caldwell's Lily Pool, or Frank Gehry's bridge and bandshell?

Constantly reexamining these "intrusions" may be appropriate, but only if we accept the proposition I discussed in chapter 7 and have implied throughout this book: that parks are not end-state works of

Manhattan, 2008. The Central Park boathouse and restaurant is one of the many recreational additions to Olmsted and Vaux's original design.

art but rather are continually evolving products of the interaction between people and nature. From that point of view, that it is not only appropriate but essential to continue to make changes that improve public parks.

Potential improvements (or "intrusions") come in two varieties: inanimate and human. In Cental Park, for example, the inanimate additions have been many: Cleopatra's Needle (an obelisk dating from 1600 B.C., donated by the Khedive of Egypt in 1881), playgrounds, sports fields, a zoo, two ice-skating rinks, a boathouse and restaurant, the Delacorte (Shakespeare) Theater, and numerous sculptures depicting, among others, Hans Christian Andersen and Alice-in-Wonderland. There also have been proposals for hundreds of other additions that did not make it, including an exposition building (1903), an opera house (1910), a large stadium (1919), a sunken oriental garden (1920), a swimming pool, circus, and running track (1923), a garden for the blind (1955), and an outdoor café-restaurant (1960).[23] All these proposed additions drew both support and opposition. Over time, however, most of the "intrusions" that made it into the park have become beloved fixtures.

The best advice about inanimate intrusions was given by Frederick Law Olmsted in 1872: "To determine whether any structure on the Park is undesirable, it should be considered first, what part of the necessary accommodation of the public on the Park is met by it, how this much of accommodation could be otherwise or elsewhere provided, and in what degree and whence the structure will be conspicuous after it shall have been toned by weather, and the plantations about and beyond it shall have taken a mature character."[24]

He was equally wise about human intrusions. Olmsted worried about business activity that interfered with regular park usage. In 1875, writing to the president of the city's Department of Public Parks, he objected to a man who was licensed to offer children rides in goat-drawn carts in the Central Park Mall. Goat droppings had become enough of a nuisance that parents were no longer eager to bring their children there to walk.[25]

There must be a balance between the beneficiaries of any activity that is a park asset and its impact on everybody else. Managing this balance among

Manhattan, 2008. Excellent management and maintenance has transformed Bryant Park into one of the most popular places in midtown Manhattan.

competing activities in a park is no easy task. It may even involve litigation. In November 2008, for example, the Bryant Park Grill initiated legal action to stop competition from another concession that had opened to serve people who came to skate at the park's temporary winter rink.[26] More common are conflicts between adults seeking quiet enjoyment of the park and boisterous children playing games, pedestrians taking a stroll and inline skaters using the same sidewalk, and horse-drawn carriages, recreational motorists, and cyclists riding on the same roadway.

ENTREPRENEURIAL MANAGEMENT

Revenue does not materialize on its own, and plans do not implement themselves; personnel require inspired leadership to be at their best; and many difficult decisions must be made to distribute resources equitably and respond with foresight to changing user demands. For a century nobody thought Bryant Park was anything special. When it went into decline in the 1970s the general consensus was that it was a failure. Suddenly, under Daniel Biederman's entrepreneurial management, it has become a great park. In most cases, however, successful park stewardship cannot be accomplished in a short period of time. It requires ongoing entrepreneurial management. Nowhere is this more evident than in the history of Central Park.

Central Park became a great park from the start because of the public entrepreneurship of Frederick Law Olmsted, whether acting as superintendent (1857–1862), adviser, landscape architect of the city's

Manhattan 2004. Robert Moses used federal WPA money to pay for the creation of the Great Ellipse in Central Park.

Department of Parks, or member of the board of commissioners (1871–1873). During the middle of the twentieth century its greatness was enhanced by parks commissioner Robert Moses. But it might have died if, after two decades of accelerating decline, its administrator, Elizabeth Barlow Rogers, had not developed the mechanisms that restored it to greatness.

It is worth exploring further how public entrepreneurs make their mark. Entrepreneurs often do not intentionally choose the role; rather, it is imposed on them by the situations in which they find themselves. Olmsted wanted to select a workforce that was prepared for its tasks. Instead, on his first day as superintendent he went on a tour of the park and found about five hundred workers, each appointed as a result of political patronage—"not because of his supposed fitness to serve the city on the park, but . . . with a view to the approaching election."[27] What Olmsted accomplished with this workforce is almost incredible.

When Rogers took on the job of park administrator, she already knew that the staff assigned by the Park Department was incapable of restoring the park but that there would not be money to hire the necessary people. Rogers created the Central Park Conservancy because she needed a mechanism that could receive private contributions. She used some of its first donations to hire "horticulturists" and train them to do jobs that had not been done there in many years.

Public entrepreneurs often cannot assemble all of the necessary information, analyze it, and devise the best possible course of action. They must act on the facts that are available to them at the time. When Moses became parks commissioner, four years had passed since the Lower Reservoir had been drained, and it had become a squatter community. There was considerable disagreement about what to do with the site, and proposals came from every civic organization interested in the park and editorials in all the major newspapers. Moses did not waste time commissioning studies or holding public competitions. As he had done with Bryant Park, he adopted an existing scheme, which resembled the recommendations of the American Society of Landscape Architects, and had it adjusted by landscape architect Gilmore Clarke. A year later the Great Lawn was in use.[28]

Public entrepreneurs often cannot allot all the time they want to understand the situation they are in; they must act while the opportunity exists. Olmsted did not expect to be asked to clean up the damage to Central Park that the Tweed machine had done, but he had to accomplish whatever he could before the city government changed hands again. Neither Moses nor anybody else sought the Great Depression, but he understood that its circumstances provided a rare opportunity to hire and pay for tens of thousands of relief workers. A year after becoming commissioner, he had had 2,600 people working on a $2 million renovation program paid for by the WPA.[29]

Rogers knew that the only way to get the money to pay for a long-delayed complete renovation of Central Park was to demonstrate that the park could be admirably restored. Like Moses, she had to use whatever money was available. So she began with projects for which the city and state had appropriated funds: the rehabilitation of the Sheep Meadow, the Dairy, and Bethesda Fountain.

Public entrepreneurs rarely have the luxury of developing the best possible plans, hiring the best possible staff, or relying on sufficient funds to meet any contingency. Olmsted was not able to determine what tools and equipment would be most appropriate; he had to use what was available in New York City during the late 1850s. Moses did not spend years carefully studying the characteristics of the best play equipment available during the 1930s; he had only enough money to install the same swings, slides, and seesaws in all Parks Department play-

Manhattan 2007. Elizabeth Barlow Rogers obtained state and city funds to renovate the Bethesda Fountain.

grounds. By 1937 Moses had added twenty-two playgrounds to Central Park.[30] Rogers did not run a public design competition for a new luminaire and lamppost for Central Park; she commissioned sculptor Kent Bloomer to design it and then installed the luminaires throughout the park.

These talented public entrepreneurs often operated among people who were uncertain about the best procedures. They had to coordinate the activities of people who sometimes disagreed with them and even opposed what they were trying to do. They had to stimulate interest in and support for what they believed had to be done. It was a particularly tough task because public entrepreneurs rarely get more than one bite of the apple. These trailblazers had to be willing to risk failure and, most important, try things that nobody had ever done before. That they have succeeded so well and so often is a testament to the power of imaginative and entrepreneurial management.

Boston, 2008. Post Office Square is financed by revenues from an underground garage and an aboveground café.

TEN

FINANCE AND GOVERNANCE

The life of a public park begins on the day it opens. From that moment its success depends on stewardship, and that stewardship is, in turn, a function of the way the park is financed and governed. Everything—whether urgent necessities or frivolous desires—has to be paid for. And while ill-conceived park design may cause problems, adequate funding, capable personnel, and enterprising management can overcome even the most egregious design errors. Thus, the people involved and the methods used in deciding which expenditures to make and which actions to take will play a major role in the success or failure of every park.

Finance and governance are two sides of the same coin. Parks, like other properties in market-based, pluralistic democracies, are controlled by whoever pays for them. In most American communities, mayors, town managers, or county executives decide on levels of taxation and budget allocations for municipal services with the approval of local legislative bodies (and often state legislatures as well). Parks compete for resources with police, sanitation, traffic management, and every other government service. They are also subject to the political demands of the local administration and the legislators who decide where and how to direct spending.

Priorities change with changing times. During the 1960s and 1970s, for example, local governments began delivering services that previously had not been thought to be their responsibility. They often paid for new and expanded services by changing the proportion of the budget allocated to specific agencies. Park departments were almost always allocated a smaller portion of the pie—with the inevitable accompanying decline in the condition of public parks. During periods of prosperity, while park users may complain about inadequate services, funding is rarely in jeopardy. As soon as there is a downturn in the economy, and therefore in government revenues, decision makers look for budget and service cuts, and park departments invariably suffer more cuts than most other agencies.

Park advocates have devised many different models and mechanisms for effectively financing and governing parks without having to rely entirely on political decisions, some dealing with daily operations and others with long-term park development. What may work in one locality, however, may be inappropriate elsewhere. In considering what will work best for the park system in any community, decision makers have sometimes followed the unfortunate trend of relying too much on experts (in the nineteenth century "high-quality" designers, in the twentieth century "impartial" consultants, in the twenty-first century "scientifically correct" environmentalists). Even the best of these experts sometimes make mistakes, and that is why the many constituencies involved in the stewardship of parks should be included in the decision-making process.

It is essential to maintain a wise balance of roles. If park officials and employees are not involved in the decision-making process, there will surely be problems of implementation; if park users are not involved, there will surely be dysfunctional sections of the park; if area voters are not involved, the regional role of the park (particularly with regard to air and water quality) will receive insufficient attention; and if elected public officials are ignored, many decisions will be undermined and others reversed.

If there is a historically effective model for dealing with park finance and governance, it is the Minneapolis Park System. When the city decided to create a park system, it established an elected park board with three at-large representatives and six from defined districts, all serving four-year terms. It also set aside a portion of the city's real estate tax exclusively for parks, thus insulating the park system from competition for money with other government functions. This measure also insulated the board from having to consider anything other than the welfare of the park system. The independently elected park board and its guaranteed revenues are arguably the reason that Minneapolis has the finest park system in the United States.

Whatever the form of governance or the source of revenues, the entity responsible for a park must consider operations and maintenance separately from capital investment. Operations require continuity over time: personnel who know what to do and when to do it, programmed activities that occur at the same time every year, and reliable annual revenue streams that can support both the personnel and their activities. Capital investments, which include purchasing property, designing the landscape, erecting buildings, installing expensive equipment or long-term plantings, and rehabilitating existing structures, may be just as important (especially for renovating aging structures and repositioning obsolete facilities), but these are each one-time occurrences that can be financed over the life of the investment.

OPERATIONS

A key component of every park's operations budget is—or should be—maintenance. All parks face similar maintenance requirements every year: dead branches must be pruned, dead trees removed and replaced, recent plant installations watered, grass reseeded, leaves collected in the fall, snow removed in the winter, benches and lampposts and crum-

Minneapolis, 1992. A real estate tax of $74 on each $1,000 goes directly to the city's elected Park and Recreation Board, which uses the money to run the city's 6,624-acre (2,681-ha) park system.

bling paving repaired—the list is extensive. All these annually recurring activities must be carried out by somebody, and paid for. They must be managed intelligently and implemented by staff with the appropriate skills and training, in ways that reflect each jurisdiction's local priorities and local customs.

GENERAL BUDGET APPROPRIATIONS

Annual budget appropriations at every level of government come primarily from general tax revenue, and this constitutes the major traditional form of park financing for operations.[1] Appropriations are distributed from a city's, county's, or state's general fund to a park agency *expense budget*, and the funds are then spent on maintenance, repairs, salaries, supplies, and so forth. Land acquisition, park development, and major capital improvements are usually made from a separate *capital budget* (discussed later in this chapter).

Most park systems are funded from the city's or county's expense budget. Thus, they are dependent on all the city's sources of revenue—not just on one specific tax. The agency responsible for a park will prepare an estimate of its requirements and submit it to the relevant executive and legislative body for approval. As only one among many agencies vying for allocation of funds, the park department is subject to changes in the economy, changes in government administration, and changes in both local and national priorities.

Unlike fire or police departments, many parks generate revenue. But in many places these revenues are not retained for use by the parks or the park departments but go to back into the general fund as a partial reimbursement of park expenditures. The rationale is that there may be other, more pressing priorities for public spending. But this practice eliminates any incentive on the part of park management to raise rents, make better deals with concessionaires, or increase fees for service.

SPECIFIC TAXES

As alternatives to taking money from general tax revenue, specific taxes can be levied and earmarked exclusively for the financing of parks. These taxes can be imposed by local and state governments or, in some cases, by public authorities. The usability of specific taxes depends on three factors: the willingness of the electorate to accept the tax burden; the financial capacity of the sector of the economy that will pay the taxes; and the government's authority to tax in a manner that channels the money to parks (possibly necessitating a referendum).

As we saw in chapter 2, parks benefit everybody because of their role in improving public health, incubating a civil society, sustaining a livable environment, and providing a framework for urbanization. For this reason it would not be fair to finance them through a user charge paid only by the people who go to the park, so they are paid for by taxing everybody. Four types of taxes are commonly used: real estate taxes, income taxes, sales taxes, and property transfer taxes. Obviously, poorer communities and poorer individuals may not be able to generate enough revenue to cover park expenses, while wealthier communities and wealthier individuals may be able to generate more than enough money. Thus, financing parks from a government's overall budget allows the money to be distributed where it is most needed.

Real Estate Taxes With the exception of federal and state assistance, real estate taxes are usually the major source of local government revenues. If the tax on real estate grows to a level that is much higher than that of neighboring communities, businesses and residents may move away, ultimately lowering total tax yields. Hence local officials are rarely eager to tamper with real estate taxes.

Some localities do earmark real estate tax proceeds for park use. In Davis, California, two property taxes—the Parks Maintenance Tax and the Open Space Protection Tax—charge residential units a total of $73 annually (commercial units pay a variable rate based on square footage) to support green space.[2] The Minneapolis park system has been largely dependent on a dedicated real estate tax since 1883; the Chicago Parks District since 1934. Very few places reserve money exclusively for park purposes, and (in contrast to Minneapolis or Chicago) park spending is decided by the town or city government rather than a board or commission that is solely responsible for park governance. Even so,

Boulder, Colorado, 2000. A sales tax set aside for parks pays for more than a quarter of the city's park department budget.

most local legislatures prefer to set spending priorities without having to give up revenues to targeted uses, especially parks.

Sales taxes General sales taxes apply to all goods and services, while selective sales taxes are levied against the sales of a particular type of product. Boulder is one of a very few localities that targets sales taxes to parks. These sales tax revenues account for 27 percent of Boulder's 2007 parks budget, funding the maintenance of ball fields and meadows, as well as capital construction and debt service. These taxes are voter-approved and must be renewed every few years.[3] Other cities that draw on the sales tax for park development and maintenance include Carson City, Nevada, which began charging 0.25 percent in 1996 and dedicating the revenues into parks; and Albuquerque, New Mexico, which was able to maintain 25 existing parks and purchase 9,600 acres (3,885 ha) of open land with two years' worth of sales-tax revenue.[4]

Income taxes Many U.S. states generate revenue from income taxes, but few permit local jurisdictions to levy them; in 1998 only nine states permitted a total of 4,200 cities or counties to do so.[5] Pennsylvania allows any local government to levy an income tax. Maryland permits county governments to collect income taxes.[6] Ohio municipalities can levy a flat 1 percent income tax through the legislative process, and an additional 1 percent tax with voter approval. Municipal income taxes provide substantial revenue to the budgets of Louisville, Detroit, St. Louis, and a number of other cities. Most jurisdictions, however, are neither permitted nor willing to earmark a specific portion of these revenues directly for parks. Fostoria, Ohio, is one of the rare towns that levies an 0.5 percent income tax to pay for park improvements and maintenance.[7]

Real estate transfer taxes These are one-time payments for real estate sales, which can be levied against either the buyer or the selleoopr. The tax can be limited by type of property, and progressive scaling can place more of the burden on more expensive properties. Transfer taxes can generate substantial sums, but they do not necessarily produce the same amount each year, because the revenue is dependent on the rate of sales. Maryland, Florida, Rhode Island, Washington, and a few other states use the transfer tax as a way of financing public parks.[8] But, as with each of the other forms of taxation, elected officials are rarely eager to direct the revenue from transfer taxes exclusively to parks rather than distributing it in the manner they think best.

PARK BOARDS, SPECIAL TAXING DISTRICTS, CONSERVANCIES, AND LAND TRUSTS

From the middle of the nineteenth century, when the first public parks began to be created in the United

States, park advocates have been wary of leaving park decisions in the hands of local officials, in large part because they often mistrusted local political machines. Consequently, the Illinois, Massachusetts, and New York state legislatures established park commissions that they hoped could operate without regard to crass and often venal political objectives.

Some commissions also control funds that are directed to park use. This is the reason that the Minneapolis Park and Recreation Board, since its inception, has been primarily financed by a property tax it is authorized to levy; 74 percent of its 2007 budget came from this tax and most of the rest from state and city contributions.[9] The park board retains all of the revenue it generates and is not required to contribute to the city's general fund. For the past few decades, however, it has received additional funds from the city government to cover park operations that could not be paid for with earmarked taxes.

During the twentieth century, when parks began to be underfunded in order to pay for government activities favored by other, more powerful constituencies, park advocates began to seek alternative methods of financing. They were not alone. In many cities, downtown businesses believed they were not getting the government services they needed, because they did not have the votes that could be commanded by neighborhood residents. The answer was taxation *with* representation, brought about by establishing conservancies, business improvement districts (BIDs), community improvement districts (CIDs), and other entities, to raise money that they could control.

Some critics refer to this transfer of responsibility from government to a group of interested parties as privatization. In the case of parks, this interpretation is misleading and sometimes erroneous. In many cases park ownership has remained in the hands of local government, which entered into leases or contracts with an entity that agreed to manage and maintain the facility on behalf of the public. This approach began long before the proliferation of BIDs and conservancies. In 1882 the city of Boston accepted the gift of the Arnold Arboretum from Harvard University and leased it back to the university for 999 years, with the understanding that Harvard would be responsible for management and maintenance.[10] After operating for more than a cen-

tury under this arrangement, the Arboretum is considered by everybody in Boston to be a public park. The terms of the contractual relationship between the city of New York and the Bryant Park Corporation are far more specific, the supervision by the Department of Parks and Recreation is more intrusive, and the relationship of far shorter duration, yet nobody in New York thinks of Bryant Park as anything but a public facility. Most people in Boston and New York believe these parks would be in worse condition if they were operated by city agencies.

Privatization is an appropriate term for many nonprofit conservancies that own and operate parks without any public scrutiny other than by the Internal Revenue Service. It is important to remember, however, that these private entities were formed to fill the vacuum caused by the abrogation of responsibility for public parks by government. Whether parks are funded by specific taxation and operated by the beneficiaries, or by donations and operated by nonprofit organizations, as long as they are open free of charge to anybody and designed for public use, they are really no different from government owned and managed parks funded by general taxation that also are open to the public free of charge.

Funding and governing parks by these alternative means, then, is a viable solution to the typical problems faced by parks—inadequate funding, poor management, and deferred maintenance—because it transfers responsibility for these matters to those who benefit from the park, either by having them pay directly for the park via a separate taxing district or by creating a separate agency to manage and maintain it, or both. These semi-independent entities can then act without being constrained by the politics or priorities of local government. The decision makers in these agencies can be appointed by elected politicians or voted into office by the residents or businesses within the taxing district. The staff of the new entity then can dedicate its activities only to parkland within the taxing district.

This is the approach taken in Los Angeles County. In 1992 county voters approved the establishment of a park district covering the entire county and a one-time property tax assessment that generated $540 million, which was used for property acquisition, beach restoration, tree planting, and a variety of park-related functions. In 1996 it approved

The Chicago Park District uses its independent taxing authority to finance its 7,300-acre (2.954-ha) system.

another one-time assessment that generated $319 million.[11]

The Chicago Park District is another entity with independent taxing authority. It was established by the Illinois state legislature to manage Chicago's parks and recreation facilities. Created in 1934 by combining nearly two dozen smaller authorities, the Park District is now the largest park-focused public authority in the United States.[12] It has the authority to levy property taxes and set its own budget, though some restrictions are placed on how much it can increase taxes and divide revenues. This property tax is by far the Park District's largest source of revenue, totaling 63.7 percent of its budget.[13]

It may seem odd to include the business improvement district (BID) in a discussion of park funding and governance. A BID is a membership organization of property owners and businesses within a defined area, established and operated under an agreement with the city government. While very few parks are managed by BIDs, some of the most successful examples of park stewardship are outgrowths of BIDs, particularly New York City's Bryant Park and Herald and Greeley Squares. Along with community improvement districts (CIDs) and conservancies, BIDs are devices for transferring day-to-day management from a local government with a myriad of competing demands to an entity controlled by people who benefit from the park. Consequently, a BID can devote undivided attention to the park and its maintenance and management.

During the 1970s, business districts, like parks, found themselves unable to compete as successfully as other recipients of local government funds. Local governments, under pressure from neighborhood residents to provide services, reduced allocations to commercial areas that were not inhabited by nearly as many voters as residential communities. Budget allocations for trash collection, street maintenance, and even police protection were redirected to neighborhoods that could genuinely demonstrate that they had been neglected in previous years.

Business districts, especially in downtown areas, were increasingly at a disadvantage in competing for customers with suburban shopping centers, and they decided to take control of their own future. Businesses began working together to compete against suburban shopping malls by creating a better-planned, shopper-friendly environment and providing maintenance, trash collection, public safety, group marketing, and other services routinely provided by shopping center owners. Bloor West Village in Toronto became the world's first BID in 1970. It took a while for BIDs to catch on.[14]

Manhattan, 1997 and 2008. The 34th Street Business Improvement District used a small part of its portion of real estate taxes within the district to transform Greeley Square into an extremely popular park.

They began to proliferate in the 1980s and 1990s after they had proved successful in Denver, Minneapolis, Philadelphia, and other cities. By 2008 there were more than two thousand BIDs in the United States, including sixteen in Atlanta and sixty in New York City.

Where they are allowed by local government, BIDs are established when a majority of stakeholders create a plan and budget, which in most cases requires approval by local government. Property owners (in the United States) or occupants (in England) pay an annual assessment, based on either real estate taxes or rents, to fund the services. Opponents of BIDs criticize them for generating what they consider to be an extra "tax" for services that normal taxes should already cover and for reducing the constituency will-

ing to support increasing citywide taxes because they are already paying a tax surcharge.

BID development in the United Kingdom is still in its early stages. English BIDs are different from their American cousins because they are not restricted to providing services to business districts; they also provide services to residential areas. Community improvement districts (CIDs), which are common in Georgia and Missouri, resemble British BIDs. They are geographically defined districts in which property owners vote to create a nonprofit entity established to run the CID. As in a BID, they agree on a self-imposed tax within the defined area. The revenue usually goes to pay for infrastructure and community facility improvements. In some jurisdictions the money can pay for services (such as sanitation, security, and general maintenance and operations). The Perimeter CID in suburban Atlanta, for example, has devoted substantial funds to improving pedestrian and vehicular traffic flow.[15] As with BIDs, the tax revenue collected by the local government is passed on to a board of directors elected by the property owners who pay them.

Like BIDs and CIDs, park conservancies and land trusts are established to remove parkland from competition for government funds and protect it from the vagaries of politics. The earliest conservancies, however, were not created in response to poor government management or inadequate funding. They were individually created to own, maintain, and manage property that was not at that time a government responsibility. Conservancies' financing is almost entirely dependent on donations, whether of land or money, that can be used for specific tasks, operations, or endowments. Over two centuries they have taken on a wide variety of forms. Some are adjuncts to government-owned facilities; some operate autonomously but in accordance with agreements with government agencies; others are entirely independent entities.

Sometimes a citizen-based park entity becomes a partner with the government agency responsible for park operations. The 12,000-member Golden Gate National Park Conservancy was established to in 1981 to supplement funding by the National Parks Service, create a constituency, and enrich the park experience for visitors to San Francisco's Golden Gate National Park. It raised the money to pay for the transformation of Crissy Field (see chapter 2), runs education programs for children, and generated support for a trail system.[16]

Most citizen-based organizations are classed as nonprofit entities, meaning that they do not pay taxes on the revenue they receive because they are organized and operated exclusively for tax-exempt purposes as set forth in section 501(c)3 of the Internal Revenue Code. The Western Pennsylvania Conservancy is typical of such citizen-based organizations. It is an independent, nonprofit organization formed in 1932 to protect exceptional places in nineteen counties within the state. It has received as donations or purchased a total of 225,000 acres (91,054 ha). Its mission goes beyond land stewardship; the conservancy has restored a number of very special landscapes, watersheds, and ecosystems. Perhaps its most famous property is Fallingwater (1936–39), the house designed for the Kaufmann family by Frank Lloyd Wright on 1,543 acres (624 ha) in Bear Run, 50 miles (80 km) southeast of Pittsburgh, and donated to the conservancy in 1963.[17]

The nonprofit organization that manages 289-acre (117-ha) Tower Grove Park in St. Louis has some of the features of a conservancy, but is a very different legal entity, responsible for property donated to the city in 1868 by Henry Shaw, a wealthy merchant, who also contributed funds for its development. It is governed by a board of commissioners appointed by the Missouri Supreme Court. Operations are financed through a combination of city funds and private donations.[18]

The Wolf River Conservancy was established in 1985 to conserve and enhance the countryside,

Atlanta, 2004. Piedmont Park was restored by a nonprofit conservancy that has raised tens of millions of dollars to support park improvements.

wildlife, wetlands, and watershed of a 30-mile (48-km) corridor of the Wolf River that passes through the parks and towns of Shelby County, Tennessee, as it flows westward through Memphis into the Mississippi River. As of 2008 it had helped to protect more than 18,000 acres (7,284 ha). This nonprofit institution takes a broad view of its mission, which includes "public education and low-impact recreational activities." Its properties include boardwalks and pedestrian trails that wend their way through forested areas, open fields, wetlands, and wildlife habitats. Along the way are sitting areas, shelters, and educational signs explaining the natural history of the area. The conservancy hopes to create a continuous pedestrian and bicycle-friendly greenway along its entire 30-mile (48-km) length. Like the Western Pennsylvania Conservancy, it is supported by donations from corporations, foundations, and individuals and has a professional staff assisted by the activities of volunteers.[19]

Atlanta's Piedmont Park Conservancy was established for many of the same reasons as New York's Central Park Conservancy, whose example it followed. During the 1970s and 1980s the city's premier

Shelby County, Tennessee. The nonprofit Wolf River Conservancy has already helped to preserve 18,000 acres (7,284 ha) for environmental and recreational uses.

Manhattan, 2005. The nonprofit Battery Park City Parks Conservancy uses a portion of the rent paid to the Battery Park City Authority to manage the Esplanade and the other district parks.

million ha) and has worked on 330 ballot measures that generated almost $25 billion for property acquisition.[21]

LEASE REVENUE

The great estates of London (discussed in chapter 3) cover the cost of maintaining their more than four hundred landscaped squares with the money they earn from leases on surrounding property. The attractiveness of these areas to residents and businesses hundreds of years after their initial development is a testament to the exceptional nature of the ground lease as a park financing model.

A similar lease arrangement pays a large part of the cost of maintaining the 36 acres (15 ha) of open space in Manhattan's Battery Park City. All its parks, gardens, plazas, playing fields, playgrounds, and other public amenities are owned by the Battery Park City Authority. They are managed under an agreement with the Battery Park City Parks Conservancy (BPCPC), a nonprofit organization expressly created for that purpose in 1987. The bulk of the money to pay for these parks comes from a portion of rents paid to the authority by lessees of property occu-

recreational facility, 185-acre (75-ha) Piedmont Park, had deteriorated to the point that citizens decided to provide what government no longer supplied: money and tender loving care. Civic leaders established a nonprofit conservancy, raised start-up funds, and entered into a memorandum of understanding that left ownership of the park in the hands of the city of Atlanta, but transferred major responsibility for the park's restoration to the conservancy. Like the Central Park Conservancy, the Piedmont Park Conservancy began with a master plan. It has gone on to operate environmental education programs, historic tours, bird-watching walks, a green market, a botanical garden, a running track, two softball fields, and two volleyball courts.[20]

The Trust for Public Land (TPL) was established in 1972 as a nonprofit organization. It operates on a national basis on every scale from small city and suburban playgrounds to vast wilderness areas. TPL even raises money to acquire land that will ensure clean drinking water and protect scenic coastlines and waterways. During its first thirty-six years it has been involved in more than 3,500 land conservation projects that have protected 2.5 million acres (1.01

Manhattan, 2005. The Chelsea Piers Sports & Entertainment Complex makes rental payments of more than $3.75 million, which covers a large portion of the operating costs of the Hudson River Park.

pied by commercial and residential tenants. In 2007 it passed on to the BPCPC $9.5 million of the $206 million that it collected in ground rent from the lessees.[22] Donations and concession fees made up the remaining 5 percent of the BPCPC's revenue.

The Hudson River Park in New York City receives lease revenues from properties along Route 9W. In 2008 the thirty-four privately leased piers adjacent to the park generated $6.5 million in lease payments and $8 million in parking fees.[23] Piers 59 to 62 are occupied by the 28-acre (11-ha) Chelsea Piers Sports & Entertainment Complex, located between 17th and 23rd streets. This complex alone paid the Hudson River Park $3.75 million in rent during 2008.[24] It is itself a recreation facility, charging fees for its diverse attractions and activities, including a spa, a health club, and sports areas for baseball, basketball, bowling, boxing, golf, swimming, ice-skating, ice hockey, running, soccer, and gymnastics.

CONCESSIONS, FEES, AND OTHER REVENUE

Parks also can collect revenue from concessions, licensing, admission, parking, fines, and a variety of other fees. Concessions may be run directly by the park or leased to private entities, which pay either a fixed amount per year or a portion of their revenue. Obviously, heavily used facilities can generate more money than lightly used ones. In July and August a concession at Jones Beach on Long Island will have a high volume of sales, while in the dead of winter, when many fewer people go to the beach, it will probably be closed. Similarly, demand will be greater in wealthier and higher-density areas that can generate more spending. Consequently, these sources of revenue may be effective in some cases but fail to work in others.

Concessions are useful in that they usually do not incur debt for any level of government or transfer ownership of the park to another group, public or private. High-end activities—like boat moorings and golf—can be charged a premium to help keep the prices of other activities low. But potential problems may arise from overcommercialization, charging fees for services that people believe should be free, and the need to ensure that the money that is generated will be used intelligently.

One particularly successful way to generate revenues for parks is to combine them with parking facilities. This was pioneered in United States by San Francisco in 1940, when it created a 1,700-car public parking garage under 2.6-acre (1.1-ha) Union Square, which had been donated to the city in 1850. In 1951 Los Angeles dug out 5-acre (2-ha) Pershing Square for a 2,150-car underground garage. Neither of those projects, nor the garages under Grant Park in Chicago, Market Square in Alexandria, Virginia, or the Boston Common, added one square inch of new parkland. Pittsburgh was the first city to create a new park on top of a garage. In 1948 the city's public parking authority proposed reconstructing an entire block as a garage. A year later, the Mellon family agreed to pay for the site if the city cre-

Pittsburgh, 2008. Garage and store rents at Mellon Square go to the city's general fund and are not reserved for park maintenance.

Boston, 2008. Garage fees and retail rent go to pay debt service on Post Office Square, as well as operating and maintenance costs.

ated a new park on top. The top of this sloping site is level with William Penn Place, and it slopes down to Smithfield Street, which is lined with stores. This design by Mitchell & Ritchey (architect) and Simonds & Simonds (landscape architects) allows cars to slip into the 896-car garage from the streets on either side. The park on top is a popular place for office workers at lunchtime and shoppers during the rest of the day.

The Mellons made a gift of the $4.3 million needed to acquire the site, demolish existing structures, and create the park, while the city's parking authority spent $3.5 million on the garage. The city government agreed to be responsible for park maintenance. Like most cities, Pittsburgh has since had other priorities. After decades of heavy use, the park, while still popular, is not in the best shape.

Boston's Norman B. Leventhal Park, commonly known as Post Office Square, has fared better. Garage and concession fees from the 1.7-acre (0.69-ha) square cover both the capital cost of the project and day-to-day maintenance, which is why it is in such excellent condition. The site had been occupied by a number of different commercial structures before 1954, when the city erected a four-story, 950-car garage there. In 1983 Norman B. Leventhal, chairman of the Beacon Companies, a real estate development company that had property in the area, formed Friends of Post Office Square, Inc. This private group was convinced that the revenue from a replacement garage could more than cover operating expenses, debt service

on a development loan, and a reasonable return on invested capital. They were right—in 1996 the project generated a gross annual income of $8.6 million to cover $3 million in operating costs and $5.6 million in debt service and return on equity.

It took the group four years to buy the garage and three more to replace it with a 1,400-car underground facility covered by a small, privately maintained park. Funding began with $930,000 in initial stockholder contributions; then the group raised $29.5 million in equity from the sale of 450 shares of preferred stock at $65,000, carrying a return of 8 percent; and borrowed $60 million from a bank. The total raised was $90 million; the project cost $75.5 million and the rest was set aside to cover initial operating losses and contingencies.[25]

The new park and garage, designed by the Halvorson Partnership (landscape architects) and Ellenzweig Associates (garage architects), was completed in 1992. After sixteen years of operation it remains a popular haunt for office occupants on their way to and from work and at lunchtime. It is impeccably maintained—flowers are changed with the season, lawns are manicured, and anything that breaks is immediately fixed. The reasons are obvious: all revenue is earmarked for that purpose and cannot be spent on anything else, and all decisions are made by its user-owners.

Large park systems can be as adept as small nonprofit organizations in using fees to pay for the operation of stand-alone parks. Roughly 18.5 percent of the Chicago Park District's 2007 budget comes from fees, rentals, permits, and concessions. Concessionaires operate in Soldier Field Stadium and Lincoln Park Zoo, as well as at golf courses, marinas, and other facilities. In October 2006, the city and the Park District leased its four garages for $563 million, with the net revenue going to park improvements.[26]

Renting out facilities for private use has also been a consistent revenue source. The Park District runs dozens of summer camps and year-round programs for all age groups, including sports and after school programs, environmental clubs, and performing arts and writing programs. Programs for adults have higher fees to offset the low price of programs for children.

Twenty-two percent of the annual budget of the of the New York City Department of Parks and Rec-

Chicago, 2008. The Grant Park Marina is just one of the many sources of revenue for the city's parks.

reation comes from nontax sources, primarily rents and concession fees. These revenues go into the city's general fund to partially compensate for the substantial appropriations that come from the city's budget. As in Chicago, the biggest sources of revenue are parking and golf, but concession fees come from sources as diverse as hot dog carts and the Tavern on the Green restaurant in Central Park.

EVENTS, ENDOWMENTS, AND SPONSORSHIPS

Events, even though they are often one-time occurrences, can raise substantial sums for parks. These can range from small gatherings to large, from weddings and bar mitzvahs to music festivals and movie premieres. Developing a reputation for effective event-hosting can result in increased future bookings. A truly exceptional example of a park event occurred in 1995, when the Walt Disney Company premiered *Pocahontas* on four huge screens on Central Park's Great Lawn. Park Commissioner Henry Stern negotiated a deal in which Disney paid $1 million in addition to the cost of the event and the extra policing and maintenance involved.[27] Central Park is also home to Summer-Stage, an annual concert series that offers many free

concerts that are underwritten by a small number that charge an admission fee. It is not just the event that generates revenue; concessions at the concerts provide income as well.

Endowments are assets—such as stock, mutual funds, or property investments—that generate income that can be used to help finance park operations. The principal is invested and rarely spent; funding for parks comes from the return on the investment. Endowments require a large upfront source of funding and precise management that typically requires the services of an outside financial consultant. Balboa Park in San Diego, California, is partly funded by the revenue from a $2 million endowment, which was established in 1985 by a local charity and a bank with headquarters in the city.[28]

Parks and park systems that draw significant crowds may be attractive to corporate sponsors as a source of good will, advertising, and revenue. In Chicago, the White Sox and Cubs contribute money for baseball diamonds and batting cages, while the Bulls provide funds for maintaining basketball courts. Exclusive concession rights are also popular. For instance, Coca-Cola and Snyder's chips are the official drink and snack of Cleveland's Metroparks. Sponsorships may take a form closer to advertising, such as when Modell's Sporting Goods replaced the backboards on New York City basketball courts with new ones prominently featuring the company's logo. Finally, parks can be an convenient place for certain kinds of hidden infrastructure: Sprint paid $850,000 for permission, improvements, and repairs to lay fiberoptic cable under the Burke-Gilman Trail in Seattle, Washington.

In order to protect their public spaces from over-commercialization, the Chicago Park District set up its Enhancements Committee to review all private market incursions into the public realm.[29] It's important to note that as crucial as revenue streams may be to financing park development, restoration, and day-to-day operations, dependence on these revenues may go too far, detracting from a park's responsibility to serve the general interest.

CAPITAL BUDGETS AND PARK DEVELOPMENT

Many of the same financing devices used to fund park operations play a role in paying for capital expenditures, including park development or renovation. These capital costs may include purchasing property, erecting buildings, installing expensive equipment, and rehabilitating existing structures—all investments that benefit a park over the longer term. Since the amounts of money are so much larger than those for operating expenses and must be available from the start, there is usually a heavier reliance on funding from major gifts and grants, and long-term financing is often necessary,

Sums of this magnitude, whether from wealthy benefactors, government programs, or other funding and management entities, rarely come without strings. Donors may want to participate in design decisions; public agencies will have policy and program requirements; taxpayers will want to ensure they get the benefits they are paying for. Consequently, as with operations, financing and governance of capital expenditures for park development are intertwined.

MAJOR GIFTS AND GRANTS

Occasionally donors will provide enough money to pay for land acquisition and park development all at once. The Mellon family donated the entire sum for Mellon Square in Pittsburgh, for example, but most often collecting the money takes more time. Funding for Millennium Park in Chicago took six years to assemble.

Donors want to participate in decisions about spending their money every bit as much as government officials do when public funds are involved. The Crown family chose the designer of Millennium Park fountain that bears their name, and while the Pritzkers did not make their $15 million gift contingent on having Frank Gehry design the band shell named for them, one historian notes that "it was implied."[30]

In chapter 4 we saw that developers are sometimes required by a local ordinance to donate property or money for park development, or to pay a fee in lieu of the donation of land. The amount of land (and perhaps landscaping as well) that must be donated to the local government is determined by statute. The logic behind this approach is that the additional occupants attracted to the area by the new

Collierville, Tennessee, 2009. Hinton Park was acquired and is being developed with revenue from a tax on residential development.

Manhattan, 2006. In exchange for creating a privately owned public open space, the developer of I Liberty Plaza was allowed to build 20 percent more rentable floor area than would have been allowed had the site been entirely covered by the office building.

development (whether residents, office workers, or shoppers) will place an additional burden on existing park facilities. The developer provides or pays for the required additional parkland. The amount is calculated based on the area (in acres of land or square feet of building floor area) of the development, the number of residents that will occupy it, or the fair value of the land. Smaller subdivisions may warrant the donation of so little land that a fee for land purchase elsewhere may be more practical. This is the approach taken in Collierville, Tennessee (see chapter 4).

In some places, in exchange for donations of cash, open space, or land, developers may obtain a floor-to-area ratio (FAR) bonus, allowing them to build more square footage than zoning would normally allow.[31] This usually takes the form of a privately owned but publicly accessible plaza that is part of the development. Once in a while an open space that is the product of an FAR bonus functions like a public park. Zuccotti Plaza in lower Manhattan, for example, occupies an entire block, surrounded on four sides by streets and sidewalks. It

was created when the developer of One Liberty Plaza took advantage of the FAR bonus provided by the city's zoning regulations.[32] Another example is the High Line, the park the New York City government is developing on top of an abandoned 1.5-mile (2.4-km) elevated freight railway on the west side of Manhattan (see chapter 5). In this case FAR bonuses are awarded to developers in exchange for financial contributions to the park.

Occasionally the federal government decides to augment infrastructure spending by establish-

San Antonio, 2007. The Riverwalk was developed with federal funds from the Works Progress Administration (WPA).

Philadelphia, 1998. Three Bears Park was developed with federal funds from the urban renewal program established under the Housing Act of 1949.

ing programs that provide grants for park development. New Deal relief programs are a particularly vivid example. Throughout the country people can identify WPA-style projects from their distinctive period style. Some are particularly significant: the San Antonio Riverwalk and the dozen public swimming pools Robert Moses built in the 1930s might never have happened without WPA assistance.

An alphabet soup of federal grant programs exist for park development, administered by agencies that in many cases have a main focus that is something quite different. The Housing Act of 1949 is responsible for part of the funding for Three Bears Park in Philadelphia's Society Hill Urban Renewal Project, San Francisco's Sidney Walton Square and Justin Herman Plaza in the Golden Gateway Urban Renewal Project, and numerous other small city parks in redevelopment areas. The Housing Act of 1974 established the Community Development Block Grant (CDBG) program, which gives localities greater flexibility than urban renewal, but the federal money it provides is primarily intended to benefit people of low income. The Housing Act of

1949 was administered by the federal Housing and Home Finance Agency; its successor, the Department of Housing and Urban Development (HUD), administers the CDBG program. In both cases the overseeing agency's main thrust was housing, not parks. The same secondary involvement with parks and recreation is true of the Federal Highway Administration, which administered the Intermodal Surface Transportation Efficiency Act of 1991 and Transportation Equity Act of the 21st Century (1998). These "transportation" programs have paid for scenic and recreational bicycle, jogging, and hiking trails throughout the country.

LONG-TERM FINANCING

Under ordinary circumstances, park development and other major capital expenditures require such large outlays that it is difficult to pay for them all at once. Setting aside some money every year until all the money is in hand may take a decade or more. Unsurprisingly, the citizens who pay for parks (usually in the form of taxes) do not want to keep pay-

Manhattan, 1999. Riverbank State Park was built as part of a wastewater treatment facility.

ing until they have become so old that they cannot enjoy their investment. Thus, like other forms of real estate development, park development is usually financed over the long term, but with bonds rather than mortgages.

Like the federal government, local governments normally issue bonds backed by their "full faith and credit." They use the proceeds to pay for parks, schools, equipment, and all manner of infrastructure and community facilities. The total amount of debt a local government can incur is determined by state legislation and is confirmed in the marketplace by investors' willingness to purchase that debt. Local officials ordinarily propose to the executive (mayor, city manager, or county executive) what proportion of the remaining debt-incurring capacity should be spent in any one year, as well as the items and the amounts to be spent on them. The executive usually makes changes and recommends a draft capital budget to the local legislature. After negotiations and further changes, the legislature will approve the final capital budget.

Sometimes local politics intervenes in decisions about capital expenditures that have become controversial. In these instances the government often introduces parkland to mitigate opposition to a project. In the late 1960s the New York City government announced construction of the North River Wastewater Treatment Plant in the Hudson River, between 137th and 145th streets. The plant was designed to treat 125 million gallons (473 million liters) of wastewater on dry days and 340 million gallons (1.28 billion liters) per day during wet weather. Neighborhood opposition to the possible

stench was so intense that the city proposed covering the entire roof with fountains. That placated nobody. Eventually the state government agreed to pay for a 28-acre (11-ha) park covering the city sewage treatment plant. This remarkable park, which opened in 1991, was designed by Richard Dattner. It provides 3.7 million annual visitors with facilities for softball, basketball, handball, tennis, paddleball, and football/soccer, as well as a 2,500-seat athletic complex, a running tack, an Olympic-size swimming pool, playgrounds, picnic areas, a skating rink used for ice-skating in the winter and inline skating in the summer, walkways, open lawns, shade trees, a café and restaurant, and a carousel.

Robert Moses was particularly skilled in dealing with opposition to projected capital spending. During the 1930s and 1940s, he did not wait for local opposition to delay highway projects; in many cases he built constituencies for his projects by adding parkland. As commissioner of parks, it was easy for him to include parks in highway designs, and he did so routinely. The Brooklyn Heights Esplanade is just one example. He included a promenade and bicycle path as part of Brooklyn's Shore Parkway, built playgrounds over the Brooklyn-Queens Connecting Highway in Williamsburg, and created Astoria Park at the foot of the Robert Kennedy (Triborough) Bridge in Queens.

Stand-alone parks have a tough time competing within the capital budget process. Most of the available money is likely to be set aside in advance for mandated expenditures, health and safety requirements, and other items that are perceived as priorities. The discretionary spending that remains is likely to be allocated to politically attractive projects—not many of which will be park-related. For that reason, park advocates often seek to avoid the political process and attempt to finance capital projects from income streams that are dedicated specifically to parks. Many of these income streams are similar to those used to provide operating funds, such as BID revenue. The construction of the rent-paying restaurant in Bryant Park, for example, was financed largely by using a portion of BID revenue to guarantee debt service on a mortgage paid from restaurant rent (now paid off) that covered the restaurant's development cost.

Most states have enabling legislation that authorizes *tax increment financing* (TIF): the local government designates a district for redevelopment and assigns any increase in real estate taxes within the area to an entity that is responsible for capital spending there. Existing tax revenues continue to flow into the taxing jurisdictions' budgets at the same amount collected at the time of the formation of the TIF district. The *incremental* (increased) tax flow from existing and new development is used to cover the cost of capital improvements.

There are two ways to approach this. The first is a "pay as you go" strategy, where an outside revenue source or tax is used to pay for the initial stages of a project and successive increases in revenue are used to finance later stages. A second strategy is to calculate the expected increase in tax revenue, or tax increment, before beginning the project and sell bonds that will be paid off from that future increase

in revenue. In that way the TIF district collects the entire sum up front, and no taxes from outside the district are used to pay for items that benefit the properties within the district.[33]

One way of looking at this kind of financing is to say that "projects, not general tax payers, pay for development costs."[34] Chicago is one of the most active users of TIF. It has set up 130 TIF districts since the mid-1980s, and these have helped to finance schools, infrastructure, and many other city projects, including a part of the cost of Millennium Park.[35] In Georgia a TIF district is called a tax allocation district (TAD); as of 2007, there were 27 TADs in the Atlanta metropolitan area.[36] The most important park-related TAD is the BeltLine Tax Allocation District, which is expected to generate, over twenty-five years, approximately $1.7 billion of its total project cost of $2.8 billion.

Memphis, 2008. Hundreds of dedicated park advocates participated in a public process that led up to Shelby County Mayor A C Wharton's opening an exhibition of three proposed master development plans for the transformation of a 4,500-acre (1,821-ha) former penal farm into a great regional public park.

ELEVEN

THE ROLE OF THE PUBLIC

By the start of the nineteenth century an increasing number of Europeans and Americans believed that parks were an essential component of healthy urbanization. As we saw in chapter 1, given the growing intensity of that belief, it was only a matter of time before governments would have to respond to public demand by investing in parkland. The role of the public was significant, particularly in Britain, where thirty thousand East End petitioners accelerated the process of acquiring land for recreational purposes, forcing the government to create Victoria Park. Similarly, a decade later, when Savannah and Philadelphia were on the verge of creating public parks, civic leaders in New York succeeded in persuading the state legislature to create America's first public park.

After two centuries of citizen activism, the American public believes it has the right and the ability to decide what property should be acquired for recreational purposes and how it should be designed, financed, and managed. We have seen in previous chapters that there is a long history of public activism forcing government to invest in parkland. Citizens in San Antonio put pressure on government to transform a regularly flooding river into a popular park. In Washington, D.C., citizens played a major role in turning an abandoned canal into a national park. In Minneapolis activists led the

effort to transform railroad property into a park trail. In Memphis park advocates, who had prevented a 4,500-acre (1,821-ha) penal farm from becoming a real estate venture, led an effort to transform it into one of the nation's largest regional parks. This activism also extends into park design, finance, stewardship, and governance.

SHAPING PARK DESIGN AND EVOLUTION

Public parks are to some degree the product of elite designers like Frederick Law Olmsted or autocratic public officials like Robert Moses. But they also are every bit as much the product of public action. Even the work of such extraordinary figures as Olmsted and Moses reflects the interests and involvement of the voters, politicians, and park employees who influenced their initial designs, as well as changes that occurred long after they had left the scene. Moreover, both lost many battles during the initial design and development stages.

The rationale for the single most brilliant aspect of the design of Central Park, its separation of crosstown traffic from circulation within the park, cannot be ascribed to either Olmsted or Vaux. It was a requirement that the board of commissioners gave to all thirty-three designers who entered the com-

Manhattan, 2009. The Olmsted and Vaux plan for Central Park did not include any playgrounds; most were built during the 1930s by Robert Moses. But the Heckscher Playground was added as early as 1926, and it has since been reconstructed to meet the demands of later generations of children.

petition for the master plan, and Olmsted and Vaux came up with the idea of cutting into the landscape to create a depressed roadway and then masking it from parkgoers with berms and plantings.

Olmsted's writings are filled with angry comments about his conflicts with Andrew Haswell Green (1820–1903), who served on the Board of Park Commissioners as a member, comptroller, and eventually chairman. When Olmsted returned to work on the park in the 1870s, he quarreled with the park's superintendent over landscaping issues, losing on major issues as well as minor details.[1]

The park's Delacorte Theater is but one example of the many things that Robert Moses could not prevent. In 1954 he permitted open-air performances of Shakespeare in Central Park. When Joseph Papp, the man behind Shakespeare in the Park, proposed building a theater for permanent summer use, the city appropriated $250,000, but Moses, who had become disenchanted with the project, stalled development by imposing requirements that increased its cost by another $225,000. In 1961 Newbold Mor-

ris, Moses's successor as commissioner, accepted a $150,000 gift from philanthropist George Delacorte, and announced that the city would build the theater.

Moses was also often unable to realize projects he thought were important. In 1960, just before stepping down as commissioner, he announced that the entrepreneur and philanthropist Huntington Hartford had donated $800,000 to construct a large café in the southeastern corner of the park. Civic organizations and newspaper editorials denounced the idea. Finally, six years after Moses had retired as commissioner, Mayor John Lindsay killed the project and the comptroller returned the money.[2]

Similar conflicts abound in the evolution of neighborhood playgrounds, community gardens, district-wide recreation facilities, metropolitan systems, and virtually all public parks in pluralistic democracies. While these conflicts underscore the significance of the roles designers, park officials, and employees play, as well as the ever-present centrality of financing, they are also evidence of the importance of citizen involvement.

STEWARDSHIP

The enthusiastic engagement of the public in caring for Central Park is one of the most important aspects of its contemporary success. Park users believe it is their park, take pride in their ownership, and are now in the habit of making financial contributions to its continuing improvement. Obviously, many park users do not have sufficient money to donate or do not wish to spend it on the park. Fortunately, enough residents, workers, and corporations near the park contribute to fund 85 percent of the operating costs, and the park remains free of charge for anybody who wants to go there. As its endowment grows, the Central Park Conservancy eventually will be able to cover 100 percent of the park's operations and, like some great museums, pay for itself with endowment income.

Few parks can or ever will be economically self-sufficient, particularly those that are not surrounded by a wealthy constituency. For that reason the Central Park Conservancy does not provide a model for financial self-sufficiency that can be widely duplicated; rather, it serves as a model for community engagement that is being copied throughout the

Manhattan 2004. The citizens of New York City have embraced Central Park and made it their own.

United States. The citizens of New York City were able to embrace Central Park as their own. Only when the citizens of a city take ownership of their park can it become a great park.

FINANCE AND GOVERNANCE

The care of public parks requires thoughtful approaches to financing and governance. The citizens of nineteenth-century Minneapolis understood this and created a system that ensured their parks would remain healthy. Chicago followed suit in the 1930s. During the latter part of the twentieth century, in response to the failure of local governments to provide satisfactory park stewardship, many communities began experimenting with methods that would achieve similar results.

There is no single correct way to finance and govern a park. In St. Louis, for example, citizens came to the rescue of declining Forest Park, forming Forest Park Forever, a nonprofit organization established to restore what had become a truly run-down facility. The group attracted hundreds of residents to participate in workshops on the park's future, brought in experts to recommend action, raised the money to pay for renovation, and persuaded the city government to increase funding. Forest Park Forever was founded in 1986; today the park is once again in good repair and playing the role for which it had been created.

Parks have become so important to the health of our communities that as many citizens as possible should be—and are—playing ever larger roles in their creation and stewardship. The financial and governance methods described in chapter 10 are among the most common models for planning, developing, or operating public parks. Every community that includes public parks should be familiar with these approaches. To be effective, however, each community must adapt or invent models that are appropriate to its situation.

THE POWER OF CITIZEN ACTION

Public parks are buffeted by the same political and financial winds that affect cities and suburbs every-

where. Although designers, public officials, and donors certainly play important roles, public parks are creations of the public, by the public, and for the public. When things are going well, the silent majority of park supporters swells; when things get out of hand, a vocal minority usually comes forward with demands that must be considered.

There are countless instances of the effectiveness of citizen action. In 1923, for example, Chicago's Field Museum, then located in Jackson Park in what had been the Palace of Fine Arts at the 1893 World's Columbian Exposition, moved to its present site in Grant Park. The South Park Commission announced it was going to demolish the old site, the former Palace of Fine Arts. Six thousand citizens protested, and each of them contributed $1 to repairing the building. The following year this "Save the Arts Palace" movement helped to get approval of a referendum that authorized a $5 million bond issue for its restoration.[3] Together with another $3 million donated by Julius Rosenwald, president of Sears, Roebuck and Company, it was enough to completely renovate the building, which has remained in Jackson Park ever since.

In 1964, when the Shelby County Government decided to close a 4,500-acre (1,821-ha) prison farm on the eastern edge of Memphis, Tennessee, there were no specific plans for its reuse. A 1975 announcement that the county would sell the property for the development of a new town provoked widespread opposition. A broad-based citizen coalition, which evolved into the Friends of Shelby Farms Park, came together to keep the site in public hands. County officials yielded to their efforts and announced that the property would be used as parkland. In 2006 citizens spearheaded a thirty-month effort that resulted in the creation of the Shelby Farms Park Conservancy, which is now responsible for park development and maintenance, and a design competition for master plan for the creation of a great regional park, won by the landscape design firm field operations (see chapter 6 for more on this park).

The role of the public in the success of its parks becomes particularly important during downturns in the economy, when parks are most at risk for reduced funding and consequent decline. We have seen the effects of deteriorated public spaces on neighborhoods during the budget crises of the 1970s and 1980s, but we can also learn from that period the power of citizen action to reverse those effects. Neighborhood residents in countless cities complained about deteriorated parks that had become dangerous areas. They wanted the parks to be available for their children rather than for increasing numbers of gang members, pushers, and addicts. The action taken by the 12th Street Block Association in New York's East Village is typical of what was happening throughout the country.

The Joseph C. Sauer Memorial Playground, which occupies 0.4 acres (0.16 ha) on East 12th Street in Manhattan's East Village section, had been among nine small recreational areas created by Robert Moses in 1934 with money from a World War I memorial fund. But by the 1970s it had become the object of neighborhood controversy, following four decades of active use but stringent park department budgets and deferred maintenance. The *New York Times* later reported: "No one remembers exactly which affront finally ignited the eight-year crusade. Was it the addicts shooting up and selling

syringes? Was it the prostitutes—four in a three-block radius—turning tricks in broad daylight while the children walked to school? Was it the out-of-state cars lined up to buy drugs on Friday nights? Or was it the Krazy Glue the pimps and crack dealers poured in the locks so that the people couldn't get into their own playground?"[4]

Beginning in 1985, neighborhood residents organized clean-up crews, started letter-writing campaigns, telephoned public officials, appeared at public meetings, and collected five hundred signatures on a petition demanding action by the city—eventually succeeding in obtaining a budget allocation for the restoration of the playground. Based on recommendations from neighborhood residents, when the Sauer Playground reopened in 1993 it contained an area with a spray shower, modular play equipment, and corkscrew slides; benches where parents could sit while keeping an eye on their children; and community gardens for both children and adults. The 12th Street Block Association was not about to let it deteriorate all over again. By informal agreement,

Manhattan, 1934. The Sauer Playground on East 12th Street was one of the first playgrounds Robert Moses erected after taking office.

Manhattan, 1988 and 2009. By the late 1980s, Sauer Playground was in terrible condition and had been taken over by junkies and prostitutes. Once Sauer Playground had been rehabilitated it was once again a neighborhood asset.

residents lock playground gates every night and unlock them in the morning. Sauer Playground truly has become their neighborhood park.

Whether in New York, Chicago, Memphis, or other cities and towns across the country, the role of the public in the stewardship of parkland has been growing steadily. Citizens in increasing numbers have understood what political leaders are only slowly coming to understand: that public parks have become an integral part of urban and suburban life.

The public's growing involvement with the design, development, and stewardship of public parks is evidence that they understand their importance and care deeply about them. More important, they will do whatever they can to insure that public parks continue to play major roles in enhancing personal well-being and improving public health, sustaining a livable environment, incubating a civil society, and shaping regional development.

Manhattan, 2008. After renovation, Sauer Playground resumed its role as a recreational facility for neighborhood residents.

Manhattan, 2009. Central Park.

TWELVE

SUSTAINABILITY: THE KEY TO SUCCESS

It is no accident that Central Park appears in every section of this book. I grew up nearby and have spent more time in the park than anyplace else in the world. As a toddler I went there to play; as an adult visiting the park remains one of my most cherished pleasures. For the first few years of my life I was under the misapprehension that the word "park" meant Central Park, because I did not yet know there were any other parks in the world, but I have since come to know and love hundreds of other wonderful public parks. Many are great works of art, magnificent places adored by the people who go there. But Central Park has remained my great love and, after studying public parks for decades, the one I consider the greatest of them all.

Because I know Central Park best, it has provided insights that I have used throughout these chapters. But the deepest insights it provides have to do with what makes a great public park. When Calvert Vaux and Frederick Law Olmsted first considered this question, they had never worked together, and they had never designed a park. At that time, there were so few public parks in the world that they only had a handful of examples on which to base a design. So they invented a place that was and continues to be a model for park development.

In the course of studying Central Park and many other successful parks from different eras and

Manhattan, 1862 and 2004. Olmsted and Vaux foresaw that Central Park would be surrounded by "a continuous high wall of brick, stone, and marble." Despite the continuing reconstruction that surrounds it, the park has remained a source of recreation for millions of people since it opened more than a century and a half ago.

locales, I have come to feel that the key to the creation and maintenance of great parks is threefold: public entrepreneurship, active community participation, and sustainability. All these concepts have been explored in previous chapters, but the last—sustainability—is what provides the key to success.

In their original proposal for the plan of Central Park, known as the Greensward Plan, Olmsted and Vaux wrote: "The town will have enclosed the Central Park. Let us consider, therefore, what will at that time be satisfactory, for it is then that the design will be judged.... No longer an open suburb, our ground will have around it a continuous high wall of brick, stone, and marble."[1] At that time, in the late 1850s, the northern edge of the built-up sections of New York City was 3.5 miles (5.6 km) south of the new park. Part of the genius of Olmsted and Vaux lay in their ability to predict the city's growth and project the form it would take. But their greater genius lay in designing a park that would be as usable in the twenty-first century as it was in the nineteenth. Photographs taken at the same place in very different eras demonstrate their success.

The reason for the continuing success of the Greensward Plan is that it could become sustainable in six ways: socially, functionally, environmentally, financially, politically, and aesthetically. When the park opened, it was not yet fully sustainable, nor had sustainability become a part of the public dialogue. That concept entered public discourse in 1987, with the publication of a report by the United Nations' World Commission on Environment and Development titled *Our Common Future,* popularly referred to as the Brundtland Report in honor of the commission's chair, Gro Harlem Brundtland, the prime minister of Norway. The commission defined sustainability as development that "meets the needs of the present without compromising the ability of future generations to meet their own needs."[2] Even today, many devoted park advocates do not concern themselves with more than one or two aspects of sustainability. But sustainability has broad application to parks and is key to a park's success over time. There is no better site for a more specific exploration of these interwoven aspects of sustainability than Central Park.

SOCIAL SUSTAINABILITY

A park is socially sustainable if, throughout its existence, people of every age, ethnicity, and income want to be there. Olmsted and Vaux had the foresight to realize that there would be no lack of potential parkgoers coming from the residences and offices that would surround the park in the future. The problem, as they saw it, was to create a place those people would want to go to, and they solved it by providing something for everyone.

In 2003 the *New York Times* reported that Central Park attracts "more or less permanent and overlapping communities of folk dancers, horseback riders, bird-watchers, storytellers, dog walkers, nannies, chess fans, volleyball players, softball leagues, joggers, cyclists, tennis players, ice-skaters, soccer teams, ultimate Frisbee devotees and pint-size fishermen."[3] The reason they are attracted is that the park offers so many different destinations. Most destinations are not intended for one specific use; with a few exceptions, such as the zoo, the carousel, the tennis courts, and the

Manhattan in the nineteenth and twenty-first centuries: the places Olmsted and Vaux designed for recreation have continued to be used in the same manner for generations.

Manhattan, 2004 and 2008. Almost every sort of recreational activity is easy to accommodate in Central Park.

fenced-in playgrounds, the landscape is so flexible that it can be adapted to their needs and used simultaneously by others. In fact, the park was designed to bring together rich and poor, young and old, "each individual adding by his mere presence to the pleasure of all others."[4]

Some parks are not socially sustainable because they consist exclusively of single-function facilities: baseball diamonds, basketball courts, swimming pools, and so forth, and thus are useful only to people who come especially for that activity. Those people consider the park a success, but the rest of the time it is empty. Because nobody else uses these parks, they are not socially sustainable. In contrast, most of Central Park was specifically designed for a

wide variety of users at any time of day or season of the year.

The key to the park's social sustainability is that the landscape itself is the destination. The various open meadows are used simultaneously by people who want to lie in the sun, picnic, play ball, read the paper, or meet their friends. Joggers may choose to run around the reservoir or make a complete circuit around the park on the circumferential road, which they share with people on bikes and skates. Some visitors go to the rough, rocky Ramble because it is a gay hangout, others go there for bird-watching, but for most people it is just a wonderful place to go for a walk. Visitors may be headed to the Sheep Meadow, the Lake, the Ramble, or merely a bench

Manhattan, 2000 and 2004. Central Park is designed to be enjoyed during daylight in every season of the year, in any weather.

under a shady tree—but whatever the destination, people think of it as their very own special place, yet they are not at all surprised to be sharing it with total strangers.

As Central Park demonstrates, social sustainability depends on having a large enough user population that can easily get to the park and lots of places that they want to go to once they have arrived. Move Central Park to the steppes of central Asia or the rain forests of Brazil and it will fail utterly. But in high-density New York City, with its millions of daily workers, residents, and tourists, it is the park's flexible, landscape-based destinations that make it socially sustainable.

FUNCTIONAL SUSTAINABILITY

The adaptability of the different destination landscapes of Central Park certainly contributes to its usability. Places where people once danced around a maypole are as easily used today for tossing around Frisbees. When the park opened, there was neither a Metropolitan Opera nor a New York Philharmonic Orchestra; now they perform in the park every summer for audiences of tens of thousands.

A park's functional sustainability is dependent on people's continuing ability to get to and enjoy those destinations without interfering with everybody else in the park. It begins at the dividing line between the park and the surrounding city. The new landscape that Olmsted and Vaux put into place was enclosed by a wall with carefully selected entry points and surrounded on all four sides by a double row of trees that covers the bounding streets with a canopy of leaves. This landscaped promenade provides people walking along the adjacent sidewalks with a natural transition into the park and helps to screen out much of the view of the surrounding city for people inside the park. Perhaps the most brilliant elements of the new landscape are its four circulation systems: transverse crosstown roads, a circum-

Manhattan, 2006. The tree canopy on Fifth Avenue along the edge of the park begins the park experience.

ferential carriageway, pedestrian walks, and bridle paths for horses. Forty-six bridges or tunnels pass over or under the roadways.[5]

The design competition required four transverse roads connecting streets on the east side of the park with those on the west side. Olmsted and Vaux made them sunken arteries. Vehicles using them have a quick, uninterrupted drive across town. Inside the park one is virtually unaware that these crosstown arteries exist. Their sides are enclosed in berms that are heavily planted with trees and shrubs. Within the park, roadways and pedestrian paths that cross over the sunken transverse roads take the form of land bridges also enclosed in heavily planted berms.

The circumferential roadway was initially intended for recreational use by horse-drawn carriages. It crosses the transverse roads on eight overpasses. But thanks to creative landscaping, drivers on this roadway are completely unaware that they are traveling on bridges. In critical locations, the circumferential roadway is crossed by underpasses that allow pedestrians to avoid traffic. In addition a separate bridle path for horses and a complex network of pedestrian paths were created.

Manhattan, 2009. The four crosstown transverses in Central Park were mandated by the Board of Park Commissioners in 1857. Olmsted and Vaux devised an ingenious design that hides them from people using the park.

Manhattan, 2002. Pedestrians use underpasses to avoid traffic on the circumferential roadway.

During the nineteenth century, this circulation system separated carriage and horse traffic from pedestrians. The plan has proved to be equally usable during the twentieth and twenty-first centuries, when motor vehicles rather than horses and carriages use the sunken, crosstown roadways. During the first two-thirds of the twentieth century, automobiles dominated the circumferential carriageway. After 1966, on weekends and during all but a few hours on weekdays when the road is open to motor traffic, its use is restricted to skaters, cyclists, and joggers. As a result, the rest of the park is free almost entirely for pedestrians.

ENVIRONMENTAL SUSTAINABILITY

Although the concept did not yet exist when Olmsted and Vaux were creating Central Park, their creation is nevertheless environmentally sustainable. This is not because they devised ecosystems whose plantings and wildlife were self-perpetuating; rather, the park's sustainability is a product of a design and an attitude that assumes human beings are an integral part of nature.

The territory occupied by the park had been an ungrateful landscape shorn of its tree cover decades earlier. In 1858 it contained two reservoirs, a few dramatic rock outcrops, several unpleasant swamps and bogs, thin-soiled, boulder-strewn fields, and some scattered squatters' shacks. The design required regrading the topography, digging out the swamps and bogs to create lakes and ponds, installing a complex of underground water-supply and drainage pipes, replenishing the topsoil, removing

some trees and shrubs and planting thousands of new trees, shrubs, and meadows, and transforming the rock outcrops into prominent dramatic features.

Despite this careful environmental engineering, during the nineteenth and much of the twentieth centuries Central Park was environmentally challenged. Raw sewage from the park's rest rooms flowed into its waterways until a sewer system was installed in 1905. High levels of air pollution persisted into the 1970s, dropping layers of particulate matter throughout the park. Periods of drought and erosion, as well as rough treatment by generations of parkgoers, destroyed the turf, washed away pavement, exposed tree roots to damage, and killed many of its original shrubs and decorative plants.[6] Because of the environmentally sustainable design, each time conditions got really bad park managers were able to make them better.

Although the park experienced serious environmental problems during extended periods, a century and a half after the landscape was put in place it contained 26,000 trees (American elms, pin oaks, Norway maples, and all sorts of others), as well as hundreds of species of understory and groundcover vegetation. The waterways and vegetation provide homes for squirrels, rabbits, bats, woodchucks, raccoons, frogs, turtles, fish, ducks, hawks, owls, egrets, herons, and 270 species of migratory birds.[7]

The complex underlying engineering of Central Park is only one reason it remains a hospitable environment for all this flora and fauna. A second is that Olmsted and Vaux formed large enough areas with quite different characteristics to support different ecosystems. These include landscapes that are shaped by the created waterways, woods, and mead-

Manhattan, 2009. Even in the more rugged sections of the Ramble, the paths in Central Park are graded and paved so that they simultaneously allow both human beings and wildlife to flourish.

ows. That heterogeneity of large enough ecosystems is central to any single park's environmental sustainability; other diverse smaller areas also play a role in the broader environmental sustainability of the entire park.

Aquatic life is supported in different forms in the Harlem Meer in the northeast, the Pool in the northwest, the Pond in the southeast corner, the Lake in the middle of the park, and two small streams. These waterways may look natural, but they were created for aesthetic and recreational purposes and had to be lined with clay to ensure that they could retain enough water. During the nineteenth century, water levels fluctuated because the natural water supply was subject to the weather. Since the completion of the Catskill Aqueduct in 1915, however, these waterways no longer suffer from periods of drought because the water in each of them can be supplemented from the city's supply of drinking water.

Two boulder-strewn, woodsy sections occupy 136 acres (55 ha) of the park: the Loch that extends into the North Woods, and the Ramble, in the center of the park. The Loch contains a steep, natural stream valley that runs from the Pool, artificially dug and extending roughly from West 101st to 103rd streets, into the Harlem Meer, created from the swamp at the northeastern corner of the park.

Vermont, 2009. Continuous pedestrian use of the unpaved paths in the 1,600-acre Grout Pond Recreation Area of Green Mountain National Forest has turned them into drainage ditches that had to have wooden rails placed over them to enable people to avoid the mud.

Manhattan, 2008. The waterways of Central Park were carefully designed to support different forms of wildlife while providing popular recreational resources for the city's population.

Tree cover in both the Loch–North Woods and the Ramble is so dense that, except for a few clearings, everything is in shadow. When I was six years old, the Ramble was my favorite part of the park. I could wander in the shadows and imagine I really was in the deep woods. I thought I might encounter a bear or a wolf, but the only creatures I ever saw were birds and squirrels. Olmsted wrote that the Ramble "should be more or less rough and rude, the trees and shrubs should grow more or less in bunches, there should be a great variety of character in them, some standing up and some struggling along the ground; instead of a smooth turf surface . . . there should be varied sorts of herbage one crowding over another and all running together without any order, or there should be vines and creepers and mosses and ferns."[8]

Perhaps the Ramble was consistent with the later English picturesque aesthetic of Humphry Repton; perhaps it was a way of creating an awesome place out of the area's seven rocky outcrops; perhaps it was intended as a vivid contrast with meadowlands in other parts of the park. The result, however, was to help provide the heterogeneity of ecosystems that allows the park to sustain a greater range of flora and fauna.

The 250 acres (101 ha) of open grassland in Central Park are perhaps the most heavily used sections of the park. Their manicured lawns, inspired by the gardens of Capability Brown, attract large numbers of people during good weather. Because they are of differing sizes and are located throughout the park, they provide microhabitats for many different creatures and make possible the dispersal of small forms of wildlife; they also absorb runoff.

Manhattan, 2008. The Ramble in Central Park was designed to provide a sublime, "rough and rude" contrast to the smooth undulating lawns of the park's open spaces.

Manhattan, 2008. The lawn at the top of the Great Hill in Central Park is a convenient place for informal, interactive games and sports.

The most significant aspect of Olmsted's approach to environmental sustainability is that he always considered people to be an important part of the environment. In Central Park and in all his later work, he took great care to design for large crowds of unruly people in a manner that would preclude their destruction of the natural landscapes he created. He knew that a great park had to accommodate "great numbers of people . . . many ignorant, selfish, and willful, of perverted tastes and lawless dispositions, each one of whom must be led as far as possible to enjoy and benefit by the scenery without preventing or seriously detracting from the enjoyment of it by all others. . . . For this and other obvious reasons, a great extent of ground must be prepared expressly for the wear of feet and wheels."[9]

His solution was to establish convenient points of entry for those coming by private carriages, public transportation, on horseback, or on foot; a prominent circulation system that allowed people to get to clearly visible destinations; and routes that led them from these destinations through the park. Pedestrian paths, for example, directed visitors through places with especially lovely views of the landscape but kept them from trampling what they came to enjoy. Thus Central Park's circulation system provided not only the functional sustainability I discussed earlier, but also the means of environmental sustainability—keeping horses on the bridle path rather than trampling the underbrush and meadows, preventing crosstown traffic from interfering with ecosystems, and guiding most people to walk along paved walkways rather than cutting desire lines through the meadows.

FINANCIAL SUSTAINABILITY

Sustainable businesses consider both revenues and expenses: their financial sustainability depends on having something left over (return on equity) after operating costs, taxes, debt service, and depreciation are deducted from the revenues they generate. A park is not a for-profit business, however, and a truly public park is one that is open to the public free of charge. While we have explored various potential sources of revenue and methods of quantifying value, the revenue directly attributable to a park can be difficult to calculate. Expenses, too, can be difficult to calculate: a park's operating costs and debt service on bonds that finance capital investments are usually paid for by the local government; it pays no taxes; and it grows in value and rarely depreciates in value. So how does one determine a park's financial sustainability?

Olmsted believed that the tax yield from properties surrounding the park should be thought of as revenue. Thus for the park to be financially sustainable, the difference between what the city collected as a result of the existence of Central Park and what it would have collected without it had to be enough to more than cover its cost. In 1856, before work on the park began, the assessed value of property in the three wards surrounding the park was $26.4 million.[10] According to Olmsted, twenty years later it was $253 million.[11] He ascribed all of the $226.6 million increase to Central Park. At that time the tax on real estate was $2.50 per $100 of assessed value, and thus the annual "park revenue" in 1876 was $5.7 million. As of 1873, $13.9 million had been spent on the park.[12] Even if one ascribes some of this increase to other factors, twenty years of annual park revenue would have been enough to pay for the entire cost of the park, plus interest on the money borrowed to pay for it, plus the annual cost of maintenance and management, and still produce a surplus to cover city expenditures having nothing to do with the park. Surely that is financial sustainability.

The initial investment in Central Park also could be looked at as an infrastructure investment that provided a financially sustainable mechanism for creating jobs. An expenditure of that sort seemed a bargain to many political leaders in the 1850s. New York was teeming with men and women who needed work and with businesses with products to sell. By satisfying their needs, political leaders could harvest thousands of votes and donations, not to mention possible kickbacks. According to Olmsted, the park provided work for the equivalent of one thousand laborers over sixteen years, and it paid local business for thousands of cartloads of materials.[13] That job creation mechanism has continued unabated. The administration of Franklin Roosevelt provided thousands of WPA-paid employees, whom Moses put to work replacing the reservoir with the Great Lawn, catching up on decades of deferred maintenance, installing the zoo, and erecting playgrounds. Today, when Central Park is in excellent condition, it is responsible for hundreds of permanent jobs.

Although the park generated hundreds of millions of dollars in tax revenue for New York City, there were many decades during which it appeared

Manhattan, 1967. The largest number of people to use the Sheep Meadow in Central Park came for a concert by Barbara Streisand. The litter after the Streisand concert was almost as legendary as the concert itself.

to be financially unsustainable because the city was experiencing fiscal problems and chose to decrease spending for all city parks, not just Central Park. This changed when Elizabeth Rogers established the Central Park Conservancy. But her success would not have been possible if Olmsted and Vaux had not created a great plan—in other words, a sustainable plan that then became the conservancy's vehicle for raising the money needed to pay for the park's restoration. By identifying each component of the plan and the steps need to accomplish it, they were able to develop fund-raising targets and schedule the orderly rehabilitation of the park.

Like the other components of sustainability, financial sustainability is realized only over time. It has taken a century and a half of hard work by thousands of people to put Central Park on the road to financial sustainability.

POLITICAL SUSTAINABILITY

Starting in 1850, when Central Park had been an issue in the mayoral campaign, and for almost a century thereafter, public parks were a potential political asset. Leaders of Republican and Democratic political machines wanted the patronage jobs they could distribute. Reformers wanted the opportunity to eliminate the power of those machines that independent park commissions provided. Property owners wanted the increases in market demand that accompanied park development. Elected officials wanted the added tax revenue that parks generated.

Once public parks were in place, however, other priorities began to replace them as major elements of the political agenda. After World War II, the flight to the suburbs was accompanied by decreasing support for city parks. Most suburban voters lived in houses with backyards where they could have a barbeque and with driveways where their children could play basketball. As new homeowners, they were not eager to pay additional taxes for park development and maintenance. Consequently, city and suburban governments alike had other budget priorities. With budget cuts came the inevitable decline in maintenance—even in Central Park.

In the 1960s, at the start of park's worst period of decline, public support was slipping away. Some pundits thought the condition of Central Park was evidence of the inevitable death of an obsolete relic of nineteenth-century planning: the public park. Mayor Lindsay and the city's parks commissioner, Thomas Hoving, thought they were wrong. But they understood that if Central Park continued to lose public support, there would be no way to reverse its decline, so they initiated a program to revive the park's latent constituency.

They closed the circumferential carriageway to motor vehicles on weekends and started a series of public "Happenings" to restore attendance. Citizens responded by staging "spontaneous performances and planned spectacles . . . war-protest marches, gay-liberation rallies, a lunar eclipse watch," and any number of invented, impromptu festivals. In 1967, 130,000 people, the largest audience ever assembled in Central Park, attended a concert by Barbara Streisand on the Sheep Meadow. August Heckscher, then

Manhattan, 2004. The elm trees that line the Central Park Mall provide an ever-changing landscape, giving shade from the sun for park-goers during hot summers, while in winter, when the leaves are gone, the branches allow warming sunlight to reach pedestrians.

commissioner of parks, later wrote: "The occasion seemed to go off perfectly. There were no disorders, no tensions in that vast human sea. The crowd dispersed rapidly when it was over. . . . I was stopped by people who wanted to thank me for the pleasure they had experienced. . . . The next day it became apparent that we had a price to pay. Tons of litter lay scattered over the Sheep Meadow and the surrounding areas."[14]

The price was very high indeed: it accelerated the park's deterioration. But it was a bargain because the concert helped to regain the constituency that was vital to the park's later restoration. Millions of

Manhattan, 2006. The formally designed Conservatory Water, on the east side of Central Park, is a favorite spot for launching model sailboats.

people who had avoided Central Park because of its bedraggled appearance or out of fear of mugging became avid parkgoers. When Elizabeth Rogers established the Central Park Conservancy, they were eager to support her efforts. The outpouring of support from individuals, foundations, and corporations proved to be overwhelming: contributions from 25,000 members generated $400 million dur-

![image](Manhattan, 1997.)

Manhattan, 1997. Olmsted and Vaux transformed the rock outcrops in Central Park into attractive destinations by adding rustic structures from which visitors could enjoy panoramic views.

ing the twenty-nine years between the conservancy's founding and 2008. By then Central Park had a staff of 275, of which 235 were employees of the conservancy, which provided $23 million of the park's $27 million operating budget.

The Central Park Conservancy has restored political sustainability to the park. But it provides more than money and staff; it has re-created a constituency that political leaders cannot ignore and reinvigorated the park-related jobs, market demand, and tax revenue that can make parks a continuing political asset, during good economic times and bad.

AESTHETIC SUSTAINABILITY

Aesthetic sustainability is central to any work of art, and Central Park is a living work of art evolving in front of our eyes and the eyes of generations both before and after ours. During its first sixteen decades the plan was just what Daniel Burnham thought every plan should be: "a living thing, asserting itself with ever-growing insistency." Olmsted and Vaux were responsible for the plan that established the park's initial and most fundamental character. But as we've seen throughout this book, Central Park, like any park, exhibits the transformations of countless others.

Great works of art never lose their appeal. You can return to them time and time again. Every time I attend a performance of *The Marriage of Figaro* or read *The Great Gatsby*, I discover something new and

Manhattan, 2008. The meadow at the top of the Great Hill is a lovely place for picnicking or just lying on the grass.

wonderful. The same thing is true of Central Park, even though I have spent my entire life exploring every nook and cranny.

Another reason for the park's aesthetic sustainability is that each place changes with the weather, the time of day, and the season of the year. This is also true of nature. But Central Park is designed to provide different aesthetic experiences that make the most of those changes. A promenade under the elm trees in the Mall affords a wonderful way to cool off in the shade of summer. In the late fall and winter, that walk can be just as pleasant because the warming sun is filtered through the branches. On nice days children of all ages go to the Conservatory Water, the formal pool on the east side of the park, to sail model boats. When I was a small boy, before Robert Moses erected two ice skating rinks elsewhere in the park, I learned how to skate there.

Manhattan, 2005. The circumferential carriageway has provided carriages, automobiles, and bicycles with a lovely way to move around the park.

Manhattan, 2009. For nearly 150 years Central Park has been a model for public parks everywhere.

Each activity that takes place within the park's different destinations is appropriate to that place, appropriate to the "capabilities" of each site, as Capability Brown would have said and as Olmsted had admired in the eighteenth-century estate gardens of England. The park's design may have required blasting and cutting though 300,000 cubic yards (229,000 m³) of gneiss rock veined with granite, but the resulting landscape transformed these major rock outcrops into focal points. In some cases they are crowned with rustic pergolas, designed by Calvert Vaux, from which visitors can enjoy the view.

Olmsted and Vaux not only altered the topography, they created places that were fitted to it. The Great Hill at West 106th Street, for example, is a 35-acre (14-ha) knoll with a 1.1-acre (0.45-ha) oval meadow at the top, which can be reached by steep walks and stairs going up the heavily wooded hillside. That secluded meadow is just the right size for tossing a ball around, lying in the shade of a tree, or picnicking.

The ongoing pleasure of the different landscape destinations in Central Park is not just a matter of their having been made the right size and shape, or having been fitted into the topography. Olmsted believed that visiting the park should be a carefully

choreographed experience, displaying aesthetics of movement. He described this best when he wrote of Prospect Park that "it should be a ground which invites, encourages, and facilitates movement, its topographical conditions such as make movement a pleasure; such as offer inducements in variety, on one side and the other, for easy movement, first by one promise of pleasure then by another, yet all of a simple character."[15]

Those who took a ride around the park on its circumferential roadway in a carriage during the nineteenth century, or in a car during the twentieth century, or on a bicycle in the twenty-first century have all had that orchestrated sequence of pleasant surprises. Before tall buildings surrounded the park, once you started the ride you would have been completely unaware of the city around you. That is still true in many places, because the roadway is embedded inside the park, often enclosed in trees, or at a lower elevation than the surrounding city. As you ride through the park, a vista may open onto a grove of trees, a verdant valley, a playing field, a body of water, or the Tavern on the Green.

Central Park includes places that have changed since it was opened to the public. Keeping it as it looked when Olmsted and Vaux finished their work in the 1860s would have been foolishness. They designed the park not only for the people who visited at that time but also for trees that would grow and for generations that would follow. In 1872 Olmsted wrote: "The people who are to visit the park this year or next are but a small fraction of those who must be expected to visit hereafter. If the park had to be laid out, and especially if [it] had to be planted with reference only to the use of the next few years, a very different general plan, a very different way of planting and a very different way of managing the trees, would be proper."[16] While not all changes will be acceptable over time, a flexible design that allows for changes in future years is very much part of a park's aesthetic sustainability.

GREATNESS

The extraordinary intertwining of these aspects of sustainability provides the explanation for the success of Olmsted and Vaux's design for Central Park. That success is also the work of Robert Moses, Elizabeth Rogers, and the thousands of others who have been involved or continue to be involved in sustaining it. All of them understood instinctively what I have argued from the beginning: that public parks are not finished works of art when they are opened to the public. They are the evolving product of a living natural landscape and its interaction with the generations of people who use them.

After going to Central Park over and over and over again for nearly seven decades, I have concluded that it excels at performing the roles that every great park must play: enhancing well-being and improving public health, incubating a civil society, sustaining a livable environment, and providing a framework for urbanization. This is what makes New York livable. And only by continuing to invest in the development and maintenance of fine public parks can we be assured of livable communities.

NOTES

The following volumes of *The Papers of Frederick Law Olmsted*, under the general editorship of Charles E. Beveridge and published by Johns Hopkins University Press, are cited in the notes as *Papers of FLO* followed by the volume number and page:

Vol. 3. *Creating Central Park, 1857–1861*, ed. Charles E. Beveridge and David Schuyler (1983).

Vol. 5. *The California Frontier, 1863–1865*, ed. Charles E. Beveridge and Victoria Post Ranney (1990).

Vol. 6. *The Years of Olmsted, Vaux & Co., 1865–1874*, ed. David Schuyler and Jane Turner Censer (1992).

Supplementary series, vol. 1. *The Writings on Public Parks, Parkways, and Park Systems*, ed. Charles E. Beveridge and Carolyn F. Hoffman (1997).

INTRODUCTION

1. S. N. Behrman, *Duveen* (Boston: Little, Brown, 1972), 31.
2. Frederick Law Olmsted, "Public Parks and the Enlargement of Towns" (1871), *Papers of FLO*, supp. ser., 1:190.
3. See Ricky Burdett and Deyan Sudjic, *The Endless City* (New York: Phaidon, 2007).

I. THE EMERGENCE OF PUBLIC PARKS

1. Spiro Kostof, *The City Assembled: The Elements of Urban Form through History* (Boston: Little, Brown, 1992), 166–72; Ben Weinreb and Christopher Hibbert, eds., *The London Encyclopaedia* (London: Macmillan, 1993), 436.
2. Ehrenfried Kluckert, *European Garden Design: From Classical Antiquity to the Present Day* (Cologne: Konemann, 2000), 117.
3. See Pankraz Freiherr von Freyberg, ed., *Der Englische Garten in München* (Munich: Knurr, 2000).
4. See Neville Braybrooke, *London Green: The Story of Kensington Gardens, Hyde Park, Green Park, and St. James Park* (London: Gollancz, 1959).
5. See the sources cited in *Papers of FLO*, supp. ser., 1:237n21.
6. Charles Dickens, *Sketches by Boz* (1837; repr., Oxford: Oxford University Press, 1982), 184.
7. Henri Lecouturier, *Paris incompatible avec la République* (Paris, 1848), 20–21, trans. Nicholas Papayanis in *Planning Paris before Haussmann* (Baltimore: Johns Hopkins University Press, 2004), 121.
8. Jacob Riis, *The Battle with the Slum* (1902; repr., New York: Macmillan, 1912), 39.
9. *Report from the Select Committee on Public Walks*, Parliamentary Paper (London: Her Majesty's Stationary Office, 1833).
10. Ibid.
11. Joseph Strutt, address to the Town Council of Derby, September 16, 1840, quoted at www.derbyarboretum.co.uk/about_the_arboretum.htm.
12. I thank John Hopkins, the landscape architect responsible for the restoration of the Derby Arboretum, for guiding me through Loudon's design when I visited the park in February 2008.
13. Melanie Louise Simo, *Loudon and the Landscape: From Country Seat to Metropolis* (New Haven: Yale University Press, 1988), 191–205.
14. See Clifford E. Thornton, *The People's Garden: A History of Birkenhead Park* (Birkenhead: Williamson Art Gallery & Museum, 2006).
15. Samuel Stansfield, Report of the Sanitary Condition of Birkenhead (Liverpool, 1843), quoted in Thornton, *The People's Garden*, 3.
16. Ibid., 4.
17. Robert Moses, "What Happened to Haussmann," *Architectural Forum* 77 (July 1942): 58–59.
18. Wendell Cox Consultancy, "Ville de Paris: Population & Density from 1365," www.demographia.com/dm-par90.htm.
19. See Pierre Pinon, *Atlas du Paris haussmannien* (Paris: Parigramme, 2002).

20. Charles-Adolphe Alphand, *Les Promenades de Paris* (1873), (Paris, France: Conaissance et Mémoires, 2002), 15.

21. Georges-Eugène Haussmann, *Memoires du Baron Haussmann,* vol. 3 (1893; repr., Paris: Elibron Classics, 2006), 237.

22. Ibid., 207.

23. Frederick Law Olmsted, *Walks and Talks of an American Farmer in England* (1852; repr., Amherst: University of Massachusetts Press and Library of American Landscape History, 2002), 93.

24. Mayor Ambrose Kingsland, "Message to the Common Council," April 5, 1851, quoted in Frederick Law Olmsted, *Forty Years of Landscape Architecture: Central Park,* ed. Frederick Law Olmsted Jr. and Theodora Kimball (Cambridge: MIT Press, 1973), 25.

25. Frederick Law Olmsted to the President of the Commissioners of the Central Park, New York, August 12, 1857, *Papers of FLO,* 3:76.

26. Francis R. Kowsky, *Country, Park, and City: The Architecture and Life of Calvert Vaux* (New York: Oxford University Press, 1998), 11.

27. This figure was reported by the Trust for Public Land, a national parks conservationist organization, in "Total Parkland as Percent of City Land Area" (2008), available on their Web site, www.tpl.org.

2. KEY ROLES

1. Frederick Law Olmsted, "Public Parks and the Enlargement of Towns" (1871), *Papers of FLO,* supp. ser., 1:180.

2. Olmsted, Vaux & Co., Report to the Chicago South Park Commission (March 1871), *Papers of FLO,* supp. ser., 1:217.

3. See the Web site of the Memorial Park Conservancy, Houston, www.memorialparkconservancy.org.

4. From Jacob Riis, *The Children of the Poor* (1892), repr. in *Jacob Riis Revisited: Poverty and the Slum in Another Era,* ed. Francesco Cordasco (New York: Anchor, 1968), 127.

5. Ibid., 209.

6. Jane Addams, *The Spirit of Youth and the City Streets* (New York: Macmillan, 1909), 103.

7. Both quotes in this paragraph are from www.healthypeople.gov/implementation/nrpa/.

8. Ibid.

9. Statistics from www.ihrsa.org/industrystats/attendance.

10. Reported in Terry Matlin, "A Walk in the Park Helps ADHD Symptoms," www.healthcentral.com/adhd/c/57718/50962/park-helps-symptoms.

11. Olmsted, "Public Parks and the Enlargement of Towns," 186.

12. Olmsted to William Robinson, May 17, 1872, *Papers of FLO,* 6:551.

13. Olmsted to gardeners, 1872, *Papers of FLO,* 6:539.

14. I thank Douglas Blonsky of Central Park Conservancy for providing this data.

15. Jacob Riis, *The Peril and the Preservation of the Home* (1903), quoted in Alexander Alland, *Jacob A. Riis: Photographer and Citizen* (Millerton, N.Y.: Aperture, 1974), 210.

16. Douglas Blonsky of Central Park Conservancy supplied these figures.

17. I thank Tupper Thomas of the Prospect Park Alliance for providing this data.

18. Olmsted, "Public Parks and the Enlargement of Towns," 182.

19. Letter from Park Commissioner Adrian Benepe to the author, November 18, 2009. This figure is for all federal, New York State, and New York City parkland within city limits, including the 20.624 acres of the National Gateway Recreational Area, which includes upland areas, wetlands, and land under water in its Jamaica Bay portion. The figure used by the Trust for Public Land is 20 percent; see Peter Harnik, ed., *2009 City Park Facts* (San Francisco: The Trust for Public Land, 2009), 9. By either reckoning New York has the largest percentage of any American city's territory devoted to parkland.

20. New York City Department of Environmental Protection, *Harbor Water Quality Survey, 1998.*

21. Silvia Pettem, *Boulder: Evolution of a City* (Niwot: University Press of Colorado, 1994), 47–48.

22. Frederick Law Olmsted Jr. and Charles Eliot, *The Improvement of Boulder, Colorado,* (Boulder: Boulder City Improvement Association, 1910), 59.

23. Prospect Park Alliance, *A Guide to Nature in Prospect Park* (Brooklyn: Prospect Park Alliance, n.d.).

24. Keith Schneider, "To Revitalize a City, Try Spreading Some Mulch," *New York Times,* May 17, 2006.

25. Joshua Laird (Assistant Commissioner for Planning and Natural Resources, NYC Department of Parks and Recreation), interview by author, February 29, 2008.

26. On the Newtown Creek facility see NYC Department of Environmental Protection, www.water-technology.net/projects/newtown/.

27. See www.nps.gov/goga/naturescience/crissy-field.htm.

28. Olmsted and Vaux, "Preliminary Report Respecting a Public Park in Buffalo," *Papers of FLO,* supp. ser., 1:158.

29. Ibid., 158, 170.

30. Figures are taken from the U.S. Census, 1880 and 1900.

31. Theodore Wirth, *Minneapolis Park System, 1883–1944* (Minneapolis: Board of Park Commissioners, 1946), 39, 59.

3. QUANTIFYING VALUE

1. Jonathan Miller, head of the property-appraisal firm Samuel Miller, quoted in S. Jhoanna Robledo, "Because We Wouldn't Trade a Patch of Grass for $528,783,552,000," *New York Magazine,* December 18, 2005, nymag.com/nymetro/news/reasonstoloveny/15362/.

2. Tom Fox, *Urban Open Space: An Investment That Pays* (New York: Neighborhood Open Space Coalition, 1990), 11.

3. Frederick Law Olmsted, "Report of the Landscape Architect on the Recent Changes in the Keepers' Service" (July 8, 1871), *Papers of FLO,* 6:614.

4. T. R. Hammer, R. E. Coughlin, and E. T. Horn, "The Effect of a Large Urban Park on Real Estate Value," *Journal of the American Institute of Planners* 40, no. 4 (July 1974): 274–77.

5. M. R. Correll, J. H. Lillydahl, and L. D. Singell, "The Effects of Greenbelts on Residential Property Values: Some Findings on the Political Economy of Open Space," *Land Economics* 54, no. 2 (May 1978): 207–17.

6. Real Estate Board of New York and the Regional Plan

Association, "The Impact of Hudson River Park on Property Values," unpublished report, 2007.

7. I thank Daniel Biederman of the Bryant Park Restoration Corporation for this data.

8. Peter Harnik, "Philadelphia Green," in *Urban Parks and Open Space*, ed. Alexander Garvin and Gayle Berens (Washington, D.C.: Urban Land Institute, 1997), 158–67.

9. Michela Pasquali, ed., *Loisaida: NYC Community Gardens* (Milan: a+mbookstore edizioni, 2006), 17–18.

4. PARK DEVELOPMENT

1. Hillary Ballon and Kenneth T. Jackson: *Robert Moses and the Modern City* (New York: W. W. Norton, 2007), 158–60 and 222–23.

2. Robert Moses, *26 Years of Parks Progress, 1934–1960* (New York: Department of Parks, 1960), 52–53.

3. Elizabeth Barlow Rogers, "The Landscapes of Robert Moses," *Site/Lines* 3, no. 1 (Fall 2007): 3.

4. For NYC see Chapter 2, footnote 19; for other cities see Peter Harnik, *Inside City Parks* (Washington, D.C.: Urban Land Institute and the Trust for Public Land, 2000), 126.

5. Roy Rosensweig and Elizabeth Blackmar, *The Park and the People: A History of Central Park* (Ithaca, N.Y.: Cornell University Press, 1992), 445.

6. Ibid., 445–91.

7. Lucy Lawliss, Caroline Loughlin, and Lauren Meier, eds., *The Master List of Design Projects of the Olmsted Firm, 1857–1979,* 2nd ed. (Washington, D.C.: National Association for Olmsted Parks, 2008), 48–49.

8. Population figures are from the 2000 U.S. Census or were supplied by the Collierville Chamber of Commerce.

9. James Wilhelm (Collierville town administrator) and Chip Peterson (assistant town administrator), interviews by author, July 29, 2008.

10. Frederick Law Olmsted, *A Journey through Texas* (New York: Dix Edwards & Co, 1857), 149–50.

11. Lewis F. Fisher, *Crown Jewel of Texas: The Story of San Antonio's River* (San Antonio: Maverick Publishing, 1997), 31–63.

12. Clare A. Gunn, David J. Reed, and Robert E. Cough, *Cultural Benefits from Metropolitan River Recreation—San Antonio Prototype* (College Station: Texas A & M University, 1972).

13. See Fisher, *Crown Jewel of Texas,* 65–75.

14. Robert Moses, *Six Years of Parks Progress* (New York: Department of Parks, 1940), 10.

15. Ibid.

16. Cleveland Rodgers, *Robert Moses, Builder for Democracy* (New York: Henry Holt, 1952), 83–84.

17. F. Scott Fitzgerald, *The Great Gatsby* (1925; repr., New York: Charles Scribner's Sons, 1953), 23.

5. SITE SELECTION AND ADAPTATION

1. Frederick Law Olmsted, "Preliminary Report to the Commissioners for Laying Out a Park in Brooklyn, New York" (January 24, 1866), *Papers of FLO,* supp. ser., 1:90; Frederick Law Olmsted, "Preliminary Report in Regard to a Plan of Public Pleasure Grounds for the City of San Francisco," *Papers of FLO,* 5:519–20.

2. Janice Lee, David Boutros, Charlotte R. White, and Deon Wolfenbarger, eds., *A Legacy of Design: An Historical Survey of the Kansas City, Missouri, Parks and Boulevard System, 1893–1940* (Kansas City: Kansas City Center for Design Education and Research, 1995), 41–52.

3. Olmsted, Vaux & Company, "Report of Landscape Architects and Superintendents" (January 1, 1869), *Papers of FLO,* 6:325.

4. Francis R. Kowsky, *Country, Park, and City: The Architecture and Life of Calvert Vaux* (New York: Oxford University Press, 1998), 171.

5. Frederick Law Olmsted, letter to Salem H. Wales (president of the board), October 11, 1873, *Papers of FLO,* 6:651–57.

6. Frederick Law Olmsted and Calvert Vaux, "General Plan for the Improvements of Morningside Park" (1887), repr. in Albert Fine, ed., *Landscape into Cityscape* (Ithaca, N.Y.: Cornell University Press, 1968), 451.

7. Olmsted, "Notes on the Plan of Franklin Park and Related Matters" (1886), *Papers of FLO,* supp. ser., 1:469.

8. Frederick Law Olmsted, "Seventh Annual Report of the Board of Commissioners of the Department of Parks for the City of Boston for the year 1881" (City Document no. 16, 1882), repr. in *Civilizing American Cities: A Selection of Frederick Law Olmsted's Writings on City Landscapes,* ed. S. B. Sutton (Cambridge: MIT Press, 1972), 222.

9. Olmsted, "Notes on the Plan of Franklin Park and Related Matters" (1886), *Papers of FLO,* supp. ser., 1:464.

10. The phrase "a sense of enlarged freedom" comes from Olmsted, "Preliminary Report to the Commissioners for Laying Out a Park in Brooklyn," 83.

11. Fredrick Law Olmsted, letter to Asa Gray, October 8, 1857, *Papers of FLO,* 3:102.

12. Quoted in Charles E. Beveridge and David Schuyler, introduction, *Papers of FLO,* 3:17.

13. Roy Rosenzweig and Elizabeth Blackmar, *The Park and the People: A History of Central Park* (Ithaca, N.Y.: Cornell University Press, 1992), 150.

14. Frederick Law Olmsted, "Public Parks and the Enlargement of Towns," *Papers of FLO,* supp. ser., 1:192–93.

15. Robert Moses, *Public Works: A Dangerous Trade* (New York: McGraw-Hill, 1970), 11.

16. Hilary Ballon and Kenneth T. Jackson, *Robert Moses and the Modern City* (New York: W. W. Norton, 2007), 161–64.

17. Chuck Davis, ed., *The Greater Vancouver Book: An Urban Encyclopedia* (Surrey, B.C.: Linkman Press, 1997), 52.

18. See en.wikipedia.org/wiki/Stanley_Park#_note-31#_note-31.

19. Peter Harnik, *Inside City Parks* (Washington, D.C.: Urban Land Institute and the Trust for Public Land, 2000), 123; www.fairmountpark.org.

20. Sarah West, *Rediscovering the Wissahickon* (Philadelphia: Westford Press, 1993), 48.

21. Roy Kitt, *Tour the Ruhr* (Essen: Klartext Verlag, 2008), 37–39.

22. Ibid., 49.

23. Alan Tate, *Great City Parks* (London: Spon Press, 2001), 114–22.

24. See Rails-to-Trails Conservancy, *1000 Great Rail-Trails,* 3rd ed. (Guilford, Conn.: Globe Pequot Press, 2004).

25. Peter Harnik, "Cedar Lake Park and Trail," in *Urban Parks and Open Space,* ed. Alexander Garvin and Gayle

Berens (Washington, D.C.: Urban Land Institute, 1997), 58–69.

26. See www.ci.minneapolis.mn.us/bicycles/.

27. See National Park Service, *Chesapeake and Ohio Canal* (Washington, D.C.: U.S. Department of the Interior, 1991).

28. Waterfront Development Corporation, "The Impact of Louisville's Waterfront Park" (2007), www.louisvillewaterfront.com/documents/Economic_Impact_2007.pdf.

6. DESIGN INFLUENCES

1. See Francesco Negri Arnoldi, *Villa Lante in Bagnaia* (Rome: Edizioni Palatino, 1963).

2. Clemens Steenbergen and Wouter Rey, *Architecture and Landscape: The Design Experiment of the Great European Gardens and Landscapes* (Munich: Prestel, 1996), 104–11.

3. Hilary Lewis and John O'Connor, *Philip Johnson: The Architect in His Own Words* (New York: Rizzoli 1994), 140–45.

4. Alan Tate, *Great City Parks* (London: Spon Press, 2001), 32–38.

5. Vincent Scully, *Modern Architecture and Other Essays* (Princeton: Princeton University Press, 2003), 292.

6. See Thierry Mariage, *The World of André Le Nôtre*, trans. Graham Larkin (Philadelphia: University of Pennsylvania Press, 1990).

7. Steenbergen and Rey, *Architecture and Landscape*, P151–85.

8. Tate, *Great City Parks*, 56–65.

9. Ibid.

10. Ibid., 39–46.

11. Field Operations, "Shelby Farms Park Master Plan Executive Summary" (2008), 10. Available at www.shelbyfarmspark.org.

12. See Nikolaus Pevsner, *Studies in Art, Architecture, and Design* (New York: Walker, 1968), 77–155.

13. See Roger Turner, *Capability Brown and the Eighteenth-century English Landscape* (New York: Rizzoli, 1985), and Edward Hyams, *Capability Brown and Humphry Repton* (New York: Charles Scribner's Sons, 1971).

14. Frederick Law Olmsted, "Park" (*American Cyclopedia*, 1875), *Papers of FLO*, supp. ser., 1:326.

15. Caroline Loughlin and Catherine Anderson, *Forest Park* (Columbia: University of Missouri Press, 1986), 10.

16. Ibid., 3–21.

17. August Heckscher, *Open Spaces: The Life of American Cities* (New York: Harper & Row, 1977), 177.

18. Jens Jensen and Ragna B. Eskil, "Natural Parks and Gardens," *Saturday Evening Post*, March 8, 1930, 19.

19. Ibid.

20. Robert E. Grese, *Jens Jensen: Maker of Natural Parks and Gardens* (Baltimore: Johns Hopkins University Press, 1992), 158.

21. In the mid-1950s Caldwell worked with Mies and Hilberseimer on Lafayette Park, a housing redevelopment project in Detroit. See Alexander Garvin, *The American City: What Works, What Doesn't* (New York: McGraw-Hill, 2002), 24–25 and 257–59.

22. Alfred Caldwell, "The Lily Pool, Lincoln Park" (1942), in *Alfred Caldwell: The Life and Work of a Prairie School Landscape Architect*, ed. Dennis Domer (Baltimore: Johns Hopkins University Press, 1997), 158.

23. George Hazelrigg, "Peeling Back the Surface," *Landscape Architecture* 96, no. 4 (April 2006): 112–19.

7. PARKS AS EVOLVING ARTIFACTS

1. I thank Dennis McClendon of Chicago CartoGraphics for providing this information.

2. See Harold M. Mayer and Richard C. Wade, *Chicago: Growth of a Metropolis* (Chicago: University of Chicago Press, 1969); and Lois Wille, *Forever Open, Clear, and Free: The Struggle for Chicago's Lakefront* (Chicago: University of Chicago Press), 1972.

3. Wille, *Forever Open*, 71–81.

4. See John A. Peterson, *The Birth of City Planning in the United States, 1840–1917* (Baltimore: Johns Hopkins University Press, 2003); and William H. Wilson, *The City Beautiful Movement* (Baltimore: Johns Hopkins University Press, 1989).

5. See Timothy J. Gilfoyle, *Millennium Park: Creating a Chicago Landmark* (Chicago: University of Chicago Press, 2006).

6. John S. Wright, quoted in Daniel Bluestone, *Constructing Chicago* (New Haven: Yale University Press, 1991), 20.

7. Julia Sniderman Bachrach, *The City in a Garden* (Santa Fe: Center for American Places, 2001), 5.

8. See Pamela Bannos, "Hidden Truths: Couch Tomb," hiddentruths.northwestern.edu/couch_main.html.

9. Charles Beveridge and Paul Rocheleau, *Frederick Law Olmsted: Designing the American Landscape* (New York: Rizzoli, 1995), 85.

10. Frederick Law Olmsted, "A Report upon the Landscape Architecture of the Columbian Exposition to the American Institute of Architects," *American Architect and Building News*, September 9, 1893, 151–54. On the exposition see Eric Larson, *The Devil in the White City* (New York: Crown, 2003).

11. Daniel Burnham and Edward Bennett, *Plan of Chicago* (1909; repr., New York: Da Capo Press, 1970), 50.

12. Ibid.

13. Dennis McClendon, *The Plan of Chicago: A Regional Legacy* (Chicago: Chicago CartoGraphics, 2008), 8.

14. Burnham and Bennett, *Plan of Chicago*, 110.

15. Timothy J. Gilfoyle, *Millennium Park: Creating a Chicago Landmark* (Chicago: University of Chicago Press, 2006), 49.

16. Burnham and Bennett, *Plan of Chicago*, 2.

17. Douglas Bukowski, *Navy Pier: A Chicago Landmark* (Chicago: Metropolitan Pier and Exposition Authority, 1996), 87.

18. Ibid., 35.

19. Ibid., 33.

20. Gilfoyle, *Millennium Park*, 170–71.

21. Ibid., 277–93.

22. Keith Schneider, "To Revitalize a City, Try Spreading Some Mulch," *New York Times*, May 17, 2006.

23. Carl W. Condit, *Chicago, 1910–29: Building, Planning, and Urban Technology* (Chicago: University of Chicago Press, 1973), 196.

8. PARKWAYS AND PARK SYSTEMS

1. Frederick Law Olmsted, "Preliminary Report to the

Commissioners for Laying Out a Park in Brooklyn, New York" (January 24, 1866), *Papers of FLO*, supp. ser., 1:83.

2. Frederick Law Olmsted, "Letter to the Park Commissioners of Minneapolis" (1886), in Theodore Wirth, *Minneapolis Park System, 1883–1944* (Minneapolis: Board of Park Commissioners, 1946), 35.

3. Olmsted & Vaux, "Report of the Landscape Architects and Superintendents to the Board of Commissioners of Prospect Park, Brooklyn" (January 1, 1868), *Papers of FLO*, supp. ser., 1:133.

4. Olmsted, "Letter to the Park Commissioners of Minneapolis," 36.

5. Daniel Bluestone, *Constructing Chicago* (New Haven: Yale University Press, 1991), 20.

6. Figures are courtesy of Dennis McClendon, Chicago CartoGraphics.

7. Henri Malet, *Le Baron Haussmann et la renovation de Paris* (Paris: Editions Municipales, 1973), 162.

8. Pierre Pinon, *Atlas du Paris haussmannien* (Paris: Parigramme, 2002), 180.

9. Olmsted, Vaux & Co., "Preliminary Report Upon the Proposed Suburban Village at Riverside, Near Chicago," *Papers of FLO*, 6:286.

10. H. W. S. Cleveland, "Suggestions for a System of Parks and Parkways for the City of Minneapolis," in Wirth, *Minneapolis Park System,* 29.

11. Board of Park and Boulevard Commissioners of Kansas City, Resolution of October 12, 1893, in George Kessler, *Report of the Board of Park and Boulevard Commissioners of Kansas City, Mo.* (Kansas City: Hudson Kimberly Publishing, 1893), 14–15.

12. Alexander Garvin, *The American City: What Works, What Doesn't* (New York: McGraw-Hill, 2002), 64–66.

13. See Christopher Tunnard and Boris Pushkarev, *Man-made America: Chaos or Control?* (New Haven: Yale University Press, 1963), 159–276.

14. Norman T. Newton, *Design on the Land: The Development of Landscape Architecture* (Cambridge: Belknap Press of Harvard University Press, 1971), 597–604.

15. Robert Miller, "The Long Island Motor Parkway," in *Robert Moses: Single-minded Genius,* ed. Joann P. Krieg (Interlaken, N.Y.: Heart of the Lakes Publishing, 1989), 151–58.

16. Olmsted Brothers and Bartholomew Associates, "Parks, Playgrounds, and Beaches for the Los Angeles Region" (1938), in Greg Hise and William Deverell, *Eden by Design: The 1930 Olmsted–Bartholomew Plan for the Los Angeles Region* (Berkeley: University of California Press, 2000), 95.

17. Robert Moses, *Public Works: A Dangerous Trade* (New York: McGraw-Hill, 1970), 79.

18. Frederick Law Olmsted, letter to William Dorsheimer, Esq. (October 1, 1868), *Papers of FLO*, supp. ser., 1:158.

19. See Cynthia Zaitzevsky, *Fairsted: A Cultural Landscape Report for the Frederick Law Olmsted National Historic Site* (Boston: National Park Service, 1997).

20. Cynthia Zaitzevsky, *Frederick Law Olmsted and the Boston Park System* (Cambridge: Belknap Press of Harvard University Press, 1982), 58–64.

21. Frederick Law Olmsted, "Paper on the (Back Bay) Problem and Its Solution Read before the Boston Society of Architects" (April 2, 1886), *Papers of FLO*, supp. ser., 1:441.

22. Frederick Law Olmsted, Seventh Annual Report of the Board of Commissioners of the Department of Parks for the City of Boston for the Year 1881 (City Document no. 16, 1882), quoted in *Civilizing American Cities: A Selection of Frederick Law Olmsted's Writings on City Landscapes,* ed. S. B. Sutton (Cambridge: MIT Press, 1971), 227.

23. Olmsted, "Paper on the (Back Bay) Problem," 442.

24. Zaitzevsky, *Olmsted and the Boston Park System,* 54–58.

25. Frederick Law Olmsted, "Notes on the Plan of Franklin Park and Related Matters" (1886), *Papers of FLO*, supp. ser., 1:468.

26. Boston Department of Parks, *Twenty-first Annual Report of the Board of Commissioners for the Year Ending January 31, 1896* (Boston: Office of the Commissioners, 1896), 50.

27. See Olmsted, "Notes on the Plan of Franklin Park."

28. The figure for Franklin Park is from Boston Department of Parks, *Twenty-first Annual Report.* The figure for Prospect Park was calculated, with help from David P. Colley, by deducting the $1.5 million that was expected from the sale of the eastern lots (which Calvert Vaux had argued should be sold to cover the price of better located property), as stated in the report of Frederick Schroeder, Brooklyn comptroller, "How We Stand: City Debt and City Taxation," reported in the *Brooklyn Eagle,* May 29, 1874.

29. Frederick Law Olmsted, "General Plan of Franklin Park," in Zaitzevsky, *Olmsted and the Boston Park System,* 49.

30. Olmsted, "Notes on the Plan of Franklin Park," 483.

31. See Charles W. Eliot, *Charles Eliot, Landscape Architect* (1902; repr., Amherst: University of Massachusetts Press and Library of American Landscape History, 1999).

32. William H. Wilson, *The City Beautiful Movement* (Baltimore: Johns Hopkins University Press, 1989), 147–92.

33. Figures courtesy of the Minneapolis Park and Recreation Board.

34. Cleveland, "Suggestions for a System of Parks and Parkways for the City of Minneapolis," 28–34.

35. Ibid., 28–29.

36. Wirth, *Minneapolis Park System,* 219.

37. See www.lccmr.leg.mn/Parks.

38. See www.fpdcc.com.

39. Daniel Burnham and Edward Bennett, *Plan of Chicago* (1909; repr., New York: Da Capo Press, 1970), 47.

40. See www.chicagoparkdistrict.com/index.cfm/fuseaction/parks.home.cfm.

41. Peter Harnik, *Inside City Parks* (Washington, D.C.: Urban Land Institute, 2000), 121, 123.

42. U.S. Bureau of the Census, 2006.

43. Figures courtesy of the Boulder County Parks and Open Space Department.

44. Figures courtesy of the City of Boulder Sales/Use Tax Division.

9. STEWARDSHIP

1. Frederick Law Olmsted, letter to the board of commissioners of the Department of Public Parks, October 23, 1872, *Papers of FLO*, 6:579.

2. Frederick Law Olmsted, letter to Howard Potter, March 16, 1883, quoted in Charles Beveridge, "Planning the Niagara Reservation," in *The Distinctive Charms of Niagara*

Scenery: Frederick Law Olmsted and the Niagara Reservations, ed. Beveridge (Niagara Falls, N.Y.: Niagara University, 1985), 21.

3. "Report of the St. Louis Department of Parks" (1915), quoted in August Heckscher, *Open Spaces: The Life of American Cities* (New York: Harper & Row, 1977), 177.

4. Jens Jensen, "Reforms in the West Park System of Chicago," *Park and Cemetery* 15, no. 6 (August 1905): 329–30.

5. Robert E. Grese, *Jens Jensen: Maker of Natural Parks and Gardens* (Baltimore: Johns Hopkins University Press, 1992), 69.

6. Ibid., 187–88.

7. Elizabeth Barlow Rogers, *Rebuilding Central Park: A Management and Restoration Plan* (Cambridge: MIT Press, 1987), 23.

8. Elizabeth Barlow Rogers, "Robert Moses and the Transformation of Central Park," *Site/Lines* 3, no. 1 (Fall 2007): 3–12.

9. These figures are taken from a report prepared by the NYC Planning Commission in 1979, when I was serving as the commission's director of comprehensive planning.

10. Budget figures are from the same report, adjusted for inflation.

11. Elizabeth Barlow Rogers, interview by author, December 16, 2008.

12. Douglas Blonsky, interview by author, December 4, 2008; and Central Park Conservancy, *Annual Report, 2008,* available on the conservancy's Web site at www.centralparknyc.org.

13. Central Park Conservancy, *The Campaign for Central Park* (pamphlet), 2005.

14. Jonathan Kuhn, "Bryant Park," in *The Encyclopedia of New York City,* ed. Kenneth Jackson (New Haven: Yale University Press, 1995), 164.

15. Christopher Gray, "An Enduring Strip of Green in an Ever-Evolving City," *New York Times,* April 22, 2007.

16. William J. Thompson, *The Rebirth of New York City's Bryant Park* (Washington, D.C.: Spacemaker Press, 1997), 8.

17. Information on Bryant Park between 1980 and the present is based on material given to the author by the Bryant Park Corporation and on a series of interviews with Daniel Biederman during 2008.

18. William H. Whyte, *The Social Life of Small Urban Spaces* (Washington, D.C.: The Conservation Foundation, 1980), 58.

19. President Dwight D. Eisenhower, Speech to the National Executive Reserve Conference, Washington, D.C., November 14, 1957.

20. Walmsley & Company, Inc., "First Historic Landscape Report for the 'Ravine,' Prospect Park, Brooklyn, New York," unpublished report, City of New York Department of Parks and Recreation, 1986.

21. Robert Moses, "The Budget Must Go Up" (an open letter to Lazarus Joseph, comptroller of the City of New York), *Atlantic Monthly,* November 1951.

22. Central Park Conservancy, *Campaign for Central Park.*

23. Henry Hope Reed and Sophia Duckworth, *Central Park: A History and Guide* (New York: Clarkson N. Potter, 1967), 42–43.

24. Olmsted and Vaux, "Communication from Landscape Architects," quoted in Frederick Law Olmsted, *Forty Years of Landscape Architecture: Central Park,* ed. Frederick Law Olmsted Jr. and Theodora Kimball (Cambridge: MIT Press, 1973), 475.

25. Frederick Law Olmsted, "Concessions in the Park" (October 6, 1875), quoted in *Forty Years of Landscape Architecture,* 418–20.

26. Charles Bagli, "Two Restaurants, a Big Tent and a Fight in Bryant Park," *New York Times,* November 26, 2008.

27. Frederick Law Olmsted, "Introduction to the Duties of Superintendence," in *Forty Years of Landscape Architecture,* 39.

28. See Roy Rosenzweig and Elizabeth Blackmar, *The Park and the People: A History of Central Park* (Ithaca, N.Y.: Cornell University Press, 1992), 439–63.

29. Ibid., 451.

30. Ibid.

10. FINANCE AND GOVERNANCE

1. John L. Crompton, *Financing and Acquiring Park and Recreation Resources* (Champaign, Ill.: Human Kinetics, 1999), 18.

2. Goodwin Consulting Group, Inc., *UC Davis Neighborhood Master Plan – Public Review Draft, Fiscal Impact Analysis* (May 20, 2003), 61. Available at cityofdavis.org/meetings/finance/NMP_Public_Review_Draft_Fiscal.pdf.

3. Information supplied by the City of Boulder Sales/Use Tax Division.

4. Kim Hopper, *Increasing Public Investment in Parks and Open Space,* vol. 1 of *Local Parks, Local Financing* (San Francisco: The Trust for Public Land, 1998), 9–10.

5. Ibid., 14.

6. See Henry J. Raimondo, *Economics of State and Local Government* (Westport, Conn.: Praeger, 1991).

7. Hopper, *Increasing Public Investment,* 14.

8. Ibid., 10–12.

9. These figures courtesy of the Minneapolis Park & Recreation Board.

10. Cynthia Zaitzevsky, *Frederick Law Olmsted and the Boston Park System* (Cambridge: Belknap Press of Harvard University Press, 1982), 63.

11. Hopper, *Increasing Public Investment,* 6.

12. Peter Harnik, *Paying For Urban Parks without Raising Taxes,* vol. 2 of *Local Parks, Local Financing* (San Francisco: The Trust for Public Land, 1998), 4.

13. Chicago Park District, *2007 Budget Summary,* 9. Available at www.chicagoparkdistrict.com.

14. Howard Kozloff and James Schroder, "Business Improvement Districts (BIDS): Changing the Faces of Cities," *The Next American City* 11 (Summer 2006), americancity.org/magazine/article/web-exclusive-kozloff/.

15. Alex Garvin & Associates, Inc., *A New Public Realm for DeKalb County* (2007), 86–87; available at www.livablecommunitiescoalition.org/uploads/100012_bodycontentfiles/100627.pdf.

16. See www.parksconservancy.org.

17. See www.paconserve.org.

18. See Carol Grove, *Henry Shaw's Victorian Landscapes: The Missouri Botanical Garden and Tower Grove Park* (Amherst: University of Massachusetts Press and Library of American Landscape History, 2005).

19. See www.wolfriver.org.

20. See www.piedmontpark.org.

21. See www.tpl.org.

22. Battery Park City Authority, *Annual Report*, October 31, 2007, and Battery Park City Parks Conservancy, *Financial Statement*, 2007.

23. Hudson River Park Trust, Financial Statement, March 31, 2008, available at www.hudsonriverpark.org/organization/financial.asp.

24. Figures courtesy of the Chelsea Piers Sports and Entertainment Complex.

25. Peter Harnik, "The Park at Post Office Square," in *Urban Parks and Open Space*, ed. Alexander Garvin and Gayle Berens (Washington, D.C.: Urban Land Institute, 1997), 146–57.

26. "City, Park District Close Deal to Lease Garages," *Crain's Chicago Business*, December 15, 2006.

27. "'Pocahontas' Premiere Free in Central Park," *New York Times*, February 1, 1995.

28. "Balboa Park Endowment Fund" (2007), City of San Diego, www.sandiego.gov/endowment-program/balboa-park/index.shtml.

29. Harnik, *Paying For Urban Parks*, 20.

30. Timothy J. Gilfoyle, *Millennium Park* (Chicago: University of Chicago Press, 2006), 117.

31. Alexander Garvin, *The American City: What Works, What Doesn't* (New York: McGraw-Hill, 2002), 440–46.

32. Jerold S. Kayden, *Privately Owned Public Open Space* (New York: Wiley, 2000), 100–101.

33. Crompton, *Financing and Acquiring Park and Recreation Resources*, 35–38.

34. John L. Crompton, *Parks and Economic Development* (Chicago: American Planning Association, 2001), 27.

35. Neighborhood Capital Budget Group, "Tax Increment Financing" (2007), www.ncbg.org/tifs/tifs.htm.

36. The Livable Communities Coalition, *Survey and Analysis of Tax Allocation Districts (TADs) in Georgia: A Look at the First Eight Years* (2007), available at www.beltline.org.

II. THE ROLE OF THE PUBLIC

1. David Schuyler and Jane Turner Censer, introduction, *Papers of FLO*, 6:40–41.

2. Elizabeth Barlow Rogers, "The Landscapes of Robert Moses," *Site/Lines* 3, no. 1 (Fall 2007): 7–8.

3. Lois Wille, *Forever Open, Clear, and Free: The Struggle for Chicago's Lakefront* (Chicago: University of Chicago Press, 1972), 94–95.

4. Patricia Leigh Brown, "Reclaiming a Park for Play," *New York Times*, September 12, 1993.

12. SUSTAINABILITY: THE KEY TO SUCCESS

1. Frederick Law Olmsted and Calvert Vaux, "The Greensward Plan" (1858), *Papers of FLO*, 3:120.

2. The World Commission on Environment and Development, *Our Common Future* (Oxford: Oxford University Press, 1987), 8.

3. Joseph Berger. "Where Village Meets Green," *New York Times*, April 30, 2003.

4. Frederick Law Olmsted, "Public Parks and the Enlargement of Towns," *Papers of FLO*, supp. ser., 1:186.

5. Frederick Law Olmsted, "Park" (*American Cyclopedia*, 1875), *Papers of FLO*, supp. ser., 1:326.

6. Elizabeth Barlow Rogers, *Rebuilding Central Park: A Management and Restoration Plan* (Cambridge: MIT Press, 1987), 44–73.

7. Information courtesy of the Central Park Conservancy.

8. Frederick Law Olmsted, "Superintended of Central Park to Gardeners" (c. 1873–74), in Frederick Law Olmsted, *Forty Years of Landscape Architecture: Central Park*, ed. Frederick Law Olmsted Jr. and Theodora Kimball (Cambridge: MIT Press, 1973), 358.

9. Olmsted, "Park," 311.

10. Tom Fox, *Urban Open Space: An Investment That Pays* (New York: Neighborhood Open Space Coalition, 1990), 11.

11. Frederick Law Olmsted, letter to A. C. Dalton, January 18, 1877; I thank Charles Beveridge and Peter Harnik for passing this unpublished letter on to me.

12. According to the *Third General Report of the Board of Commissioners of the Department of Public Parks for the Twenty Months from May 1st, 1872, to December 31st, 1873* (New York: William C. Bryant and Co., 1875), the amount spent was $5,028,844 for land and $8,873,671 for construction.

13. Frederick Law Olmsted, "Superintendent of Central Park to Gardeners" (April–May 1872), *Papers of FLO*, 6:537–38.

14. August Heckscher, *Alive in the City: Memoir of an Ex-Commissioner* (New York: Scribner's, 1974), 216–17.

15. Frederick Law Olmsted, "Address to Prospect Park Scientific Association" (May 1868), *Papers of FLO*, supp. ser., 1:151–52.

16. Olmsted, "Superintendent of Central Park to Gardeners" (April–May 1872), 539.

INDEX

[Page numbers in italic refer to captions.]